For Glory and Bolívar

For Glory and Bolívar

The Remarkable Life of Manuela Sáenz, 1797–1856

PAMELA S. MURRAY

Foreword by FREDRICK B. PIKE

UNIVERSITY OF TEXAS PRESS, AUSTIN

Copyright © 2008
by the University of Texas Press
All rights reserved
Printed in the United States of America
First edition, 2008

Requests for permission to reproduce
material from this work should be sent to:

Permissions
University of Texas Press
P.O. Box 7819
Austin, TX 78713-7819
www.utexas.edu/utpress/about/
bpermission.html

♾ The paper used in this book meets
the minimum requirements of ANSI/NISO
Z39.48-1992 (R1997) (Permanence of
Paper).

Library of Congress Cataloging-in-
Publication Data

Murray, Pamela S.
  For glory and Bolívar : the remarkable
life of Manuela Sáenz / Pamela S. Murray ;
foreword by Fredrick B. Pike. — 1st ed.
      p.   cm.
  Includes bibliographical references and
index.
  ISBN 978-0-292-72151-7

  1. Sáenz, Manuela, 1797?–1856.
2. South America—History—Wars of
Independence, 1806–1830—Biography.
3. Mistresses—Ecuador—Biography.
4. Bolívar, Simón, 1783–1830—Relations
with women.   I. Title.
  F2235.3.S152M87   2008
  980'.02092--dc22
  [B]
                        2008024175

For Edward B. Deacon—at long last!

With thanks also to Fredrick B. Pike.

CONTENTS

FOREWORD

FREDRICK B. PIKE

LIKE THE LADY whom Bing Crosby sang about in 1931, Manuela Sáenz came along from "Out of Nowhere." Crosby, as a smitten troubadour, fears that his lady will return to her nowhere and disappear. This, alas, is how it has been with Manuela. A vast majority of male observers wanted her, expected her, to return to nowhere after the sort of brief interlude that Andy Warhol would refer to, in a different context, as her "fifteen minutes of fame."

There was never any real likelihood that Manuela would disappear totally, but she did recede into some of the dark corners of history, and might have been scourged even there had it not been for her close relationship with a heroic man — Simón Bolívar, "El Libertador" — a role that evoked occasional reference to her as "La Libertadora."

In Latin America, not until the twentieth century was well along, did Evita Perón, among others, help to make a feminine role in history acceptable and, at least to some, even laudable. Manuela bestrode the world in her own day, but only in a way that made it clear to most observers that her day would be ephemeral at best. With the struggle for independence under way, exceptions to the rules of conduct were allowed. But once normalcy was restored, the Latin American world expected to return to its old ways, in which women could aspire to social but not political power — unless they remained discreetly behind the scenes. Apparently, no one had informed Manuela. Certainly, she was not noted for her discretion, and so she was as likely to be dubbed a villain as a heroine.

An illegitimate child (a fact sufficient in itself to disqualify her from acceptance, let alone admiration, by respectable society), Manuela grew up in her native Ecuador. In due time, her father managed to arrange her marriage to a solid, stolid gentleman of good background, who often found his headstrong bride a bit more than he could handle. She, in turn, found her mate exceedingly dull, however grateful she might have been for the economic security marriage provided.

When the Latin American struggle for independence reached serious proportions in the nineteenth century's late teens, Sáenz devoted her formidable energies to the patriot cause. Eventually, in 1822, she met El Libertador himself, and the pair embarked on an often-interrupted eight-year relationship. In short, she became his mistress—at least, the one he generally preferred above others. However, even the love-smitten Bolívar found her a mite eccentric, referring to Manuela as the "amiable madwoman." No doubt, he found her a little less mad when, in 1828, her remarkable courage and ingenuity saved him from assassination. Their relationship lasted until Bolívar's death from tuberculosis in 1830.

Increasingly discouraged and dismayed by the course of events in South America, confined to a wheelchair as a result of an injury, and in financial distress following her husband's death in 1847, Manuela found herself forced to depend increasingly on the hit-or-miss largesse of others. Nonetheless, she continued for a while to indulge her passion for behind-the-scenes political manipulation. Had she been able to foresee the future, she surely would have found nothing really remarkable about a North American politico who, in the 1930s and early 1940s, dominated his mighty country and a good part of the world from a wheelchair. Nor, projecting ahead, would she have found anything surprising about women serving as presidents of Chile and Germany in the early twenty-first century, and before that, of the Philippines and elsewhere. Undoubtedly, she would have been astonished that it took until 2007 for a woman to mount a serious campaign for the U.S. presidency. High time, she might have thought, that reality caught up with her own worldview.

Previously, most readers, even those at home in the Spanish language, would have known Manuela only through her heroic role as Simón Bolívar's protector against a gang of would-be assassins. Now there is no danger of her having to "go back to nowhere." She is reclaimed in Pamela Murray's richly researched and enchantingly written biography as one of the hemisphere's greatest women, one who paved the way for so many other women in modern times to manifest their own greatness. In a way, Sáenz has helped to lead a new revolution in Latin America, one of true woman's emancipation and equality, that is every bit as important as the one Simón Bolívar mounted against Spain. Manuela Sáenz died in 1856 in the backwater coastal town of Paita, Peru, far from the political firestorms she adored, but what a life she left behind.

Fredrick B. Pike
Professor of History Emeritus
University of Notre Dame

THIS BOOK HAS been a long time in the making. While a desire to write it first came to me some ten years ago, fulfillment of that desire has been a prolonged, at times, seemingly endless, process. It has been the fruit not only of research in books and documents but of engagement with people and places, including libraries and archives in various countries over the years. It has been the result of persistence. Indeed, persistence was indispensable in the task of recovering one of modern Spanish America's most remarkable and maddeningly elusive historical figures.

Numerous individuals deserve recognition for their support and assistance during my efforts to trace a life closely intertwined with the early histories of the "Bolivarian" nations—Ecuador, Peru, and Colombia, in particular. In Colombia, these individuals include Juan Escobar and his wife, Berta Arango de Escobar, along with their two gracious and talented daughters, Karla and Yohanna. The Escobar Arango family ensured that I always had a place to stay in Bogotá. For someone who was, at the time, still new to the city, their warm, generous hospitality—including once letting me monopolize their personal computer for two weeks—made all the difference. I also thank Hedwig Hartmann, the Archivo Central del Cauca's undisputed one-of-kind director, who made my first research trip to Popayán (in 1998) both a pleasant and a fruitful experience.

In Quito, Ecuador (first briefly in 1996 and again in 1998), historians Guillermo Bustos, Jorge Villalba, S.J., and Fernando Jurado Noboa helped orient me. My research also benefitted from the gracious assistance of Grecia Vasco de Escudero, director of the Archivo Nacional de Historia del Ecuador. My attempt to learn more about contemporary views of Sáenz and her significance included a tour of the Museo Manuela Sáenz in downtown Quito. This led to an interview with the museum's founder and director, retired businessman and local Sáenz aficionado, Don Carlos Álvarez Saá. Both experiences gave me insight into the public cult that now surrounds Bolívar's mistress as well as the ways in which the work of academic historians can be overshadowed, even trumped, by seductive nationalist myths.

In Lima, I benefitted greatly from my acquaintance with historians Jorge Ortiz Sotelo and Susana Aldana Rivera. Jorge and Susana both offered indispensable early guidance while introducing me, from their unique perspectives, to aspects of Peru's rich early republican history. Susana, in addition, became a friend and companion. She helped me make the most of a planned trip to northern Peru—and Sáenz's adopted hometown of Paita—through her rich knowledge of that region, especially the Department of Piura.

On my arrival in the city (and departmental capital) of Piura, I found people willing, even eager, to help with advice and information. These people included Isabel Ramos Seminario, curator of the Casa Museo Grau; amateur historian Manuel Antonio Rosas; and young Juan Carlos Adriazola Silva. It was Isabel who wisely advised me to focus on and thus make the most of Sáenz's extant correspondence. Juan Carlos, for his part, accompanied me on the hour-long bus ride from Piura to Paita, gallantly volunteering to serve as my personal guide around the small, hot, and dusty port city.

I also wish to thank the helpful staffs of Quito's Archivo Nacional de Historia del Ecuador and the Archivo Histórico del Banco Central del Ecuador; the Archivo General de la Nación and Biblioteca Nacional de Colombia in Bogotá; the Archivo Central del Cauca in Popayán; the Archivo General de la Nación and Biblioteca Nacional del Peru in Lima; the Vatican Film Library of St. Louis University in St. Louis, Missouri; and the United Kingdom's National Archives (formerly Public Record Office) in Kew. I thank Eddie Luster and the staff of the Interlibrary Loan Department at the University of Alabama at Birmingham's Mervyn Sterne Library for their dedication and diligence.

The moral support and cooperation of U.S. colleagues, including fellow historians of Latin America, have been important, as well. A special word of thanks thus goes to Angela Thompson, to whom I first confided the idea of writing Manuela Sáenz's life story and placing it within the context of the larger history of Spanish American women. Angela not only encouraged me to "go for it" but, generously, proofread some of my first attempts to put my findings on paper.

J. León Helguera, Vanderbilt University professor emeritus of history and one of this country's most distinguished (and few remaining) Colombianists, enthusiastically endorsed the project from the beginning. More important, he steered me toward many of the documentary sources needed to realize it. He also read the draft of the manuscript submitted to the University of Texas Press, raising pertinent questions and exhorting me toward greater bibliographic punctiliousness. For all this, I am grateful.

I am grateful, too, for the expert advice and encouragement of Jane Rausch as well as for the interest, goodwill, and supportive words over the years of

Helen Delpar, Larry Clayton, George Lauderbaugh, and Karen Racine. Although she is not a professional historian, I also thank former *St. Louis Post-Dispatch* editor Sally Bixby Defty for her many encouraging and enthusiastic e-mails, all of them appreciated.

Writing a historical biography, especially for the first time, is not easy. Indeed, it proved harder than I ever imagined. I am deeply indebted, therefore, to Lyman Johnson. Lyman's thorough reading and constructive criticism of the first draft made me see what was missing. It also pushed me to do better and to undertake much-needed revisions. Thanks to this, Sáenz's life story found its wings.

I am equally indebted, albeit in a different way, to Fredrick B. Pike, University of Notre Dame professor emeritus of history. Ever since our serendipitous meeting over dinner in Miami's Little Havana some ten years ago, Fred has cheered me on in my quest to grasp fully my elusive subject. An exemplary pen pal (of the traditional, non-e-mail, sort), he has been a source of both inspiration and epistolary companionship. He somehow knew I could write this; I am forever grateful for his friendship, wisdom, rare confidence, and encouragement.

I acknowledge, too, the vital material support received from my home institution, the University of Alabama at Birmingham (UAB). This support has included two UAB Graduate School Faculty Research Grants, one for research in Colombia, the other for research in Peru, and a UAB Faculty Development Program Grant for research in Quito. Two National Science Foundation–sponsored ADVANCE Faculty Research Awards (administered by the NSF-UAB ADVANCE program) were crucial for the final stage of the project. By providing me with two successive course releases, one in spring 2005, another in spring 2006, these awards gave me the time needed to make important revisions. A sabbatical leave during the 2006 fall semester gave me the chance to prepare a final version of the manuscript for publication.

I thank editor-in-chief Theresa May and the University of Texas Press editorial team for their patience, support, and cooperation. I also wish to express appreciation for the careful reading and suggestions made by the Press's two outside readers and by my copy editor, Kathy Bork. Thanks, too, to Craig Remington and his staff at the University of Alabama's Cartographic Research Lab for their mapmaking assistance.

I close these acknowledgments with a few words about the person who bore much of the cost of my long years of obsessive intellectual labor: my husband, Edward Bixby Deacon. Ted gamely, if not gladly, endured my absences during months-long research trips to South America. As I ground through two drafts of the book manuscript, he endured my virtual (emotional, if not physical) absence on evenings and weekends. He has stoically taken up chores and cheerfully cooked dinners. At the same time, Ted has been in my corner. He has served as a sounding board, cheerleader, and critic, often reminding me to avoid distractions and to write "faster." He reminds me that life does not always wait for a book to be finished. He has been a reality check and author's blessing.

For Glory and Bolívar

Introduction

MANUELA SÁENZ (1797–1856)—FRIEND, lover, and ally of Spanish American independence hero Simón Bolívar and, today, an icon of nationalists and feminists throughout the region—has been largely ignored by professional historians. In the United States, she remains unknown among most scholars of Latin America. My own introduction to her was by accident. It happened decades ago when, as a graduate student browsing the book stacks of Tulane University's Latin American Library (preparing for the requisite Ph.D. prelim examinations), I came upon *The Four Seasons of Manuela: The Love Story of Manuela Sáenz and Simón Bolívar* (1952) by popular author Victor W. Von Hagen.[1]

A distraction from my usual dry reading, Von Hagen's story captivated me. Here was the tale of a strong-willed, passionate woman who had defied convention and raised controversy in order to pursue an affair with Bolívar, a.k.a. the "Liberator"—renowned commander of the largest and most successful patriot army in Spanish South America, creator of republics, and, for a time, the world's most celebrated revolutionary leader. Here, too, was a woman who had participated in the epic Spanish American struggles for independence and whose abilities, enthusiasm, and commitment to the patriot cause had won her Bolívar's confidence. Proof of that confidence was her eventual acceptance into the ranks of his closest followers, including her emergence as his personal archivist, confidante, and, in the last years of his life, his most ardent defender. More broadly, and as Von Hagen reveals in his vivid storyteller's fashion, Sáenz had carved a place for herself in a man's world; she had learned to ride the crest of war and revolution and had wielded political influence. Why, then, given the modern history profession's growing interest in women's experiences, had I and other graduate students never heard of her?

The answer to this question is complicated. One part of it lies in biography's quasi-pariah status among academic historians. Author of two widely acclaimed biographies and of the Pulitzer Prize–winning *Founding Brothers: The Revolutionary Generation,* Joseph Ellis refers to this status when he describes the genre as "a bastard, or . . . orphan periodically adopted as a welfare case by History or English departments."[2] He also explains some of the reasons for biography's predicament. He notes, for example, the "hegemonic" influence of social history, whose approach to the past sees groups or collectivities rather than individuals as the proper focus of study. This same influence, he adds, "privileges the periphery over the prominent figures at the political center, who become 'dead white males' and their respective stories elitist narratives casually dismissed as 'great man history,' even when the subject is a woman or, even when the story told undermines the entire notion that [only] men make history."[3]

One wonders what Ellis might have to say about the "new biography." He almost certainly would look upon it with some dubiousness. New biographers, after all, are less interested in understanding a life on its own terms and making it intelligible to readers than in elucidating the contested process of identity construction—of "inventing selves," more particularly. Indeed, their genre stems from postmodern epistemological insights and premises that have contributed to a new hegemony within the profession and that inevitably conflict with, as Jo Burr Margadant has put it, "a narrative strategy designed to project a unified persona."[4]

Today's historians of Latin America are not immune to the bias that prevails among their disciplinary brethren, at least in the United States. In an essay in *Latin American Research Review,* Michael Monteón puzzles over Latin Americanists' tendency to shun traditional life-writing. He then offers an explanation similar to Ellis's, noting that biography is "academically unfashionable" and "does not lend itself to social science modeling." The genre "presents numerous difficulties in research and composition," he adds, perhaps thinking of the concerns of postmodernist scholars.[5]

As others before him have noted, however, tackling such "difficulties" can be worthwhile. This is certainly the case for the vital subfield of women's history (now increasingly being subsumed, it seems, into the history of gender), to which biography can offer, as Donna Guy once put it, "invaluable" insights into the influences and motivations underlying the actions of individual historical agents.[6]

This brings us to yet another factor that has worked against the telling of Manuela Sáenz's life story, one exemplified by the general silence that, until around the middle of the twentieth century, was long maintained by Spanish American historians. The silence was especially noteworthy in the case of authors in Sáenz's native Ecuador. In a survey of national histories published between 1860 and 1940, for example, María Mogollón and Ximena Narváez found only three books that even acknowledged the existence of Bolívar's Quito-born mistress. Those three limit their attention to what most authors have regarded as her main accomplishment: her thwarting of the attackers who, on September 25, 1828, broke into the presidential palace in Bogotá in an attempt to assassinate the Liberator. They also downplay that accomplishment; their brief accounts say almost nothing about the bravery and quick thinking with which Sáenz met the attackers (nor about the beating she took from them) but dwell, instead, on her physical beauty. Above all, they display the deeply conservative male gender bias that long has characterized both Ecuadorian and Spanish American historical writing. Most evident in works such as the once-popular children's textbook, *Leyendas del tiempo histórico* (1901), by Manuel J. Calle—a work that, in condemning Sáenz's illicit affair with Bolívar, portrays her as a "fallen woman"— this bias includes the assumption that women have no role to play on the stage of national history.[7]

Although Manuela Sáenz is known widely today in Spanish America, historians in the region are still largely silent. While national histories in both Colombia and Ecuador now acknowledge her existence, for example, their acknowledgment remains severely limited. In some cases, they say even less than earlier narratives. The latest, most comprehensive, work on Ecuadorian history, the fifteen-volume *Nueva historia del Ecuador,* edited by Enrique Ayala, for one, notes Sáenz's role on the night of September 25 only in passing and offers no further discussion of her or of her place in the history of the nation's women.[8] The forty-volume *Historia extensa de Colombia* does little better, paying only brief homage to Sáenz's success in saving Bolívar from the clutches of his would-be assassins. A newer survey, the *Nueva historia de Colombia,* omits mention of our protagonist altogether.[9]

Memory of Manuela Sáenz, of course, has been preserved in other writings. These include a few articles by gentleman-scholars who, in the first half of the twentieth century, took an interest in preserving her papers. Since around the mid-twentieth century, such writings have included reams of more popular publications including newspaper essays, poems, and historical novels. Overall, however, this literature has had only a loose connection with the historical personage. Indeed, it often has projected a distorted, semimythical image of her. One reason for this is that, as with Argentina's controversial Eva Perón, opinions about Sáenz (known to many in her own time as the "Libertadora") have been polarized—divided into two opposing camps of historical interpretation.[10]

Originating in the criticism of her contemporaries, including her and Bolívar's political enemies, one camp, for instance, sees her as a "bad girl." Its authors focus on her unorthodox behavior, highlighting her violation of gender norms or boundaries that prohibited women from participating in government and the public sphere, including, in the wake of independence, the raucous world of competitive politics. This camp also echoes the discomfiture of some of Sáenz's male acquaintances who, on seeing her willingness openly to confront her and Bolívar's opponents and her habit of appearing in public dressed in a military-style uniform, characterized her as "indecent" or "crazy."[11]

Some authors within the "bad girl" camp, moreover, have interpreted the Quito native's "crazy" conduct as evidence of a confused sexual or gender identity. An example of this appears in the work of popular Peruvian author Ricardo Palma. In an essay penned around the turn of the twentieth century, Palma classifies the Libertadora as a "manly woman" (mujer-hombre). Contrasting her with her well-known friend, Lima socialite Rosita Campusano, whom he classifies as a "feminine woman" (mujer-mujer), he claims that Sáenz preferred the world of army camps and barracks to the urban refinements and luxuries of Lima. She "did not know how to cry" and had "renounced her sex," he concludes.[12] Possibly inspired by the memoirs of one of Sáenz's acquaintances, French scientist Jean-Baptiste Boussingault (who met her in Bogotá in the late 1820s), Palma also pronounces her "a mistake of nature whose masculine spirit and aspirations were embodied in feminine forms."[13]

Palma would be joined by Colombian author Alberto Miramón, whose 1944 *La vida ardiente de Manuelita Sáenz* elaborates on the theme of Sáenz's supposed gender deviance. Miramón's book offers a unique, Freudian-inspired explanation for Sáenz's bold—and, thus, seemingly unfeminine—public conduct, arguing that such conduct stemmed largely from the effects of an overactive libido. Indeed, in stating that his protagonist "belonged to a certain erotic category of women that has been identified by modern science," the author suggests she was a nymphomaniac. Her excess sexual energy, he continues, led her not only to indulge in "continuous infidelities" but also to invade the manly realms of war and politics, working zealously on behalf of her lover's political interests.[14]

Other authors have simply condemned the Libertadora for her transgressive behavior. Eschewing any attempt to understand the historical woman (perhaps unsure of what to make of her), they portray her as disreputable. In his 1951 two-volume biography of Bolívar, for example, Salvador De Madariaga claims Sáenz's relationship with the Venezuelan-born hero was based on little more than personal ambition, greed, and crass convenience. He states that Sáenz "tolerated" Bolívar's affairs with other women in exchange for "a generous pension, not a little political power, and the freedom to indulge in [numerous] romantic adventures." Characterizing her conduct as low class or boorish, he also suggests she was a liability for her prestigious lover. Sáenz's love of port wine combined with her habits of smoking, "dressing and acting like a hussar," and telling "dirty jokes," Madariaga asserts, coarsened the atmosphere around Bolívar, thereby tarnishing his reputation along with that of his Bogotá circle, or "court."[15]

Pilar Moreno de Ángel tends to agree, offering a similarly negative assessment of both Sáenz and her influence. In her two well-documented biographies, one of José María Córdova, the other of Francisco de Paula Santander (Bolívar's main Colombian rival and Sáenz's antagonist), Moreno portrays Sáenz as an opportunistic camp follower. She depicts her, too, as someone who lacked a sense of propriety or female respectability—who "rode horseback like the men and smoked and drank like a soldier."[16] She implies that this same quality led to Sáenz's later difficulties (in 1828–1830) with her Bogotá neighbors; her "free and easy ways" (costumbres libres y desenfadados), Moreno asserts, offended the city's pious, puritanical residents. Moreno also agrees with De Madariaga's suggestion that Sáenz was a political liability, alleging that she contributed "notably to an increase in Bolívar's rising unpopularity." She particularly condemns Sáenz's political activism, or habit of, as she puts it, "intervening openly in politics without the ability or experience to do so." Such a habit, she concludes, poisoned the atmosphere by increasing the tension that had come to exist by the late 1820s between Bolívar and his rivals.[17]

Yet others have seen Manuela Sáenz as a heroine. Reflecting the impact of twentieth-century nationalism and the secular cult of Bolívar, especially strong in Venezuela and its immediate neighbors (Colombia and Ecuador), their writings celebrate her commitment to independence, personal bravery, and love for as well as devotion to the revered founder of five nations. An example of such writings may be found in the work of well-known Venezuelan scholar and Bolívar panegyrist Vicente Lecuna. In an essay entitled "Papeles de Manuela Sáenz" (1945), Lecuna praises Sáenz, highlighting her courage and compassion as well as her stoicism in the face of misfortune. He especially lauds her thwarting of the notorious September 25, 1828, attackers and, in paying homage to her sangfroid and bold action that night, states that she "saved" the Venezuelan nation from "the shame of assassinating its greatest hero." For this reason alone, he adds, she ought to be remembered always "with respect and sympathy."[18]

Yet, as in the case of works associated with the "bad girl" school of interpretation, Lecuna's portrait of Sáenz is one-dimensional. Indeed, in dismissing unflattering myths or claims about her, for example, that she was less than totally faithful to Bolívar, his article suggests the Libertadora was less a real person than a kind of saint or Mary Magdalene—a woman who transcended her supposed moral weakness through love for and devotion to the Liberator-Messiah. Sáenz's "noble conduct . . . purified her life and redeemed all her sins," the article piously concludes.[19] Lecuna's view has been largely echoed by other Spanish American authors since the 1940s, especially nationalist authors in Ecuador who, like Ángel I. Chiriboga, see Sáenz as a romantic "martyr of love and glory."[20]

The present work seeks to transcend such simplified, stereotypical images. It offers a more balanced, nuanced view of Sáenz, portraying her not as "bad," deviant, or transgressive, or as romantic or heroic (much less saintlike), but as a complex person rooted in the equally complex and changing world of her time. Above all, it seeks to recover the historical person.

It has been preceded in this by two older biographies: one by Alfonso Rumazo González, another by Von Hagen. In his now-classic *Manuela Sáenz: La libertadora del libertador* (1944), Rumazo seeks to trace Sáenz's life in a serious manner, relating it to historical developments that shaped it, such as the 1808–1809 crisis of Spanish colonial authority and ensuing Spanish American struggles for independence. He examines not only her romantic affair with the Liberator but her alliance with him and involvement in events marking the early years of the new Spanish American republics, Peru and Colombia, in particular.[21]

Rumazo's book suffers from serious flaws, however. It tends to offer conjecture as fact. Indeed, it fails to substantiate key claims about its protagonist and her activities. One example of this is the claim that Sáenz joined Bolívar's army in combat and participated in the decisive December 9, 1824, Battle of Ayacucho, an assertion based more on legend that on any archival or documentary evidence.[22] Another, ultimately greater, flaw is the book's tendency to overlook key parts of its protagonist's life experience. While lavishing attention on her eight-year relationship with Bolívar (devoting over half of roughly three hundred pages to the subject), Rumazo fails to examine her subsequent trajectory. He devotes only one short, twenty-one-page chapter to the twenty-six years by which she outlived her famous lover (who died in December 1830). He gives especially short shrift to the two decades she spent in the northern Peruvian port town of Paita, where, from 1835 on, Sáenz lived out the rest of her life as a political exile.[23]

Von Hagen's *The Four Seasons of Manuela* (1952)—until now, the only biography available in English—suffers from similar weaknesses. Its narrative focuses almost exclusively on Manuela's affair with the Liberator, with fourteen of its eighteen chapters (these arranged into four parts: "Spring," "Summer," "Autumn," and "Winter") devoted to charting the couple's eight years together. It acknowledges other aspects of her life only briefly. Despite its inclusion of several new details about her years in Paita, for example, it says little about the friendships Sáenz formed with local residents or about the role she came to play in the town's tiny Ecuadorian émigré community. Like Rumazo's book, *The Four Seasons of Manuela* also overlooks Sáenz's continued involvement in the world of politics; it says nothing about her post-1835 efforts to collaborate with two-time Ecuadorian president General Juan José Flores or about her ties to other important national figures, nearly all of them, like her, old followers of Bolívar. It also tends to fictionalize or, at least, to make broad use of poetic license and, beyond a helpful bibliographical essay, avoids scholarly documentation. It suggests, too, that, with Bolívar's death, Sáenz's life was over—a suggestion that reflects both authors' tendency to see her life primarily as part of an epic love story.[24]

The present work differs significantly from these older biographies. It deromanticizes its subject, offering readers the first critical, comprehensive study of a remarkable, if still little known and poorly understood, woman. It builds on recent scholarship, both on Sáenz and on nineteenth-century Latin American women generally. Above all, it presents the results of my visits to archives, libraries, and historic sites in the countries in which Sáenz resided—Ecuador, Peru, and Colombia—and consultation of a wide array of primary sources. Belonging to manuscript collections located in Quito, Lima, Bogotá, and elsewhere, these sources have been preserved by scholars and, thanks to publications that have appeared over the last century, gradually have been made available to a wider audience. They include Manuela Sáenz's extant personal correspondence—a source that, despite its many gaps, allows a biographer to reconstruct her life story.[25] Combined with other surviving documents of the period, for example, the reports and recollections of those who knew her, they also allow for a reassessment of the historical woman.

Crucial to this reassessment have been the letters Sáenz exchanged with General Juan José Flores from the mid-1830s through the mid-1840s.[26] Ignored by (or unavailable to) earlier biographers, these letters reveal not only Sáenz's friendship with Flores—and enduring ties to other old Bolivarians—but also her growing interest and involvement in Ecuadorian national politics, facilitated by the alliance she chose to form with a friend who also happened to be her country's main strongman, or caudillo. Such interest and involvement, of course, belie older biographers' assumption that, after Bolívar's death, the Libertadora faded away into sad obscurity.[27] It shows that Sáenz learned to adapt to new circumstances and that, in the wake of her exile to Paita, she reinvented herself, finding new sources of pride and self-respect as well as personal influence.

More generally, this biography also shows that for all her seeming exceptionalism—that is, the fame (or notoriety) and influence she achieved in the course of her brief career as Bolívar's follower and mistress—the Libertadora cannot be understood apart from her time, place, and generation. The time, of course, was Latin America's "Age of Revolution," an age that witnessed the impact of the European Enlightenment as well as the French, British North American, and Haitian revolutions; collapse of Iberian colonialism; and birth, by around 1840, of some sixteen fledgling Latin American nations.[28]

Like others born in the last years of the eighteenth century, Manuela Sáenz grew up and matured in the midst of these changes. She learned to navigate and negotiate them, adopting, for example (and as the coming chapters illustrate), the vocabulary of Spanish America's new liberal-republican order, with its universalist promises of freedom, constitutionally based law, and citizenship. She also formed part of a unique storm-tossed generation, one marked by the new century's most intense and violent moment: the wars for independence that, between 1810 and 1825, raged across Spanish America. It was as a member of this generation that the Libertadora burst onto the public scene and new post-independence political arena—an arena in which, largely because of her sex, she would be transformed at once into both an icon and a partisan lightning rod.

The subject of this biography also cannot be understood apart from her gender or from the broader history of Spanish American women. She was, of course, no ordinary woman. She was a relatively pampered and privileged city girl—a member of Quito's small, exclusive, white (or *criollo*) elite or upper class. She had little in common with the darker-skinned (Indian and mixed-race) peasant or working-class members of her sex, who predominated in poor urban neighborhoods as well as in the Andean countryside. Her experiences, nevertheless, may offer insight into the changes women throughout the region—in small towns, villages, and cities—underwent as a result of their involvement in the struggles for independence and in what Sylvia Arrom describes as a broad process of civic and political "mobilization."[29] They offer insight into the limits of this mobilization and into the gender boundaries that, after independence, would, among other things, exclude women from formal participation in the young Spanish American republics. They demonstrate one woman's tendency to chafe against those boundaries and, above all, to search for her own path and destiny.

ONE

Beginnings, 1797–1822

ALTHOUGH LITTLE IS known of Manuela Sáenz's childhood, available sources offer a glimpse of the world that shaped it. They shed light on circumstances that affected her girlhood. These circumstances included her illegitimate origin and official, baptismal, status as a foundling, or *hija expósita*—that is, a child of "unknown parents," a designation meant to disguise the fact of her parents' illicit union.[1] They also included an upper-class social background. Sáenz's December 1797 birth to parents of elite status (a status based on wealth, access to public office, and noble or "pure" Spanish lineage) helped mitigate the dishonor that usually haunted a bastard child.

More important was her father's willingness to provide for her and, however informally, recognize her as his offspring. Because of this, young Manuela enjoyed many of the same privileges enjoyed by her half-sisters, the legitimate daughters of Simón Sáenz de Vergara; like them and other upper-class women in Spanish America, she would have the right to be addressed as "Doña" (Madame or Lady), for instance. She was also to be incorporated into her father's legitimate family and into strategies designed to advance family interests. An example would be her arranged marriage to one of Sáenz de Vergara's business acquaintances, a prosperous British-born businessman named James Thorne. Yet the young woman also would venture out beyond the paternal orbit. She would embrace the cause of Spanish American independence—a cause that would put an end to her relatively secure and conventional existence and, in time, open new doors for her.

Manuela Sáenz's illegitimacy was not quite what it might seem to a casual observer, someone unaware of the factors that determined its meaning for her. For Sáenz and other late-colonial upper-class Spanish Americans, the question of out-of-wedlock birth hinged on several variables. One variable was the precise definition or degree of illegitimacy. Spanish canon law recognized two main categories of illegitimacy: *hijos naturales* (offspring of single parents who could, in theory, marry each other), and *hijos espurios* (those born of incest, adultery, or a union involving a member of the clergy). *Espurios* embodied the more unfortunate category. The greater amount of sin or depravity associated with their parents' sexual behavior translated into a correspondingly greater degree of dishonor and, thus, a heavier social stigma than that suffered by *naturales*.

Other birth-related variables could attenuate the disgrace that was to some extent attached to all categories of illegitimacy. One was a child's baptismal status, that is, the description of its race and natal condition (legitimate, *hijo natural,* or *expósito*) given at the time of baptism and recorded in the local church's baptismal registry.[2] As suggested already, the practice of designating a child as a foundling could help hide parental peccadilloes and thus allow elite parents to save face, that is, to maintain their honor and reputation. In cases in which the child was an *espurio,* designating it as a foundling or *expósito* was especially vital for preserving the ever-fragile honor and reputation of the mother.

A final crucial variable was parental recognition; on this depended a child's future status and life chances. Yet, as with virtually all things affecting the lives of illegitimates, this recognition was seldom a cut-and-dried matter. Parents often chose to recognize an out-of-wedlock child informally and in private. As research has shown, under certain conditions, they also might recognize the child formally and in public.[3] Yet, in the case of Manuela Sáenz and her mother, Joaquina Aizpuru, circumstances mitigated against any kind of recognition.

Joaquina Aizpuru was the unwed daughter (and second-to-youngest of ten children) of Don Mateo José de Aizpuru y Montero and his wife, a native of Quito, Gregoria Sierra Pambley. A native of Panama, Don Mateo José (1717–1803) had established himself in Quito as an attorney (or *relator*) for the region's highest court and governing body, the Audiencia of Quito, and as head of a respectable creole family that resided in the oldest, most prestigious part of the city.[4] His daughter's out-of-wedlock pregnancy, fruit of an affair with a local gentleman and family acquaintance, must have been upsetting to him. As available sources show, it remained "private"—arranged so as to help Joaquina avoid the scandal usually associated with unwed motherhood.

As was customary among the region's upper classes, this arrangement allowed a woman to keep her maternity a secret to all except a few close relatives; the mother-to-be had to stay out of sight, often by going away to a place in the country where she could come to term and give birth far from the curious eyes of friends and neighbors. More important, a private pregnancy allowed her to preserve her reputation for virginity and, thus, both her and her family's honor and respectability. It exacted a heavy price, however, for it included the expectation that the unwed mother give her infant up to a foster home—in many cases, kin who became the child's surrogate parents. The mother also was to avoid acknowledging the child; to do otherwise would be to risk her secret and the very honor she and her family had sought to salvage.[5]

While no doubt torn by her predicament, Aizpuru (around thirty years old at the time) did what the circumstances, as well as honor and custom, demanded of her. After first trying to place her infant with a local family, she agreed to entrust her to one of the nuns at Quito's La Concepción convent, an institution known for taking in the occasional "orphan."[6] We can only guess to what extent she acknowledged the child later. It is clear she had little time or opportunity to extend acknowledgment; extant sources indicate that Aizpuru was dead by 1804 and that she may have died in (or shortly after) childbirth. They also show no sign that her daughter ever knew or met her.[7]

The loss of her mother left Manuela Sáenz dependent not only on the care of her designated nun-guardian but also on the support of her sole remaining parent: her father. A native of the village of Villasur de Herreros in the northern Spanish province of Burgos, Simón Sáenz de Vergara y Yedra (1755–1825) arrived in the colonies around 1780 and, in the manner of many a hungry immigrant of his era, quickly contracted an advantageous marriage. Indeed, his 1781 marriage by proxy to the aristocratic Juana María del Campo Larrahondo y Valencia of Popayán (the southern New Granadan city where he had landed a year earlier) sealed the friendship and business alliance he apparently already had formed with her father, fellow peninsular Spaniard Francisco del Campo y Larrahondo, a local magistrate, director of Popayán's important royal aguardiente monopoly, and knight of the Order of Charles III. His marriage no doubt allowed him to benefit from del Campo's social connections, the most important of which was his marriage to María Ignacia Valencia Fernández del Castillo, younger sister of Pedro Agustín Valencia—one of the city's most illustrious citizens and scion of one of the region's wealthiest and most prominent families.[8]

Sáenz de Vergara soon emerged as a merchant involved in the fairly lucrative trade between New Granada (modern-day Colombia) and the Audiencia
of Quito, a jurisdiction that included both Popayán and the Audiencia capital
of Quito, where, in 1786, he and his family settled. Available sources suggest he
became an exporter of Quito-made woolens; in 1823, he still owned a textile mill
in Guaytacama, a nearby town whose Indian residents produced wool cloth and
other products destined for New Granadan markets. Sáenz de Vergara's business success may be gleaned from the fact that, in addition to the mill, he owned
four houses in Quito proper as well as a retail store not far from the city's main
plaza (today's Guayaquil Street); the store likely served as an outlet for European
fabric and other goods imported through Cartagena, Guayaquil, and Panama.
Sáenz also owned several lots in the neighboring town of Tanicuchi.[9]

A further sign of Sáenz de Vergara's ambition and fortune was his pursuit of
positions within the Spanish colonial military and government bureaucracies.
Along with the standard requirement of proof of "blood purity," that is, pure
Spanish/white ancestry, such positions usually required advance payment or
purchase; they thus tended to go to only the most affluent or well connected
individuals. Thanks to the prestige traditionally associated with royal (especially
military) service, moreover, they also offered a chance to increase one's honor
and respectability, qualities which Sáenz de Vergara seems to have avidly sought.
In 1786, he acquired a coveted commission as a lieutenant in the second company
of Quito's militia regiments; five years later, he began petitioning for a promotion to captain in the regular army. He then won a number of local civil offices.
These included, by 1796, the potentially lucrative post of chief tithe collector
(*juez colector de rentas decimales*) for Quito's archbishopric and an honorific appointment to a permanent seat on the Quito city council (*regidor perpétuo de cabildo*).[10] For a man eager to join the region's political establishment—and whose
ambitions seem to have inspired the resentment of local creole aristocrats—this
last award must have been deeply gratifying.

It also suggests the extent to which, in his pursuit of bureaucratic office,
Sáenz de Vergara enjoyed certain political advantages over his rivals. In the last
decades of the eighteenth century, Spanish colonial authorities adopted a clear
preference for appointing peninsular-born, as opposed to creole (locally born),
candidates to office. This preference was taken to an extreme in the case of Quito's Audiencia officials. Since the time of Bourbon visitor-general, later Audiencia president, José García de León y Pizarro (1778–1884), Audiencia government
had become the monopoly of a political machine that distributed appointments
mainly to García de León's peninsular allies and their friends, relatives, and
cronies.[11] Simón Sáenz may have been one of these. There seems no reason to

doubt, in any case, that he benefitted from the prevailing pro-peninsular bias in appointment policies.[12]

In sum, Sáenz's bureaucratic career reflected not only his wealth and ambition but also his privileged upper-class status. It reflected, above all, his membership in the Audiencia's small but politically influential peninsular minority.

The same may be said of his place of residence. By the year of his illegitimate daughter's birth, the successful Spaniard and his family (including his wife and six legitimate children, three slaves, and two Indian servants) resided in a home close to the main plaza, the symbolic and administrative heart of Quito. Indeed, their home was but a few blocks away from that of the Aizpurus.[13]

More important, Sáenz de Vergara used his wealth and advantages for his daughter's benefit. He provided the one thousand–peso minimum dowry needed to ensure her acceptance at La Concepción convent and thus her care and proper upper-class upbringing.[14] The nuns of this convent, Concepcionistas, belonged to one of the oldest and most popular of the female religious orders in Spanish America. Since arriving in Mexico in the mid-sixteenth century, they had established themselves throughout the colonies, including in Quito, where, in 1577, they had founded a motherhouse before spreading to the smaller cities of the Audiencia's region. They also were closely identified with the region's elites. Their Quito convent, the oldest, largest, and richest of the six female monasteries in the city, had a tradition of admitting only the daughters of the Audiencia's "most noble families."[15]

The Concepcionistas' relative affluence was evident in their facilities. Unlike the cramped dwellings of most of the city's twenty-two thousand or so inhabitants—small, one-story mud and adobe houses that, like Quito itself, stood at the foot of a dormant volcano—the convent was luxuriously spacious. It rambled for more than a block, an elegant arched passageway connecting its main building off the northwest corner of the plaza with a large house on Mejía Street.[16] La Concepción also embodied a world of its own; with its own houses (the nuns' private cells), patios, chapel, kitchen, gardens, workshops, and bakery, it resembled a small, self-sufficient town. It mirrored the city's socioethnic hierarchy, as well. In the mid-eighteenth century, its one hundred nuns, women of elite white or creole origin, presided over an army of some thirteen hundred mostly Indian and mestiza maids and servants.[17]

In addition, thanks to this army, the cloister buzzed with activity. Indeed, while the members of other religious orders, for example, the Reformed Carmelites, stood out for their piety and strict observance of the rules of monastic discipline, the Concepcionistas stood out for their practicality and devotion to industry; they manufactured lace and fine embroidery as well as enameled wood objects and other handicrafts sold as far away as Lima, Guayaquil, and Panama.[18] They also devoted some of their time to educating the city's most privileged young ladies, teaching them how to read, write, sew, and embroider as well as how to concoct various delicacies (e.g., candy and other sweetmeats) for special occasions. It is here that, under the tutelage of Sister Josefa del Santísimo Sacramento, young Manuela Sáenz must have received her first lessons in literacy and acquired her skill in candymaking and other domestic arts associated with female gentility.[19] The Concepcionistas' lasting importance to her may be gauged, in part, by the fact that, as an adult, Sáenz remained in touch with them and continued to rely on their advice and assistance.

As in the case of many illegitimate children (i.e., *hijos expósitos* who had lost their mothers through death or separation at infancy), moreover, Manuela Sáenz was introduced to her father's home.[20] She came to know her Sáenz del Campo half-siblings—María Josefa, José María, María Manuela, and Ignacio, in particular—and to regard them, unreservedly, as her true relatives. Although time and circumstances were to separate her from them, she would remain in touch with several of these siblings. She corresponded in her later years with younger half-brother Ignacio, for instance, and, as scattered sources hint, developed a special bond with José María.[21] By contrast, Sáenz had relatively little contact with the Aizpurus. Given the difficulties she was to encounter in her adult dealings with her maternal aunt (to be discussed later), it is possible that, as a child, she was never recognized, much less accepted, by them.

Through her arranged marriage, Manuela Sáenz became an integral part of her paternal family's social and business network. Marriage had not been her only option. The young woman might have chosen to become a professed nun—a highly respectable vocation for a woman at the time and one that made sense in light of Quito's severe shortage of eligible bachelors.[22] She apparently was disinclined to do so, however. A popular legend claims that Sáenz once fled the nunnery in order to meet a young Spanish officer with whom she allegedly wished to elope; soon thereafter, to forestall scandal, her father forced her to marry someone else. While its truth is hard to verify, the legend hints at the young woman's desire to live her life outside the sheltered world of the cloister.[23]

It also highlights the fact that Simón Sáenz had other plans for her. Having already married his oldest legitimate daughter, María Josefa, to a fellow Spaniard and (by 1822) Audiencia judge, Sáenz Sr. must have seen marriage as the best course for his illegitimate daughter as well. It is doubtful that he was thinking primarily in terms of Sáenz's personal happiness. For most upper-class Spanish Americans of the time, marriage was less about fulfilling the emotional needs of individuals than about ensuring the welfare and interests of their families. From the standpoint of elite heads of household especially, it long had been a vital means of advancing and consolidating those interests and thus a key part of a family's sociopolitical strategies. Its importance in this sense no doubt had increased as a result of the 1778 Real Pragmática, a law designed to boost parental authority over marriage by giving parents the right to legally challenge a child's choice of marriage partner.[24]

Arranged marriages, moreover, required a parent to find the most appropriate or eligible partner for a child. They required considering a child's actual marriage prospects. Sáenz Sr. no doubt knew that his illegitimate daughter was unlikely to contract the sort of union possible in the case of her two legitimate half-sisters, both of whom ultimately married high-ranking Spanish officials. He certainly could not expect her to marry a gentleman whose prestige—and chances for future promotion—almost certainly would suffer from the whiff of dishonor associated with marriage to an *expósita*. Still, with the help of her father's substantial eight thousand–peso cash dowry, young Manuela had decent prospects.[25]

One of these was James Thorne. A native of Aylesbury, England (a small town west of London, now seat of Buckinghamshire County), Thorne was one of a small number of British entrepreneurs and fortune seekers who had begun trickling into the Spanish colonies at the end of the Napoleonic Wars. While the exact circumstances of his arrival remain unknown, by 1817, he had established his residence in the Peruvian viceregal capital of Lima.[26] He also was a rich man. Thorne had secured his fortune as a shipping merchant involved in the trade between Lima-Callao and other major Pacific port cities—a trade that, due to the troubles affecting Spanish shipping, relied increasingly on foreigners like himself. He owned at least one or two sailing vessels, including a brigantine named *Columbia,* that distributed cloth and other British manufactures to markets in Valparaíso, Guayaquil, and Panama and that also may have supplied these markets with basic commodities, for example, sugar and wheat. In addition, Thorne enjoyed close personal and business relations with members of Lima's creole establishment and with wealthy landowner Don Domingo Orué y Mirones, in particular. He was not only Orué's friend but also an administrator of some of his property. Indeed, he administered the Hacienda Huaito, one of Orué's nine rural estates and, on the eve of Peru's independence, possibly the most prosperous sugar plantation in all of Chancay Province.[27]

Beyond his wealth and business connections, James Thorne had other qualities to recommend him as a potential husband for young Manuela. Some twenty years older than she, he was a solid, stable, mature individual. As a foreigner and thus an outsider vis-à-vis local creole society, he also may have been less inclined than other eligible candidates to see her illegitimacy (assuming he knew of it) as an irredeemable flaw or stain on his honor.

For Sáenz de Vergara, furthermore, Thorne—with his thriving shipping enterprise and diverse contacts—was a valuable business acquaintance. The two men apparently met after the Spaniard had left Quito, at around the time (late 1810) of the arrival of new Audiencia authorities sympathetic to his political rivals—leaders of the city's 1809 creole uprising.[28] Extant sources suggest they met in either Guayaquil or Panama, where the harried merchant-bureaucrat had hoped to escape the influence of his rivals and, above all, boost a fortune that had been threatened by the uprising and subsequent turmoil. It is likely Thorne helped Sáenz de Vergara financially; he might have provided the latter with a fresh source of credit, a loan, or, perhaps, access to new clients.[29] The Spaniard, for his part, must have been grateful. He also surely realized the advantages to be derived from deepening his relationship with a successful foreign (especially British) businessman. For Spanish subjects like him, after all, the times were uncertain. War abroad and, since 1810, the struggle between insurgents and loyalists at home had created new threats to Spanish shipping, commerce, and political authority. Sáenz de Vergara, in sum, no doubt came to see Thorne as an ally and asset—someone who could help him sustain the wealth he had accumulated. It is no surprise, then, that he would see him as a desirable future son-in-law.

Perhaps sensing its importance to her father (and having little real say in the matter, in any case), nineteen-year-old Manuela Sáenz accepted the arranged union with Thorne. She traveled to Lima to be with her betrothed and, on July 27, 1817, married him in a wedding ceremony held at the elegant parish church of San Sebastián.[30] She also must have sensed the union's significance for her. Marriage, after all, confirmed not only her link to her paternal family but also her place within an age-old strategy of elite maintenance; it thus enhanced her claim to elite status in general.

Marriage enhanced her claim to honor, as well. A concept of ancient Iberian origin, honor helped rationalize the race- and class-based social hierarchy of late-colonial Spanish America. It determined not only the distribution of prestige and power but also, on a more basic level, "who was trustworthy, who did favors for whom, who were one's friends."[31] As Ann Twinam has observed, honor also was a rather fluid quality that depended less on a person's actual traits, for example, racial or ethnic origin, than on public perceptions of that person, that is, on reputation rather than reality. Honor was negotiable and, as in the case of Joaquina Aizpuru's private pregnancy, subject to manipulation by individuals.[32]

Miniature oil portrait of Manuela Sáenz, ca. 1816 (artist un-known). Casa Museo del 20 de julio de 1810, Bogotá. Although often attributed to Colombian artist José María Espinosa, this portrait does not carry Espinosa's signature and dates from a time when Espinosa was in southern Colombia (a fugitive from Spanish authorities) and Sáenz in Quito or en route to Lima. It likely marked the occasion of Sáenz's engagement. For her help in interpreting this portrait, I thank art history consultant Frances Robb of Huntsville, Alabama. Photograph by author.

It varied with a person's sex or gender, moreover. Female honor, for example, tended to be defined mainly in terms of sexual behavior and, compared to its male counterpart, suffered relatively less from the stigma of illegitimacy. Elite women born out of wedlock, in other words, could more easily "pass" as individuals of honorable (that is, legitimate) origin; they had relatively less trouble finding an eligible partner than did elite men of similar birth status. To the extent that it confirmed her passing, or social acceptance, therefore, marriage could bolster a woman's honor-related aspirations or pretensions.[33] The dowry played a vital role in this. Beyond its material or monetary value—often crucial in attracting a partner—it remained the traditional symbolic endorsement of a bride's sexual purity and, thus, public proof of her honorability.[34]

Marriage also gave a woman respectability. It ushered her into her time-honored gender roles of wife and mother and, through its character as a religious sacrament, confirmed her place within the larger Catholic cosmos. It particularly strengthened her identification with Spanish Catholicism's powerful Marian ideal of femininity. Based on widespread reverence for the figure of the Virgin Mary, this ideal encouraged all women to adopt the latter's perceived virtues of modesty, humility, and submission to male authority.[35]

Marriage, in addition, signaled a woman's place within the patriarchal order, the system of male gender dominance characteristic of late-colonial Spanish America. Rooted in ancient, chauvinistic assumptions of male superiority (and of female weakness and inferiority), this system sought to restrict women generally. It found clear expression in Spanish law, which treated women as legal minors— and thus, like children, as ineligible for full participation in civil society or for inclusion in civic or public life. Indeed, the law specifically barred women from all positions of leadership and governance, including (with the notable exception of widows) even the position of head of household.[36] As a legal institution, marriage also placed wives under the authority of their husbands and required them to seek the latter's consent before conducting various public activities.

Yet, it also reflected a countervailing tendency, that is, the protective side of Hispanic patriarchy. No wife was required by law to stay at home or to devote herself exclusively to the domestic sphere. Unlike her counterparts in France, Britain, and the United States, furthermore (and like married women throughout the Hispanic world generally), a wife maintained her own juridical identity; she was recognized under law as a separate and distinct person rather than as someone subsumed into the being of her husband.

She also benefitted from the limits the law placed on a husband's authority. Although men had the right to serve as their wives' legal representative in most matters, married women retained a certain independence and freedom of action. They had the right to draft their own will, testify in court, and accept an unencumbered inheritance without their spouse's consent. They also enjoyed rights designed to protect them from abuse to their person and property. A wife could sue her partner for failure to fulfill legitimate husbandly responsibilities, for example, for failing to provide for her and their family. She could take him to court for physical mistreatment, for example, for habitual or severe wife beating. She had recourse to the law to retain access to her personal property. Should her spouse threaten to squander her dowry or prove incapable of administering it, a wife could sue for its return. The law also entitled her to full control of the dowry principal at his death or the couple's legal separation.[37]

In sum, despite its role as an instrument of women's restriction and gender-based subordination, marriage in Spanish America offered a propertied, upper-class woman a relatively decent bargain. Besides enhancing her claim to status, honor, and female respectability, it ensured her a modicum of justice—legal recognition of her rights as a person and marriage partner as well as property owner. In the context of patriarchy, in short, it upheld her claim to human dignity.

Marriage to James Thorne in particular brought additional benefits. It made Manuela Sáenz the mistress of a wealthy man's household. As in the case of other well-to-do upper-class women, this included command over slaves and servants. It included access to domestic luxuries such as the fine silverware with which Thorne provided her.[38]

Sáenz also became the object of her husband's love and affection. As the couple's surviving correspondence shows, Thorne cherished his young spouse. In a December 1822 letter, for example, he showered her with terms of endearment, addressing her as "most beloved wife of my heart," "darling companion," and, more familiarly, "my precious *chichita*." In it he expressed his attachment to her as well and his longing for her companionship—a longing sharpened by frustration over the circumstances that, as the letter makes clear, had forced him to be apart from her for most of the year. "A prison, in your company, would be better than a palace," Thorne told his spouse earnestly. He also assured her of his husbandly devotion. "Regardless [of your lack of response], my love is too firmly grounded . . . to be shaken," he stated after expressing hurt at her apparent epistolary silence.[39]

More important, Sáenz became her husband's confidante, someone with whom he could share his business woes and frustrations. This may be gleaned from the same letter. The letter refers to a dispute in which Thorne had become embroiled and that involved Lima's recently established Cámara de Comercio (Chamber of Commerce), a body that apparently had accused him of owing a debt of ten thousand pesos; it also reveals its author's anguish over the Chilean government's recent seizure of the *Columbia*. The letter goes on to lament Sáenz's absence, asserting that Thorne had "suffered" without her beside him and had missed the "soothing balm of her sweet advice."[40]

As was often the case with the wives of merchants and public officials in her hometown, Manuela Sáenz also became her husband's business collaborator.[41] By 1822, she had begun conducting various transactions for Thorne and, at least on occasion, acting as a retail buyer or distributor. Her purchase of over three thousand pesos' worth of imported merchandise—luxury textiles, dresses, and garments—that year serves as an example. An extant receipt shows that Sáenz purchased the merchandise in late May 1822, after she had embarked on a journey to Quito (where she was destined to arrive in June) and, possibly, just before she left the port city of Guayaquil, the usual stopover for Quito-bound travelers. Her husband's December 11 letter hints that her goal was to sell to clients in Quito and remit all or part of the proceeds to one Señor Villacis, apparently one of Thorne's business contacts in Guayaquil. It is quite possible, of course, that some of the goods were to be sold through her father's retail enterprise.[42]

Other evidence shows that, during Thorne's periodic absences on business, his wife supervised his affairs in Lima. Indeed, Sáenz possessed her husband's general power of attorney. Drafted in March 1820, on the eve of Thorne's anticipated trip that year to Guayaquil and Panama, the power of attorney authorized her to act as his agent or proxy and, in the event of his death, as his executor. It in effect licensed her to undertake activities once undertaken exclusively by her husband and thus to collect debts; hire accountants; buy, sell, and rent property (including slaves); and file lawsuits as well as engage in other legal transactions in accordance with circumstances and Thorne's personal instructions.

Thorne's power of attorney also allowed his wife to conduct her affairs autonomously. The young Señora Sáenz de Thorne wasted little time in doing so. In 1820–1821, for instance, she bought and sold a few household slaves, including a woman named Trinidad and a man named Manuel Solís; in March 1822, she emancipated one-year-old Juana Rosa, the cherished young daughter of one of the female slaves already in her household.[43]

Fortified by her new legal power and status, Sáenz also sought to claim her maternal inheritance. By June 1821, she had hired a lawyer in Quito to take charge of the necessary legal proceedings. The lawyer asked a judge in Quito, Andrés Salvador, to summon individuals capable of revealing the facts behind Sáenz's origin, including the identity of her parents and the circumstances that had led to her early separation from them (and subsequent classification as an *hija expósita*). He specifically asked for testimony to be taken from one Mariano Ontañeda, a Mercedarian friar who had known both parents and who, years earlier, had helped them find a home for their infant daughter. During his September 1821 testimony, Ontañeda revealed the once-secret identity of Sáenz's mother—a fact needed to confirm Sáenz's right to a portion of the estate of Don Mateo Aizpuru.[44] Although Spanish law clearly recognized this right, the estate's current administrator, Ignacia Aizpuru, Sáenz's aunt, had seen no reason to acknowledge her niece's claim.[45] The young woman, thus, would be obliged to resolve the impasse through a return visit to Quito. Only after a meeting with Doña Ignacia would she begin to have hope of satisfaction.[46]

Sáenz, meanwhile, reveled in her adopted city of Lima. Founded in 1534 by Francisco Pizarro, the fabled City of Kings had once been the Spanish Empire's greatest emporium, a devourer of silver extracted from the prodigious Andean mines of Oruro and Potosí and magnet for all manner of luxury merchandise brought in from Spain and the Orient. Despite economic stagnation in the eighteenth century, it remained an important and undeniably glamorous center of Spanish American power, wealth, and culture.

It also possessed an impressive population. Although less than half the size of Mexico City (and much smaller than Paris and London), Lima in 1812 had close to sixty-five thousand inhabitants—more than three times the number of people in Sáenz's native Quito.[47] Thanks to its position as a major site of international commerce, its people were cosmopolitan and heterogeneous, comprising roughly equal proportions of whites, blacks (slave and free), and racially mixed groups, or *castas*.[48]

Its women, moreover, stood out for their unusual degree of freedom and mobility. Unlike their counterparts in Spain and elsewhere in Spanish America—and, in seeming defiance of traditional Iberian norms of female seclusion—female residents of Lima (Limeñas) circulated throughout the city unchaperoned. They went about their business in public places and mingled freely with people of all classes, a habit that often astonished contemporary European visitors, men particularly. "It is not thought at all inconsistent with propriety for respectable females to sit [on benches in the plaza and public walkways] laughing and talking for an hour after dark," one British visitor, Robert Proctor, observed primly; "in fact," he added, after also remarking on Limeñas' apparent disdain for housework, fondness for smoking, "coquettishness," and apparent love of intrigue, "the ladies here regulate their own conduct."[49] Proctor also characterized women as the city's "principal actors."[50]

Such comments suggest the extent to which Limeñas' freedom and mobility stemmed from yet another of their unique habits: their use of their city's traditional female costume, the *saya y manto*. Consisting of a long, narrow, snug-fitting, and usually pleated skirt, often with decorative fringe at the ankle (the *saya*), and a thin black silk shawl pulled closely over head, face, and shoulders (the *manto*), this costume allowed a woman to in effect disguise herself; it turned her into a "*tapada*" and thus into someone who could go out into the world anonymously—virtually invisible to her husband or other male guardians.[51] Like her neighbors, the new Señora Sáenz de Thorne may have used the costume and learned to exploit its evident advantages.

Sáenz's years in Lima also witnessed her political and civic awakening. This awakening owed much to the general crisis of Spanish authority that had begun almost a decade earlier with Napoleon Bonaparte's 1808 invasion of Spain and overthrow of the Bourbon monarchy. The forced abdications of Charles IV and his son, Ferdinand VII, that year sparked not only an empire-wide resistance to the invasion but, by 1810, calls for reform in Spanish government—including in the status and treatment of Spain's New World colonies. The abdications also inspired creole bids for autonomy and, soon afterward, political independence. Above all, the 1808–1810 crisis sparked conflict over the colonies' political future and, in turn, wars throughout the region between proindependence insurgents, or patriots, and defenders of the old colonial order, or loyalists.

These wars at first favored the loyalists. Soon after Ferdinand VII's return to power in 1814, for example, Spanish authorities dispatched a large expeditionary force to northern South America, a hotbed of the recent insurgency. Commanded by General Pablo Morillo, a seasoned Napoleonic War veteran, this force succeeded in scattering the insurgents of Venezuela and New Granada and, by either executing their leaders or forcing them into exile, securing the region once more for the Spanish.

The loyalist victory proved pyrrhic, however. Over the next few years, the Spanish army's harsh crackdown on the patriots and their supporters alienated creoles generally, undermining support for the Crown and encouraging the spread of patriot and republican sympathies. Such sympathies contributed to a revival (and the eventual success) of the independence movements led by General José de San Martín, a former Spanish army officer and native of Argentina, and Venezuela's Simón Bolívar.[52]

Women participated in the overall political conflict and, after 1810, in the increasingly bitter wars that erupted between patriots and loyalists. Their participation certainly was crucial to the former. Urban upper-class women, for instance, nurtured the patriot cause in its infancy, hosting informal gatherings (*tertulias*) that had served as forums for anti-Spanish criticism—and, as in the case of Quito's Manuela Cañizares in 1809, helped hatch the first creole autonomist conspiracies. Like "La Güera" Rodríguez and Leona Vicario in Mexico, they also gave much-needed financial, material, and logistical support to the leaders of the first insurgent armies.[53]

By 1817, moreover, women of all classes were integral to the patriot struggle and involved in virtually all aspects of it. They routinely served as spies and couriers as well as nurses, arms smugglers, and provisioners of food and clothing. Although usually in disguise, they served occasionally as combatants as well. They also stood out for their role as patriot army recruiters. Indeed, the efficacy of their recruitment method—which involved bribing or otherwise persuading loyalist troops to defect to the patriot side (a process generally known as "seduction")—had become a source of worry for Spanish officials. One example is the case of Policarpa Salavarieta in Bogotá. In 1817, after discovering her key role in a plot to subvert the city's royalist garrison, officials there executed the young seamstress in the main plaza.[54]

Women's wartime mobilization also transformed them. It gave them a chance to "stake out a civic role for themselves" within the emerging republics and to act not only as mothers, sisters, and daughters but also as citizens.[55] Early republican authorities acknowledged this role—and thus women's new politico-civic identity—through their public praise for female patriotism. During his brief October 1820 visit to the Colombian Province of Socorro, for example, Simón Bolívar encouraged local patriot ranks by recognizing women's important service to the anti-Spanish struggle in the region.[56]

Women themselves asserted their status as republican stakeholders. They began claiming their rights under the law, for instance. In early republican Caracas (ca. 1811), they demanded that the constitutional principles of liberty and equality be applied to them in their legal disputes with men, and, as Arlene Díaz has shown, invoked such principles in their courtroom arguments. Women thus affirmed the legitimacy of the new republican order while defending their interests as property owners and individuals.[57]

Manuela Sáenz reflected women's politico-civic transformation. Like many others of her era, she became involved in the conflict on behalf of the patriots and a supporter of the cause of San Martín, in particular. By 1818, the intrepid Argentine general had emerged as a champion of patriots everywhere, especially those within the Peruvian viceroyalty—long a bastion of Spanish power and authority throughout the continent. After having led his followers to victory over the Spanish in Buenos Aires two years earlier, San Martín had crossed the Andes to unite with his Chilean allies and triumph over the loyalists at the Battle of Chacabuco (February 1817). He and his allies secured this triumph—and, the cause of Chilean independence—by decisively routing the Spanish expeditionary army at the Battle of Maipu the following April. They had then set their sights on driving the Spanish from Peru proper and on occupying the capital, seat and symbol of the region's remaining loyalist sentiment.

This plan had fired the imagination of Lima's patriots, who soon contacted San Martín and began cooperating with his effort to undermine local creole support for Spanish authority. Patriots also cooperated with the aggressive campaign launched against Spanish shipping in 1819 by San Martín's ally, Admiral Lord Thomas Cochrane. Above all, they began coordinating their activities with those of the general's own liberating army, particularly the forty-five hundred–man Chilean-Argentine expeditionary force, which, by September 10, 1820, had landed in the southern Peruvian town of Pisco.[58]

Surviving sources hint at our protagonist's involvement in local patriot efforts to recruit men for San Martín. They suggest that she participated in a well-
known 1820 campaign to "seduce" members of the Numancia regiment, an important and experienced unit (some seven hundred men in all) within Lima's
royalist defense arsenal. The campaign was conducted primarily by women with
ties to Lima's patriot circles, among them a known friend of Sáenz's: Rosa Campuzano.[59] It coincided with a pro–San Martín conspiracy that erupted in early
December among some of Numancia's officers. One of these officers was Sáenz's
half-brother, Lieutenant José María Sáenz del Campo—a factor that may well
explain her involvement in recruitment/seduction activities.[60] By July 1821, furthermore, Sáenz was an open supporter of the new patriot government established that month under San Martín's auspices. She answered the government's
call for private donations of fabric and clothing to resupply the patriot army
and, with other women, participated in drives to collect these donations from
residents of the city's main barrios.[61]

Sáenz's support for the patriot cause, in turn, won her public honor and recognition. This included an official award that entitled her and other female award
recipients to wear a white and red silk sash with a gold medal bearing the government's coat of arms and the phrase "To the patriotism of the most delicate."
The award in effect signaled her induction into the female section or auxiliary
of the patriots' honor society founded by San Martín in late 1821: the so-called
Order of the Sun. Although female members of the order were not eligible for
the same benefits as their male counterparts, that is, for government pensions
and offices, they did win perquisites for their male relatives who, by government
decree, were to be granted preference in applying for public office.[62]

More important, perhaps, was Sáenz's inclusion in a special roll or list of
"worthy [female] patriots" that appeared in the January 23, 1822, issue of the
government newspaper, the Gaceta del Gobierno del Perú Independiente. This
list identifies 112 women who, according to Gaceta editors, "stood out" for their
"[patriotic] sentiments." It signaled the distinction Sáenz had earned in the
eyes of local civil authorities as well as her membership in an official new civic
elite.[63]

Above all, public recognition confirmed Sáenz's growing sense of patriot
identity. This identity stemmed in part from her association with members of
Lima's creole patriot establishment, a group that included aristocrats such as
José de la Riva Agüero and other members of the local titled nobility such as the
two countesses and three marquises—of Castelhon, Casa-Muñoz, and Torre-
Tagle—whose names also appear in the Gaceta's honor roll.[64] It stemmed from
other, more personal factors as well. One of these may have been a desire to dis-

tance herself from the loyalist affiliation of her father and paternal half-siblings in Quito—an affiliation that had tended to isolate them from their creole neighbors and that, in time, would encourage them to return to Spain.[65]

Yet another factor behind Sáenz's identification with the patriot cause may have been purely practical. Like many in Lima in the months before San Martín's arrival, Sáenz no doubt saw a patriot victory as the only way to end the general suffering caused by the prolonged conflict between patriots and loyalists. This conflict—in particular, the effective patriot attacks on Spanish shipping and the blockade of Callao—had led to serious trade disruptions and, in turn, food shortages and threats of hunger throughout the city. There also had been a general breakdown of law and order, a situation exacerbated by the Spanish authorities' decision to abandon Lima (and retreat to the Peruvian highlands) in June and thus leave its residents at the mercy of escalating crime and disorder.[66]

Available sources hint, moreover, that Sáenz's early support for the patriots sprang at least partly from a desire to help win a military promotion for her brother. Such a promotion apparently had been promised him as a reward for his involvement in the Numancia officers' conspiracy and, in fact, occurred after his regiment formally defected to the San Martín camp on December 3, 1820.[67] His sister's patriot affiliation no doubt also reflected a desire for the potential rewards of such affiliation, including the possibility of exploring new horizons—and of enjoying the public honor and prestige that, so far, due to her illegitimate birth status, had been denied her.

Libertadora, 1822–1827

AROUND THE MIDDLE of April 1822, Manuela Sáenz embarked on a return trip to Quito. She sailed northward from Callao to Guayaquil—gateway to the Quito Audiencia and, for travelers from Lima, still the quickest, most direct route to the Audiencia's remote capital. She likely was accompanied by her husband, who probably had business to attend to in the northern port city. Sáenz went on to Quito without him. She no doubt took the old Spanish road by horse and mule, traveling with her servants and perhaps a friend or acquaintance as well as the usual armed escort for safety.[1]

Patriot forces in the region had helped clear the way for her. Having declared its independence from Spain over a year earlier, Guayaquil had served as the base for a new thrust, led by another patriot ally, General Simón Bolívar and his Colombian army, against the Audiencia's remaining royalist forces. In late February 1822, General Antonio José de Sucre, Bolívar's trusted subordinate, had occupied the southern city of Cuenca. Over the next few months, Sucre and his men pushed steadily northward, defeating the enemy at a battle near the town of Riobamba on April 21 and forcing them to continue their retreat toward the capital. They confronted Spanish troops on the steep slopes overlooking Quito and, between May 22 and 24, defeated them decisively at the Battle of Pichincha.[2]

Sáenz no doubt thrilled to the news of this successful military offensive and probably arrived in Quito shortly afterward, around the end of May or early June. Like many others in the city, she also must have looked forward to the festivities being planned in honor of the patriot triumph and of the anticipated arrival of the new hero: Bolívar.

Her return to Quito in 1822 was her first visit home in five years. It likely was spurred, in part, by a desire to visit her father, a man whose past support for the Crown and hostility toward his creole rivals now made him persona non grata among the city's new creole patriot authorities. Sáenz de Vergara's royalism no doubt also left him disinclined to accept the political changes about to be imposed by Sucre and his army. He chose exile and would return to Spain later that year.[3] His daughter may well have anticipated this and hoped to see him once more before his departure.

She also hoped to satisfy her pending claim to a maternal inheritance. Her aunt, Ignacia Aizpuru, Sáenz's last surviving maternal relative and sole executor of the Aizpuru estate, apparently refused to acknowledge the claim—at least not at first. She did agree to negotiate, however. As available sources show, she eventually offered to recognize her niece's right to an inheritance and to pay her a flat cash sum of ten thousand pesos, to be paid within two years and to be secured through liens on two of her haciendas: Chillo and Cotocollao. Sáenz would accept the offer, dropping her original demand for the claim's full value, as she said, "to avoid lawsuits and differences within the family."[4]

Sáenz's homecoming surely was brightened by the prospect of witnessing the arrival of the now-famous Bolívar. The thirty-nine-year-old native of Caracas was a true blue blood, the descendant of a long line of creole aristocrats. His paternal ancestors had settled in the former captaincy-general of Venezuela in the sixteenth century and, over time and through accumulation of land and slaves, municipal offices and noble titles, had established themselves as members of Caracas society's wealthiest and most exclusive stratum: the *mantuanos.* The youngest of four children (two boys and two girls), Bolívar was heir to a vast estate consisting of slave-worked sugar and cacao plantations, indigo fields, cattle ranches, and copper mines.

Despite having lost both parents while still a boy, he had benefitted from all the privileges typical of a man of his elite background. He had had access to an education at the hands of tutors, for example, Simón Rodríguez, who had encouraged him to read widely and absorb the latest ideas from the Enlightenment. He had had the opportunity to travel and as a young man had enjoyed direct exposure to contemporary European culture via visits to Spain, France, Italy, and England, in particular. Such exposure had left Bolívar fairly sophisticated and, in the context of his native creole society, unusually cosmopolitan. Beyond his familiarity with the writings of leading Enlightenment thinkers such as Montesquieu, Voltaire, and Rousseau, for example, he spoke French fluently, an ability that tended to impress both local elites and foreign visitors; he later also would master some English.[5]

Bolívar also was the Liberator, a title he had earned in 1813 for his prominent role in Venezuela's anti-Spanish insurgency and, ultimately, for his leadership of Spanish America's largest, most dynamic patriot movement. He was the supreme commander of the continent's most successful army. Since 1817, this army—in essence, a coalition of guerilla forces supplemented by a corps of more disciplined professional soldiers of British and Irish origin—had proved itself brave and enthusiastic as well as agile and effective. It had also been victorious. Indeed, with the help of Bolívar's formidable skills as an organizer, propagandist, and military strategist, it had broken the back of Spanish power in northern South America.

The army's victories over the Spanish, in turn, had allowed the Liberator to begin realizing his political vision and to consolidate his main work as a statesman: creation of the Colombian republic. Founded at the 1819 Congress of Angostura and inaugurated formally two years later at the 1821 Congress of Cúcuta, this republic (known to historians as Gran Colombia) not only filled the vacuum left by the collapse of the old Spanish regime, that is, the Viceroyalty of New Granada, but embodied the liberal-constitutionalist ideals for which most creole patriots had struggled. It also embodied Bolívar's dream of Spanish American unity. From its capital in Bogotá, it claimed jurisdiction over all the territory of the former viceroyalty, including the old Venezuelan captaincy-general and, since the army's victory at Pichincha, the Audiencia of Quito—the combined territory, in other words, of modern-day Venezuela, Colombia, Ecuador, and Panama. Bolívar had been elected its first president.[6] Rivaled only by General San Martín in Lima (whose achievements had earned him the title of Protector of the Peruvians), Bolívar was well on his way to becoming the single most powerful and prestigious man in Spanish America. Indeed, not unlike Napoleon in Europe by the late 1790s, he was at once a military hero and a revolutionary champion, destroyer of an old caste system and builder of new, independent republics.

Like Napoleon, moreover, Bolívar was a conqueror. His army's recent victory over the Spanish in Quito signaled not only the city's liberation, but also its capitulation (or resignation) to him and the Colombian republic. Only days after the victory, fully aware of the lack of alternatives, local civil and ecclesiastical leaders had, in one breath, declared their independence from Spain and

annexation to Gran Colombia. Marked by the sort of grandeur usually reserved
for the arrival of a new Audiencia president—or, were this Lima or Bogotá, a
new viceroy—the Liberator's triumphal entry into Quito on June 16 confirmed
his lofty status. Residents of Quito (Quiteños) paid homage by decorating their
homes with flowers and red, blue, and gold flags advertising their recent annexation and new identity as Colombian citizens. They welcomed Bolívar in
throngs, filling their narrow streets and balconies both to cheer and to watch
as he and his escort (some three hundred military officers and civil officials)
paraded solemnly into the city. The parade ended at the main plaza, where the
Liberator was joined by another seven hundred or so horsemen and then was
invited to ascend an elegantly decorated platform. Once on the platform, he received a formal welcome from city fathers and local maidens, the latter of whom,
dressed in classical nymph costumes, presented him with a crown of laurel.
A special thanksgiving mass followed in the cathedral. The celebration continued into the evening and included a private ball at the home of the prominent
Larrea family.[7] Overall, Bolívar's reception in Quito was just what one might
have expected for a man whom contemporaries were starting to see as a new
kind of savior—or, as some of his admirers and panegyrists suggested, a New
World Caesar Augustus.[8]

Quiteños, not surprisingly, were soon petitioning the Liberator for assistance
and favors. Señora Sáenz de Thorne was among them. She may have obtained
a personal audience with Bolívar sometime during the latter's initial two-week
stay in the city; available evidence shows that he soon learned of some of the
problems she faced with regard to her Aizpuru inheritance. Sáenz also may have
been introduced to the Liberator by her half-brother José María. Having returned to his hometown at about the same time as his half-sister (indeed, the
two may have arrived in Quito together), the young officer had just joined the
Colombian army and been promoted to the rank of lieutenant colonel; later that
same year, he obtained an appointment as one of Bolívar's aides-de-camp.[9] Still
a bachelor, he may well have asked his half-sister to accompany him to what, no
doubt, was Quito's biggest social event of the year: the formal ball at the home of
the Larreas. It was during this ball that, according to legend, Sáenz and Bolívar
first met and launched their romantic relationship.[10]

The couple's relationship, of course, was illicit. If illegitimacy rates (as high as
35 percent through the eighteenth century) are any sign, extramarital affairs—
including adulterous ones—were fairly common among elites in late-colonial
Spanish America. They were encouraged both by the widespread practice of
arranged marriages and by the gap between elites' public and private worlds.
As Ann Twinam has shown, this public/private dichotomy lowered the price of

Portrait of Simón Bolívar, Lima, 1823 (artist unknown). Post-
card reproduction from the Bromsen Collection, John Carter
Brown Library, Providence, Rhode Island. Courtesy of J. León
Helguera.

sexual transgression; as long as a person (either a man or a woman) remained
discreet about it, he or she could carry on an affair without fear of damage to
honor and reputation. The existence of a clear sexual double standard, nevertheless, required special discretion on the part of women.[11]

Such affairs, moreover, no doubt had increased in the wake of the violent
and prolonged wars for independence. War, after all, had disrupted families,

separating spouses and relatives. It had exposed communities to large numbers of military men, who, being mostly young, single, and restless, had formed attachments to local women—at least some of whom were seeking masculine protection.

The wars had fostered the well-known romantic liaison between General Francisco de Paula Santander, a twenty-seven-year-old bachelor and Gran Colombia's vice president, and Doña Nicolasa Ibáñez de Caro, a young married woman who, in 1820, became his mistress. Beyond the couple's love for each other, this liaison was abetted by the prestige of the victorious patriot army as well as the power of the new government Santander represented.[12] It was encouraged by a postwar society that had begun to witness a certain loosening of mores. In the 1820s, for example, Bogotá and other New Granadan cities witnessed a pronounced proliferation of dances, parties, gambling, and cockfights. Many of these amusements involved an unprecedented mingling of the sexes and classes and, at the same time, as Aida Martínez and others have suggested, the rise of a new, more easygoing, democratic culture and sociability.[13] Sáenz's budding affair with Bolívar must be viewed in this context, occurring as it did in a city, Quito, eager to celebrate its liberation from the Spanish and to make up for recent wartime privations.

In addition, affairs in general were nothing new to Bolívar. In the manner of many an upper-class gentleman of his day (including his famous countryman and precursor in the wars for independence, Francisco de Miranda), the slim, wiry warrior-statesman was something of a Don Juan, having had a string of lovers and girlfriends since the premature death of his wife, María Teresa Rodríguez de Toro, almost twenty years earlier. Among his known lovers had been Fanny Dervieu du Villars, the wife of a French army officer (as well as a friend and distant cousin), whom he met during his early years in Paris. After his permanent return to Venezuela, Bolívar launched an apparently more serious affair with Josefina Machado, a woman of *mantuano* background who followed him to Angostura but who later died of a sudden illness. He had courted Bernardina Ibáñez, younger sister of the aforementioned Nicolasa and in the early 1820s widely considered to be the most beautiful woman in Bogotá.[14]

Overall, while numerous, Bolívar's romantic relationships were fleeting. This was no accident. As his main biographers have observed, the Liberator was too restless and driven to let love stand in the way of his political mission (i.e., the anti-Spanish struggle) or larger quest for fame and glory. His peripatetic habits—he rarely lingered in cities and, when not absorbed in a military operation, was almost always in a hurry to get back to his troops—also made it difficult for an affair to take root and blossom.[15]

Yet, the affair with Sáenz did blossom. It grew at first from mutual attraction. Although existing portraits of her are mostly posthumous and vary widely, memoirs and other accounts of the time agree that Sáenz in her prime was beautiful. They portray her as striking: a woman with lustrous black hair, deep-brown eyes, roses-and-cream complexion, and noticeably curvaceous figure—features bound to appeal to the famously sensual Liberator. Manuela also stood out for her warm, down-to-earth personality, free-spiritedness, and vivaciousness.[16] Indeed, she seems to have loved nothing better than laughter and a good joke, a tendency that helped her avoid taking herself—and perhaps those who disapproved of her—too seriously. "I [tend to] laugh at myself," she once confessed to her husband in an effort to explain the couple's apparent incompatibility, especially the clash she saw between her own sprightliness and Thorne's more somber "English" nature.[17]

Her sense of humor, moreover, could be irreverent. An example of this would appear at a party she would throw in Bogotá several years later that included a special performance by one of her black female servants, Jonathás. An apparently talented mimic, Jonathás left guests guffawing with her impersonation of a monk preaching a Holy Week sermon, as one of Sáenz's friends would recall afterward.[18] Jonathás's mistress also possessed a mischievous playfulness and delighted in the occasional small prank or attention-grabbing gesture. In one incident recalled by a friend with whom she occasionally went horseback riding, she appeared one morning disguised as a man, complete with fake mustache and an officer's uniform; before anyone could recognize her, she took off on her horse, forcing her astonished companions to chase after her and thus confirm her identity.[19]

Beyond her other personal attributes—including the generosity and sense of compassion for which she would become well known—Sáenz's sense of humor and lightheartedness endeared her to her lover. It almost certainly helped distract him from the cares of war and politics as well as from the black moods that would increasingly plague him. As Bolívar once admitted to her, he loved Sáenz less for her "delicious attractions" than for her "delightful temperament" and "enchanting spirit."[20] Years later, in response to one contemporary's criticism of her sometimes-impulsive behavior, he would refer to her simply as "[our] dear madwoman."[21]

Sáenz, for her part, fell passionately in love with the charismatic Liberator. A sign of this is the letter she wrote her husband several years after the start of the affair. As the letter reveals, Thorne by then had learned of the affair and had tried repeatedly to persuade his wife to end it and return to him. Sáenz was determined to resist Thorne's pleas and blandishments. "No, no, no, no, for God's sake man. . . . one thousand times, NO . . . I will not go back to you," she wrote him, adding that she wished he had not "obliged" her to write and, thus, once again, go through the "anguish" of explaining her decision to leave him.[22]

Sáenz's letter also reveals her dissatisfaction with Thorne. One source of this dissatisfaction may have been his physical appearance. While admitting that Thorne was "excellent" and a man of "[many fine] qualities," for example, Sáenz noted that "as a man" he was "[rather] heavy," suggesting that, at least in comparison with the athletic Bolívar, she found him less than attractive. She had grown bored with their marriage, as well. As if trying to spare her husband's feelings, she attributed her boredom less to Thorne himself than to the spouses' mutual incompatibility—including features she associated with her husband's nationality. "A life of monotony is reserved for [those] of your nation," she informed him. Sáenz then hinted at qualities she had found missing in the couple's life together. Although the English excel "at commerce and naval matters," they "lack pleasure in love [and] grace in conversation," she stated, in apparent reference to the reasons behind her dissatisfaction with Thorne as a lover and companion.[23]

Above all, Sáenz's letter to Thorne reveals her strong desire to be with Bolívar. In it she explained that, regardless of the illicitness of her affair with the Venezuelan general, Sáenz was in love with him. Ordinary concerns about "honor" and propriety no longer mattered. Indeed, in response to Thorne's earlier warning about the need to preserve her feminine honor and reputation, Sáenz claimed to "no [longer] care about those social preoccupations that people have invented for [the purpose of] torturing each other." She also expressed confidence in Bolívar's feelings for her. She was now "sure of possessing his heart," she assured her husband. Her mind was made up, in any case. Although the decision to leave her "dear Englishman" had been a hard one, it would be useless for Thorne to try to dissuade her, she stated, explaining that she preferred Bolívar over all others. "Do you [truly] believe that after being this gentleman's [Bolívar's] mistress for seven years . . . I would prefer to be the wife of the Father, Son, and Holy Ghost?" Sáenz asked her spouse with a certain incredulity and sarcasm. "Why, not even the Holy Trinity could make me leave him!" she answered her own question, betraying both her enthusiasm for her lover and her impatience to be free of Thorne.[24]

Sáenz's passion and desire were not enough to keep Bolívar beside her. The Liberator was driven by demons and, above all, by a thirst for fame and glory—a thirst that, in the eyes of some biographers, arose in good part from his secret, longtime admiration of Napoleon. Despite having once embraced the cause of independence out of idealism, the Liberator now pursued it out of pragmatism.

Indeed, the cause had become his path to personal greatness, a means for acquiring the power needed to realize his ambitious state-building projects. These included the Andean Federation, a proposed union of the territories Bolívar had helped free from the Spanish and one that eventually (albeit more in theory than in practice) was to bring together the fledgling republics of Peru, Bolivia, and Gran Colombia.[25]

Such projects also explain Bolívar's ceaseless politico-military strategizing. In the months after his arrival in Quito, for instance, the Liberator devoted himself not only to basic matters of government administration, but also to securing Gran Colombia's claim to the port of Guayaquil, control of which was vital to his larger strategy: ensuring access to Peru. Indeed, Peru was his main objective. There, despite the efforts of San Martín, the anti-Spanish struggle had languished, and there was where Bolívar aspired to lead a campaign that would seal his renown as the independence movement's greatest leader. It was this aspiration (fostered ultimately by grand thoughts of a future federation) that led him to leave Quito for Guayaquil in early July 1822. The Liberator met with San Martín later that month in the port city to discuss the question of Colombian military assistance—assistance needed to fight the more than ten thousand Spanish troops who, from their stronghold in the Peruvian highlands, continued to threaten Lima's new patriot government.[26]

Although the question at the time remained unresolved—San Martín would return to Lima and resign two months later—it would become increasingly urgent. In March 1823, Bolívar responded to a new, more direct request for aid from the Peruvians, this time from the new Peruvian government of President José de la Riva Agüero. He sent a contingent of six thousand Colombian soldiers along with Sucre as his personal emissary. It was not until August 6, 1823, however, after having received several more appeals (these accompanied by invitations to come to Lima personally), that he finally would embark for the fabled former viceroyalty and land of the Incas. Once there, with the consent of an increasingly desperate Peruvian Congress, he would assume supreme command of the country's fractious government and military.[27]

Preoccupied with Peru and related matters, Bolívar seldom had time for his mistress; indeed, he seldom had time to return to Quito, where the latter remained through 1822. Sáenz missed him keenly. In a December 30, 1822, letter written a month after one of Bolívar's rare visits to the city, she addressed her lover as "my incomparable friend" and expressed "despair" over his absence.[28] She also betrayed frustration over the fact that she had spent most of the previous six months without him. Sáenz had seen her lover only once since his departure for Guayaquil in early July: in late October, when Bolívar had rushed back to Quito in response to the news of a new royalist guerilla uprising in the southern Colombian province of Pasto, this time led by Benito Boves. Bolívar's return visit had lasted just long enough for him to gather fresh reinforcements to help his army beat back Boves and squelch the rebellion. He had abandoned the city again toward late November in order to accompany the reinforcements northward as far as Ibarra, a town midway between Quito and the city of Pasto, capital of the troubled province. Sáenz subsequently had heard from him and in late December (a few days before Christmas) learned of his army's victory over the rebels at Yacuanquer, a site just outside the provincial capital. She also had learned of Bolívar's plan to consolidate the victory by proceeding directly to Pasto. She hated this plan or, at least, the thought of Bolívar's being farther away from her. His move to Pasto would put him "more than 70 leagues from here [Quito]," she remarked to him with some annoyance.[29]

Sáenz may well have been expecting to visit Bolívar in Ibarra or to be re-united with him for Christmas in Quito. As things now stood, she would not see him again until his return to the city toward the end of January. She was disappointed, hurt, and angry. "The [army's] victory at Yacuanquer has cost me dearly," she told her lover. Although Bolívar might think her unpatriotic for saying so, she added, she preferred "a victory for herself" over "ten [military] victories" in Pasto.[30]

An anxious, lovesick Sáenz soon found a way to resolve or at least reduce the problem of her and Bolívar's frequent and prolonged separations. Before her return to the Peruvian capital (in or around October 1823), she likely offered to assist the Liberator in some fashion, perhaps as an informant or liaison with Lima's patriot circles. She also apparently persuaded him to let her join his per-manent entourage. By December 1823, Sáenz was a member of Bolívar's staff and had assumed the role of his personal archivist. Such a role was unusual. Beyond the well-known case of her contemporary, Leona Vicario of Mexico (who rode with José María Morelos while administering the finances of his guerilla army), few women at the time occupied positions on the staffs of either the patriot or the royalist armies.[31]

Sáenz's position as archivist had additional implications. In associating her formally with the Colombian army, it signaled not only her commitment to the patriot cause, but her new public political alignment. Sáenz henceforth was to see herself—and would be seen—primarily as a Colombian (rather than a Pe-ruvian) patriot; she was to be identified, furthermore, as a "Bolivarian," a politi-cal affiliation whose significance would not be lost on the opponents of Bolívar around her. Equally important, her archivist's position also entitled her to receive payment for her services. During 1824–1825, for example, Sáenz would receive occasional disbursements from Bolívar's account, this administered by army paymaster José María Romero and, no doubt, vital to her efforts to free herself from her financial dependence on her husband.[32]

Sáenz's staff role had additional benefits. One of these lay in her interactions with Bolívar's personal secretary, young Venezuelan-born Captain Juan José Santana, who frequently sent her official letters and documents—these destined for the archive—by courier. Sáenz soon became friends with Santana. Her regular correspondence with him, in turn, helped her stay in touch with and keep track of her lover. Indeed, thanks to Santana's reporting, she stayed abreast of Bolívar's activities, health, and whereabouts during their separations.[33]

Sáenz also now had license to follow Bolívar. An opportunity to do so presented itself unexpectedly in February 1824. Bolívar was by then on his way back to Lima from Trujillo, where he had recently suppressed a rebellion led by former president José de la Riva Agüero. While he lingered in the coastal town of Pativilca, recovering from a recent bout of illness, disaster struck the Peruvian capital. On February 5, a mutiny broke out among men of the Argentine (Río de la Plata) regiment, a key component of the local patriot garrison.

The mutiny was a reaction against Lima's new patriot authorities, including the wavering leadership of the Marquis of Torre-Tagle, the country's recently elected president and a largely nominal figure. Although Torre-Tagle and his allies initially had welcomed Bolívar to Peru and proclaimed their support for his war against the Spanish—subsequently investing him, moreover, with supreme military authority—they quickly had lost enthusiasm. More important, they had failed to provide for the soldiers on which the patriot war effort now depended. Indeed, for months, they had neglected to pay the garrison its full rations and pay. Leaders of the mutiny thus demanded immediate payment. On February 10, after Torre-Tagle's refusal to accede to their demands, the mutineers freed all Spaniards from local jails and raised the Spanish flag over Callao; they then entered into negotiations with Spanish general José Canterac, paving the way for the Spanish reoccupation of Lima at the end of the month.

Impressed by this chain of events and keenly aware of his army's weaknesses (not the least of which was the fact that it was still vastly outnumbered by the Spanish), Bolívar responded by ordering Colombian troops to evacuate the city.[34] Sáenz formed part of the Colombian evacuation. About a week after the start of the Argentine mutiny, she set out northward for Pativilca accompanied by the mules and armed escort provided her by Colonel Tomás Heres, one of Bolívar's trusted subordinates.[35] She eventually rejoined Bolívar in Trujillo, where, by March, he had established a new general headquarters and launched feverish preparations for what was to be the last and greatest of his campaigns: the Andean Campaign.

Sáenz likely contributed to these preparations in some fashion. Through early April, virtually the entire city of Trujillo became involved in the outfitting and provisioning of an expanded eight thousand–man army, a project for which Bolívar—who had just been named dictator by a desperate Peruvian Congress—demanded the cooperation of all citizens. Like many of Trujillo's upper-class ladies, Sáenz may well have helped with the sewing of soldiers' clothing and uniforms.[36]

She subsequently began trailing Bolívar and the army. Archive in tow, she proceeded from Trujillo to Huamachuco, where, on April 22, 1824, Bolívar had established a new base of operations. He had begun training the army's new recruits and preparing the army as a whole for its anticipated ascent into the Andes. Sáenz then followed her lover to Huaraz, center of a rich agricultural region and the point at which the army began crossing the formidable two hundred kilometer–long Cordillera Blanca. She no doubt caught a glimpse of this crossing. She also visited Bolívar at least once before continuing toward her next destination: the lofty (over six thousand feet) town of Huánuco.

Sáenz's movements by then had assumed a discernible pattern. They included following the Liberator at a distance of at least a day's ride and along a separate route whose location remained a secret; apparently, only she, Bolívar, and Santana and their couriers knew of it. Available sources suggest, moreover, that, as the army moved into enemy territory (passing through villages whose inhabitants harbored royalist sympathies), Sáenz, probably for security reasons, increased her distance from it. An example was her journey to Huánuco. While Bolívar and his general staff took the direct route across the mountains, completing their trip from Huaraz in ten days (June 14–24), Sáenz took a longer, more roundabout route. Noted Bolívar scholar Vicente Lecuna estimates that she traveled some three hundred kilometers in order to reach her destination, passing through the villages of Chiquián, Cajatambo, and Yanahuanca before arriving in Huánuco toward the end of June.[37]

She likely stayed in Huánuco through July, meeting with Bolívar whenever feasible and waiting for the army's three divisions to finish their tortuous climb up Cerro de Pasco, the lofty "knot" (or geologic mass) that divides the northern and southern ranges of the Peruvian Andes. Cerro de Pasco was the starting point for the Andean Campaign proper—where all three divisions were to assemble in early August in preparation for their pursuit of Spanish forces. Since no evidence points to her presence there, Sáenz may have remained in Huánuco through the first week of August. Her exact location during the August 6 Battle of Junín, the army's first confrontation with the Spanish, remains uncertain.

Surviving evidence does show that she ceased to follow the army after this battle. Indeed, instead of continuing toward Peru's southern highlands—where the army would again confront the enemy at the decisive December 9 Battle of Ayacucho—Sáenz began turning back toward the coast and Lima. She settled for a time in the central Andean valley town of Jauja; after months of trekking across the frigid cordillera, she must have delighted in the town's temperate climate. Jauja was just fifty kilometers north of Huancayo, where, on August 13 (having delegated full responsibility for the rest of the Andean Campaign to Sucre), Bolívar reestablished his headquarters. In late October, Sáenz again rendezvoused with him.[38] She later followed her lover back to the Peruvian capital, where he arrived on December 7, and she, shortly thereafter. The couple no doubt rejoiced at the news of the army's victory at Ayacucho.[39]

Although content with her new role as the Liberator's personal archivist, Sáenz was only partially satisfied with her overall situation. While she had found a way to be closer to Bolívar, she began to wonder about the extent of his commitment to her. The previous May, stories had begun circulating about her lover's alleged fling with Manuelita Madroño, a pretty eighteen-year-old native of Huaylas. Sáenz's May 28 letter to Santana hints that she knew or had heard something about the fling. "The general . . . has hardly written me two letters in 19 days," she complained in reference to a lapse in Bolívar's regular correspondence. "Misfortune has befallen me, all things [must] come to an end, [Bolívar] no longer thinks of me," she added, revealing her panic and self-pity. Sáenz then asked Santana for an explanation of Bolívar's epistolary silence. At the same time, she accused Santana of withholding information that, in her view and by virtue of their mutual friendship, he owed her; "you sin by keeping quiet," she stated. Sáenz's letter to Santana also revealed her anguish and, above all, fear of romantic betrayal. "I feel miserable," she confided, adding melodramatically that she was "ready to do something crazy" and "might even die of this [suspected betrayal]."[40]

Sáenz also had to deal with Bolívar's desire to distance himself from her. On April 11, 1825, the Liberator embarked on a long, rather luxurious sultan-style tour of southern Peru and Bolivia (territory just freed from the Spanish) while leaving his mistress behind in Lima; he would not see her again for nine months. A bit over a week later, he wrote her to express doubts about their future. "I see that nothing in the world can unite us under the auspices of innocence and honor," he told her in the letter. He went on to suggest that, despite their love for each other, "duty" and conscience left the couple no choice but to part ways and put an end to their illicit relationship. Sáenz was to "reconcile" with her husband while her lover was to separate himself from the woman "whom I idolize," he stated. "A cruel but just fate [dictates] our mutual separation," he added. "Let us not be guilty any longer," his letter concluded, adding, as if to persuade himself, "no, no, we will not be."[41]

Bolívar seems to have been genuinely troubled by his and Sáenz's ongoing relationship, one that almost certainly had lasted longer than he had imagined or intended. He also apparently had begun to see it as a potential source of dishonor and embarrassment. His concerns found expression in a late November 1825 letter penned to his mistress from the distant Bolivian town of La Plata. "I wish to see you free [of your husband] but, at the same, innocent," he wrote her, the term "innocent" no doubt an allusion to the stigma associated with her adultery. "I cannot stand the idea of being the robber of a heart that was once virtuous and that, because of me, no longer is," he added in a statement whose chivalrous tone scarcely masked the uneasiness behind it. Bolívar seems to have been at a loss to resolve the dilemma of being embroiled in an affair that could no longer be considered merely private and that, instead (due largely to Sáenz's own initiative and persistence), had become open, public, and, in the eyes of at least some contemporaries, scandalous. "I don't know how to reconcile my happiness and your [happiness] with your duty and my [duty]," he admitted. He went on to compare the lovers' affair to an impossible "knot"—one that, he stated, not even "Alexander with his sword" could hope to untangle.[42]

Bolívar's frustration over the affair likely was in part a belated reaction to the protests of Sáenz's husband. Thorne was possessive and "more jealous than a Portuguese," as Sáenz herself once put it.[43] He may have swallowed his pride enough to ask Bolívar to help him obtain the return of his wife, perhaps by appealing to that same sense of "duty and honor" that Bolívar had begun to invoke in recent letters. He may have sought some form of legal recourse. What is certain is that he was loath to give up his wife and, through 1825, continued trying to persuade her to return to him.

Some evidence of this may be gleaned from Bolívar's personal correspondence, including his responses to Sáenz's apparent complaints about her husband. In one such response, Bolívar alluded indirectly to Thorne's effort to reclaim her (an effort that must have been rather heavy-handed) by mentioning "the ill treatment" Sáenz had been suffering "because of me." That effort may have included something drastic such as a threat to have Sáenz sent to a women's prison, or *divorcio,* a not-uncommon strategy employed by husbands seeking to punish a wife for perceived misbehavior. The Liberator's aforementioned letter, in any case, also suggested that his mistress escape her fears, or "dreaded misfortunes," by going to Arequipa to stay with his friends; these "will protect you," he assured her. Perhaps reflecting its author's desire to avoid being drawn into a potentially ugly marital quarrel, the letter's tone is cool and diffident.[44]

Yet, for all his apparent doubt and ambivalence, Bolívar found it hard to renounce his mistress. Even as they appealed to ideals of duty and conscience, his 1825 letters to her simultaneously recalled her beauty and charm along with her love for him — "your divine heart, that heart like no other," as one missive noted.[45] Bolívar also professed his "pure and guilty love" for Sáenz and, in concluding one letter to her, referred to her simply as "Manuela, the beautiful."[46]

Above all, he made clear his wish to hold onto her. Sometime after his early February 1826 return to his official residence in La Magdalena (a suburb of Lima that was now the site of Colombian army headquarters), Bolívar queried his mistress about a proposed trip to London, a trip she apparently had mentioned to him and that, presumably, was an idea of Thorne's. He demanded that she verify it. "My adored one: will you not answer me clearly concerning your terrible trip to London?" he wrote her, worry reflected in his hurried scrawl. "Don't be enigmatic . . . tell me the truth [about it]," he then exhorted. In the next breath, he expressed his "resolute" desire that she not go anywhere, seemingly having forgotten his earlier suggestion that she try to reconcile with Thorne. "Do not go anywhere . . . not even with God Himself," he commanded. Bolívar went on to assure Sáenz that he still cherished and desired her. "I, too, want to see you and see you again; and touch you and smell you and taste you and unite you to me through all the senses," he stated in response to her words to him. "[You are] the only woman [for me]," he added.[47]

For Sáenz, such assurances must have been gratifying. They affirmed her lover's desire for her yet they also marked a change in the couple's relationship. This change could be seen to some extent in Sáenz's move to La Magdalena, where, by 1827, she was living in a home of her own and receiving a five hundred–peso monthly stipend paid by Colombian consul and Bolivarian political agent Cristóbal Armero.[48] The move confirmed Sáenz's importance to her lover as well as the latter's apparent new willingness to acknowledge her in public. It signaled her semiofficial status as a mistress. Now able to consort openly with Bolívar, Sáenz, it appears, was triumphant.

Sáenz's residence near Bolívar's headquarters at La Magdalena also signaled her growing importance as a friend and ally. Sáenz once had described herself to Bolívar as "your best [female] friend."[49] She valued friendship generally, at one point even going as far as to suggest to a correspondent that the bonds of friends were more solid and lasting that the "[fickle] feelings" of lovers.[50] She especially valued the trust and regard of her fellow Bolivarians, that is, those men closest to

her lover. Her steadfast role in the Andean Campaign—including her willingness to fulfill her archivist's duties while tenaciously shadowing the army under
arduous, even dangerous, circumstances—had helped win her that trust and
regard. At the very least, it won her the respect of some of Bolívar's staff officers.
By the time of the Battle of Junín, for example, men such as Colonel Tomás de
Heres and General Antonio José de Sucre had begun to send her occasional well
wishes and greetings.[51]

Sáenz reciprocated. On one occasion in 1825 (while Bolívar was touring Bolivia), she asked Santana to forward her greetings to aides-de-camp Belford
Wilson and José Domingo Espinar as well as "anyone else who may remember me."[52]

She became good friends with Santana as well. Although a Caracas native,
Santana may have reminded Sáenz of her brother José María; the two young officers likely were about the same age. The secretary's extant correspondence with
Sáenz hints that, as a newcomer to Peru, he was rather lonely. No doubt sensing
this, Sáenz reached out to him. Besides confiding her romantic anxieties, she
lavished the secretary with an almost sisterly attention; she once had several
handkerchiefs made for him. She also cultivated Santana and, as his expressions of gratitude and appreciation suggest, must have bestowed on him several
practical favors, including, perhaps, speaking well of him to Bolívar.[53] Sáenz, at
the same time, expected Santana to write her regularly, keeping her informed of
the activities of Bolívar and the army as well as of his own observations. She also
apparently relied on him to forward letters sent her by her remaining relatives
in Quito. When his correspondence lagged or ceased to arrive with its usual
frequency, she chided him. "A timely little scolding is what is needed," she wrote
him once playfully in October 1825, adding that he should not ignore his "best
friend."[54] In sum, by the time of Bolívar's return to Lima, Sáenz not only was a
member of his official personal staff but, through her friendships with Santana
and others, a part of his unofficial inner circle—a group that included both
civilians and officers and that, to a large degree, functioned as a kind of itinerant
family.

Sáenz soon stood out for her personal and political loyalty. An early example
of this was her strict adherence to Bolívar's orders, including his apparent command that she not release any document from the archive without his explicit
go-ahead. Such adherence sometimes brought Sáenz into conflict with senior
army officers. One of these was the no-nonsense Colonel Heres, who, in 1825,
after the renewal of Bolívar's tenure as president of Peru (a reward for his victory
over the Spaniards), had been appointed to serve as minister of war.[55] Sáenz's
conflict with Heres arose when she refused to release a letter he had requested

of her. Her refusal ultimately moved him to write his superior and explain his need for the letter as well as to request that Sáenz be told to let him borrow it; he asked, too, that she be ordered to furnish him with any other letters he might see fit to borrow in the near future.[56]

Sáenz's loyalty also showed itself in the role she began to assume the following year at La Magdalena. This role likely included receiving some of the guests and petitioners (including political refugees from neighboring countries) who streamed in to visit Bolívar, then working to consolidate his position as Peru's and South America's single most powerful leader. It may well have included participating in the many fancy dinners and receptions held at Bolívar's official villa. Sáenz also may have met in private with certain visitors, especially those seeking some sort of special assistance or favor; it was during this time that she likely began to act as an advocate for or intercessor on behalf of refugees and other distressed individuals.[57] Available evidence suggests, moreover, that, while at La Magdalena, Sáenz began looking after the needs of Bolívar's men, especially those soldiers and junior officers who were ill or bereft of resources. It shows her efforts to intercede with Bolívar on behalf of individuals seeking his official pardon or clemency, efforts for which she eventually would become well known.[58]

Sáenz's loyalty to her lover became most evident in her willingness to stand up to his rivals and opponents. The latter had emerged largely in response to the extraordinary power Bolívar had wielded since February 1824, when, alarmed at the prospect of an imminent Spanish reconquest, Peru's Congress had first authorized him to act as dictator—hoping that he would defeat the Spanish and salvage their country's precarious independence. A year later, grateful for Bolívar's services, Congress had reauthorized the dictatorship while postponing its plans for new elections. By the middle of 1826, however, increasing numbers of Peruvians had grown tired of the dictatorship. Creole elites in particular had come to resent Bolívar's harsh, seemingly anti-Peruvian, policies. A key example of these, in their eyes, was his decision to allow the April execution of José Terón and Juan Félix de Berindoaga, two former high-ranking Peruvian government officials whom his supporters had charged with treason.

Members of the country's armed forces harbored similar nativist-type grievances, disgruntled as they were by practices that gave preference to foreign, especially Gran Colombian–born, soldiers and officers. Peruvian leaders in general also distrusted Bolívar's intentions; many suspected that his long-range goal was to keep their country under the boot of its recent liberators, the (in their eyes) insufferably arrogant Colombians.[59]

Bolívar's behavior helped fuel Peruvian resentment. For example, he tried to force Peruvians to accept the constitution he had drafted in 1825 for the new

Republic of Bolivia. This document embodied the most conservative and authoritarian aspects of Bolívar's political thinking. It included a highly restrictive, indirect form of suffrage (one elector for every one hundred citizens); a three-chamber legislature composed of tribunes, senators, and censors (the latter elected for life and responsible for the nation's moral uplift); and, above all, a lifetime (if relatively nominal) presidency.[60]

Although designed to reconcile freedom with order by balancing new republican and democratic principles of government with older hierarchical ones— or, in effect, federalist notions with centralist ones—the Bolivian Constitution alarmed its author's critics. While the Liberator saw it as an essential stepping-stone to a strong, stable postindependence political order (one to be embodied ultimately in his cherished Andean Federation), critics saw it more as an elaborate scheme for perpetuating him and his friends in power. Their view seemed justified by Bolívar's attempts to silence them and by his tendency to manipulate the country's fledgling democratic procedures. In February and March 1826, for example, as Peruvians were electing delegates to a long-anticipated constitutional convention, Bolívar sought to disqualify those delegates who opposed him or his ideas. He and his allies thereafter took the question of constitutional reform out of the hands of the Congress altogether by persuading—indeed, pressuring—a majority of its members to adjourn the body and refer the issue to the electoral colleges. Based in the provinces, the latter proved compliant with Bolívar's wishes. Indeed, in August, Peruvian electors officially adopted the Bolivian Constitution and elected the Liberator as lifetime president. In November, some two months after Bolívar had left on an emergency return trip to Gran Colombia, faithful Bolivarians shepherded the new charter through its formal ratification—a development that would further anger opponents and, ultimately, help galvanize them.[61]

Manuela Sáenz was aware of Bolívar's ideas and projects. She knew of his plan for an Andean Federation and of some of the practical challenges related to it—the need to revive the once-prosperous silver-mining industry centered in Potosí, for example. She also seems to have supported it unquestioningly.[62] Such support, however, was more personal than ideological. As was the case for many, perhaps most, of the Liberator's close friends and allies, it sprang more from love and admiration for Bolívar than from devotion to any particular agenda or set of notions.

Sáenz's support sprang, too, from a strong desire to see her love reciprocated. In a letter sent to him soon after his hurried September 3, 1826, departure from Lima en route to Gran Colombia, Sáenz apparently asked her lover to promise that he loved "no one else" but her. The ever-gallant Bolívar obliged. "The altar you inhabit will not be profaned by any other idol or image," he assured her in his response that October, adding, "you have made me an idolater . . . of Manuela," and "believe me: I love you." Bolívar also urged Sáenz not to succumb to despair in his absence. "Don't kill yourself [but instead] live for me and for you," he stated in response to her apparent intimations of suicide. "[You must live] to console the unfortunate as well as your lover."[63]

While Sáenz no doubt welcomed Bolívar's soothing words, she could not have been consoled by his opponents' increasingly visible machinations. Antigovernment plots and conspiracies had been simmering throughout Peru that year, since at least early July. On July 6, 1826, for example, there had been an uprising of two Hussar squadrons based in Huancayo. It ultimately was suppressed by Bolivian-born general Andrés de Santa Cruz, one of Bolívar's key regional allies. Another conspiracy had reared its head in Lima. It had involved both Argentine and Peruvian officers as well as Peruvian civilians opposed to Bolívar's dictatorship. This one, too, had been discovered in time and suppressed; the conspirators had been arrested and put on trial, with many later sent into exile.[64]

A new, ultimately more threatening, conspiracy arose the following January. Hatched by several Peruvian-born army officers in alliance with disgruntled Colombian colonel José Bustamante, it sought to exploit the growing discontent within the Colombian army's vital Third Division, a unit Bolívar had left behind in order to guarantee order during his absence from Lima. This discontent stemmed, in part, from rank-and-file resentment of the harsh discipline imposed by the division's chief commander, Venezuelan-born general Jacinto Lara. It also stemmed from the effects of anti-Bolivarian propaganda sown by Bustamante and his co-conspirators. Such propaganda included rumors suggesting that Bolívar had lost prestige and power and denunciations of his efforts to replace the original Peruvian and Colombian constitutions with the authoritarian Bolivian charter. It included the allegation that various battalions were to be shipped off to Havana (still a Spanish-controlled enclave) as punishment for supposed misbehavior—an idea that alarmed ordinary soldiers and caused widespread fear and indignation.[65]

The conspiracy bore fruit in late January. On the evening of January 25, 1827, soldiers of the Third Division (four battalions and a cavalry squadron) rose up against their senior commanding officers. On orders from Bustamante and his accomplices, they arrested some eighteen or so officers, including Generals Lara and Arthur Sandes, and later forced them to board a ship described by the local British consul as "one of the worst" in Callao's harbor. They then sent them to the distant Colombian port city of Buenaventura. On January 26, the mutineers also seized control of the Palace and Plaza de Armas in Lima. Among other things, they expected authorities to pay the back wages owed them along with the bonus that one of their superiors, General Aparicio, had promised them as a reward for the uprising.

More important (and largely unwittingly), the Third Division uprising paved the way for the conspirators' civilian allies. These included powerful local opponents of Bolívar who, over the next few days, proceeded to seize the reins of power in Lima. Under the auspices of a new government led by General Santa Cruz, they suspended the hated Bolivian Constitution, restored the original 1823 Peruvian charter, and announced plans for a new Congress to meet within three months—all measures quickly endorsed by Lima's city council and ratified on January 27 by a local popular assembly. Less than two months later, having acceded to the mutineers' demands, the country's new officials also arranged for Bustamante and about two thousand Colombian troops to leave Peru and return by ship to their native country.[66]

Manuela Sáenz was quick to respond to the Third Division uprising. Having remained at La Magdalena to help look after Bolívar's affairs, she likely knew of the rank-and-file grievances that lay behind it, including food shortages and inadequate wages, which had plagued the troops in recent months, making them vulnerable to the appeals of the conspirators. Sáenz worked to limit the uprising's impact and potential for damage. She tried to visit some of the arrested officers and to protect Bolívar's archive, a goal she apparently achieved, in part by arranging to smuggle out various documents.[67]

She also tried to reverse the results of the uprising. Soon after the events of January 25, according to one observer, Sáenz contacted the three battalions that had remained at La Magdalena and, armed and dressed in a colonel-style uniform, personally exhorted them to remain true to the Liberator. She then began distributing money among sergeants and corporals in the hope of persuading them to resist the rebellion and join the resistance movement (or counter-rebellion) that she and others had organized. She had some success, thanks to help she reportedly received from a local priest friend and several junior officers who had rallied behind her.[68]

Sáenz's actions alarmed the new Peruvian authorities, however. Toward midnight on February 7, these authorities sent troops to detain her at her home in La Magdalena. The troops apparently barged into Sáenz's house and, on orders from their commanding officer, tried to force her to depart for Lima immediately. Sáenz pleaded illness and persuaded the men to let her stay until the next morning—although, as she would complain later, she had to spend the rest of the night with a junior officer watching her inside her bedroom. On February 8, the soldiers escorted her to Lima and confined her at the women's prison belonging to the convent of Las Nazarenas. For the next several months, Bolívar's mistress was, in effect, a government prisoner.[69]

Sáenz refused to accept her fate quietly. She protested the treatment she had received at the hands of Peruvian authorities and, in a formal letter of complaint to Consul Cristóbal Armero, highlighted the government's apparent refusal to explain the reasons for her February 7 arrest and imprisonment. She was "neither a prisoner of war nor a criminal," she noted indignantly, going on to decry the "inquisitorial" manner in which, she alleged, government agents had detained and interrogated her.[70]

Sáenz also asked the consul to assure her right to know what if any official charges had been made against her. She reminded him of her status as a "Colombian" and thus, as a citizen entitled to be treated with the "consideration" that, under "the [universal] law of nations," was due all citizens arrested for real or alleged crimes—even those arrested within the Peruvian republic. She also invoked the protection of Article 117 of the recently restored 1823 Peruvian Constitution with its requirement that all suspects be told of the reason for their arrest within twenty-four hours or else be set free. "I don't know if there is a basis for me to be tried as a Peruvian but, if there is, [I ask] that I be convicted as one," she stated wryly.[71]

Sáenz concluded her letter by speculating on the reasons for the government's apparent "oversight" of the twenty-four-hour requirement, hinting that an anti-Colombian bias might explain it. Her only "crime," she asserted, had been to "belong to a republic that has done much good for that of Peru." She then urged Armero to speak on her behalf with Peru's new interim president, General Santa Cruz, and thus obtain her "vindication."[72] Thanks to this and other appeals made to friends and acquaintances in Lima (and in violation of the government's apparent order for her to remain incommunicado), the persistent woman eventually won her release from Las Nazarenas; by March 23, she was free.[73]

Sáenz's firm insistence on her rights had aroused the hostility of Lima's authorities. It especially provoked the wrath of the minister of foreign relations, Manuel Lorenzo Vidaurre, one of the fiercest of Bolívar's Peruvian critics and opponents. Apparently alluding to Sáenz's determined effort to obtain justice— and perhaps also to incite public opinion against his government—Vidaurre characterized her actions as "scandalous" and an "insult" to "the public's honor and morals." On or around April 9, he summoned Armero and threatened reprisals if the latter did not see to it that Sáenz left the country within twenty-four hours. Armero, for his part, must have persuaded his client to take the threat seriously.

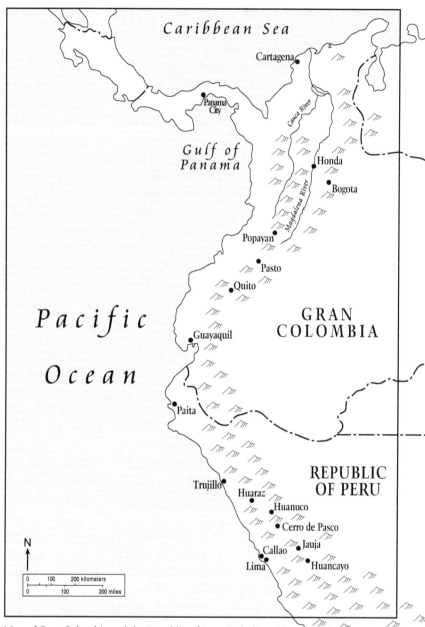

Map of Gran Colombia and the Republic of Peru, including cities Saenz lived in or traveled through from 1822 to 1830. Drawn by the University of Alabama Cartographic Research Lab, Tuscaloosa.

On April 11, Sáenz boarded a ship bound for Guayaquil, joining General José María Córdoba, some 10 other Colombian officers, and 130 convalescing soldiers—all of whom also had been asked to leave the country.[74] She had come to be known by then as the Libertadora. In the words of an observer who referred to her as such that same year, she was "a handsome and very singular woman, . . . [who was] generous in the extreme to the officers and soldiers to the last dollar in her purse and . . . ready to nurse [the sick or wounded] with the most zealous humanity."[75] Sáenz thus had gained a new public identity, one that was to evolve and to characterize her and, ultimately, to encourage her political activism.

THREE

Colombian Crucible, 1827–1830

STILL SMARTING FROM the treatment she had received at the hands of Lima's authorities, Manuela Sáenz landed in Guayaquil toward the end of April 1827. From there, she made her way back to Quito.[1] She also waited impatiently for news of Bolívar. The Liberator had hardly written her since his arrival in Bogotá the previous November and subsequent emergency trip to Venezuela. Sáenz was hurt by his silence. In a brief note to her lover, she complained of being ill in bed with a "headache" and "very angry." "Does it cost you so much to write me?" she then asked in frustration. She went on to suggest that Bolívar's epistolary neglect was the inevitable result of their long separation and a sign, above all, that his "few" feelings for her had cooled. "How true it is that long absences kill love," she told him. Her own love for him had endured, she added, noting, "I have conserved my passion for you in order to conserve my peace and happiness."[2]

Sáenz then responded to Bolívar's request—as conveyed via his personal emissary, General Arthur Sandes—that she rejoin him. She planned to leave for Bogotá on the first of December, she told her lover, adding, "I am going because you call me." "You will not tell me to return to Quito afterward," she warned him. Declaring that she "would rather die than be taken for shameless," Sáenz must have remembered well her lover's past ambivalence toward her and misgivings about their relationship.³ She was determined this time not to be brushed aside.

Nature offered an omen of the challenges that awaited her. On November 15, 1827, some two weeks before the anticipated start of her journey, an earthquake hit New Granada. The quake rattled cities, towns, and villages; it severely damaged several churches and houses in Bogotá.⁴ Sáenz nevertheless proceeded with her plans to leave in December, heading northward to Pasto, her first destination.

Long a royalist redoubt, the Pasto Province as a whole finally had been conquered—indeed, bludgeoned into submission—by Bolívar's army. Its surviving inhabitants no doubt still burned with the memory of the cruelties they had endured, and it is unlikely they would have been particularly pleased to learn of Bolívar's mistress among them. Sáenz must have been mindful of this and may well have chosen to travel in disguise. She was in the city of Pasto itself, in any case, by the fifth of January.⁵

She then proceeded to Popayán, capital of New Granada's vast, wealthy Cauca Province (later a department), after first having taken the precaution of writing to Colonel Tomás Cipriano de Mosquera, the province's top civil and military authority. Explaining that she did not know whom else to turn to, Sáenz had asked Mosquera for help in procuring a fresh team of mules. She needed the animals, she had told him, in order to proceed with the next leg of her journey—a trek across the rugged central prong of the Colombian Andes to La Plata, a village on the cordillera's eastern side.⁶ From La Plata, she apparently planned to reach the Magdalena River and continue her journey northward to Honda, gateway to the Colombian capital, via raft, or *champán*. Her request for fourteen mules—"eight for baggage and six for riding"—suggests the size of her entourage. The group likely included several servants (most of whom, like Jonathás, had followed her from Lima) along with at least one or two guards. Sáenz's letter to Mosquera also included a request that the latter help her find adequate lodging in Popayán or, in her words, a "separate house" in which she and her companions could rest during their brief stay. Sáenz likely reached Bogotá around the first week of February.⁷

Perched on the edge of an inter-Andean basin some 8,660 feet above sea level, Bogotá was guarded by the mountains of Monserrate and Guadalupe—two dark sentinels perpetually wreathed in clouds. It had been a viceregal capital just nine years earlier and, despite the collapse of Spanish authority, remained the seat of an archbishopric. It lacked the style and luxury of Lima, however. Indeed, in contrast to the latter's balconied elegance, Bogotá was plain and austere. Most of its houses were simple one-story structures, their low height and thick walls (of bricklike tapia or adobe) designed to reduce the impact of earthquakes, their heavy wooden shutters perfect for shutting out the cold night air; glass windows were still rare. There were few two-storied residences. Those that existed tended to be clustered along the Calle Real, Bogotá's main commercial district, or located here and there on a few streets close to the main plaza.[8] Sáenz eventually would settle in a rather plain two-story house on San Carlos Street (today Calle 10). The house's central location—a stone's throw away from the Presidential Palace—would serve as a symbol of her privileged position.[9]

Although larger and decorated with government seals, Bogotá's public buildings were scarcely more impressive than its private ones. Housing the cabildo, or city council, Gran Colombia's Congress, the office of the president, the national library, and the botanical garden, they resembled ordinary residences, plain and solid. Bogotá, nevertheless, had its amenities. It boasted fine streets paved with stone, a broad central plaza (site of its weekly market as well as public events), six monasteries, four convents, a theatre, and a small museum. It possessed numerous houses of worship, some quite impressive in their adornments, including the cathedral and churches belonging to the various convents (Franciscan, Dominican, Augustinian). It brimmed with chapels, or *capillas,* including the two perched on the mountains above the city.[10]

This city of some twenty-eight thousand inhabitants also was the heart of a grand, noisy experiment in self-government. Since their political independence in 1821, its people had begun to mix old colonial-era habits with new political practices, including elements of an incipient liberal-republican civic culture. They had begun to participate in what Víctor Uribe has described as "an expanded public sphere"—a realm mediating between the state, on the one hand, and the family and society, on the other, and marked by the growth of a free press, new civic organizations, and competitive electoral politics.[11]

One example of this sphere lay in the numerous informal gatherings at which residents could swap political ideas along with news and gossip. Whereas in the past *tertulias* typically had taken place in the privacy of someone's home, they now increasingly took place in more public venues, such as the store of a friend or acquaintance. By 1828, the Fonda de las Paisanas, a shop, or bodega, run by the local Torres sisters, had become an especially popular site for them.[12] By then, too, residents of Bogotá (Bogotanos) had gotten into the habit of chewing over opinions expressed in local pamphlets and newspapers—the production of which recently had soared. They had grown addicted to all sorts of news and publications. According to one contemporary observer, they enthusiastically followed each new round of *papeluchos,* that is, broadsides (usually speeches, essays, or satirical poems) that appeared frequently around the city on the walls of public buildings and regularly on Sundays. They also had grown accustomed to the writings of a new breed of opinion maker—lawyer-journalists who, like Vicente Azuero, founder and editor of *El Conductor,* were fierce champions of freedom of the press and the self-appointed guardians of republican liberty.[13]

Yet another example of the city's budding public sphere and civic culture was its participation in the recent nationwide elections for deputies to the forthcoming constitutional convention. Destined to take place in early April at the town of Ocaña (a bit over a week's journey north of the capital), the convention was to consider reforms to Gran Colombia's Constitution, that is, the Constitution of Cucutá (1821). It was to serve, too, as a referendum on Bolívar's political ideas. It also was to become a forum for the dispute that had arisen by then between Bolívar and his New Granadan opponents.

This dispute was, in part, ideological. Bolívar had grown skeptical of republicanism as a blueprint for government in Spanish America. Even in the early days of his career, he had questioned the relevance of republican institutions to a society still steeped in, as he once put it, patterns of "ignorance, tyranny, and vice" inherited from the Spanish colonial era. He had doubted that Spanish Americans were ready for such institutions, noting that they did not share the same cultural traits and traditions of the nation—the United States—that so often served as a model for them.[14] His skepticism came partly from practical experience. Having witnessed the disasters associated with the first Venezuelan republic of 1811, Bolívar had concluded that a strong centralist (as opposed to federalist) regime was vital; without it, he now believed, there could be no peace and order, no strength or national unity.

Bolívar's views on government also reflected his admiration for Great Britain and its constitutional monarchy—a form of government that offered a balance between competing claims of order and liberty and to which could be attributed that nation's remarkable strength and stability. It was this British example that he wished the fragile young Spanish American nations to emulate. As early as the time of his famous "Jamaica Letter" (1815), for example, Bolívar had proposed the adoption of a hereditary Senate and lifetime presidency, the former to function much as the British House of Lords, the latter to serve as a stand-in for the monarchy (technically forbidden within a republic). He saw the lifetime presidency as especially important and, indeed, essential to the nation's unity. Such an institution would serve, in his words, as "the sun which, fixed in its orbit, imparts life to the universe" and, within a republican or "nonhierarchical" political system, as a much-needed "fixed point . . . about which leaders and citizens, men and affairs can revolve."[15]

    As Bolívar had noted in the preface to his 1826 Bolivian Constitution, more-
over, the practice of allowing the president to appoint a vice president to succeed him would allow the nation to avoid elections—the "scourge of republics"
and, in Bolivar's view, a mechanism for "anarchy . . . handmaiden of tyranny
[and] the most imminent and terrible peril of popular government."[16] It was
for just such reasons that the Liberator now sought to have the Bolivian charter
adopted by the countries he and his army had recently freed from the Spanish.
    Yet, Bolívar's ideas alarmed liberals and republicans. They especially alarmed
those in Bogotá, where, since 1826, lawyer-journalists and politicians like Vicente
Azuero had voiced opposition to the Bolivian charter and, especially, to Bolívar's
own increasingly obvious efforts to have it replace the country's existing Constitution. Azuero and his colleagues also had lashed out at the charter's provision
for a lifetime presidency. They saw this provision as little more than a prescrip-
tion for a new kind of monarchy, a threat to civil liberties, and, above all, perhaps, proof of Bolívar's own growing "Caesarist" tendencies. They had begun
proposing their own ideas for constitutional reform, moreover. By 1828, these
included a proposal for greater restrictions on the country's existing executive
and for reorganizing the republic along more liberal, federalist principles.[17]
    The growing feud between Bolívar and his New Granadan opponents in-
volved more than ideology, however; it also reflected a basic clash of interests.
Just as the Liberator sought to realize his ambitious agenda—one that, coin-
cidentally, would enhance his power and authority—his adversaries, largely
young, upwardly mobile lawyer-bureaucrats of provincial elite origin, had
their own aspirations. They hoped to safeguard their recent access to government positions and to the honor and status traditionally associated with those
positions—a benefit that had accrued to them in their roles as the new republic's magistrates and administrators. They feared such access was to be deprived
them by the nation's powerful (and largely Venezuelan-staffed) military.[18]
    The lawyer-bureaucrats' fears were not without basis. Indeed, they were fed
by Bolívar's tendency to appoint favorite military officers to high government
posts, a tendency that had grown since his return from Peru. They were accompanied by worries over the extent of Bolívar's power. The president, after all,
wielded vast influence, thanks less to the nature of his office than to his continued control of the Colombian army and his personal prestige as the Liberator.
He also had begun to drift toward dictatorship.
    This drift could be seen in his response to the April 1826 Páez rebellion in
Venezuela. The rebellion had begun when one of Bolívar's old comrades-in-
arms, the rough-hewn General José Antonio Páez (after Bolívar, the most powerful man in the country), had refused to obey an order to come to the capital to

answer criminal charges, including allegations that he had abused the rights of local civilians. Páez's defiance had become a cause célèbre among Venezuelans tired of submitting to distant authorities in Bogotá and inclined to favor separation from Gran Colombia. It had provoked a standoff with those authorities and, above all, a crisis that threatened the nation's unity.[19]

Although Bolívar returned from Peru to resolve the crisis, he insisted on resolving it in his own highly individual manner. He, at the same time, revealed his penchant for dictatorship. Even before his return to Bogotá, for example, his closest and most faithful (and most servile) followers—army officers quick to discern the true will of their leader—had begun publicly calling on him to assume special, or "supreme," powers. Bolívar had privately suggested dictatorship as the only way to end the Venezuelan crisis as well as the country's various other problems; "dictatorship composes everything," he had told Vice President Francisco de Paula Santander while on his way back to the Gran Colombian capital.[20]

Seeing the unpopularity of this idea among Santander and his allies, however, Bolívar backtracked momentarily. After arriving in Bogotá in late November, he assured New Granadans of his intention to respect the country's existing laws and Constitution. Yet, he also demanded a renewal of the extraordinary presidential powers that, under the auspices of article 128 of the Constitution, he had exercised previously. Bolívar then went to Venezuela and, in early January 1827, struck a special deal with Páez and his followers. In exchange for a promise to lay down their arms, the latter were granted a general amnesty; in exchange for Páez's vow of personal loyalty, moreover, the rebel chieftain was recognized as his country's supreme leader.[21]

Bolívar's handling of the Páez rebellion outraged observers in Bogotá. Having expected the rebels to be put in their place, many of these viewed the general amnesty as both arbitrary and illegal. They also viewed it as deeply unfair to those who had stood up for the Constitution. Santander and his allies (the Santanderistas), in particular, saw it as a betrayal. Already wary of Bolívar's motivations, one such ally, Vicente Azuero, saw Bolívar's public pardoning of Páez as evidence of his intention to "subvert" the republic and rule, in effect, as a dictator. Before the end of the year, Azuero (and his fellow Santanderistas) began publicly referring to the Liberator as a "tyrant."[22]

The Páez incident highlighted another vital aspect of Bolívar's feud with his opponents: his growing antagonism toward and personal rivalry with Santander, who, starting in 1826, had emerged as the opposition's ringleader. What led to this rivalry? Part of it stemmed from the breakdown of the men's feelings of mutual trust and friendship, feelings that had developed during their days as wartime allies. Most of it stemmed from the effect of their accumulated political differences, including divergent attitudes toward the challenges they had come to face since independence. A native New Granadan, Santander had developed a distinctly national (and New Granadan) perspective—a product of his role, since 1821, as Gran Colombia's acting chief executive—which contrasted with Bolívar's more internationalist (and pan–Spanish American) one.

An early example was Santander's divergence from Bolívar on the issue of Colombian involvement in Peru's struggle for independence. Whereas the Liberator had deemed that involvement to be of the utmost importance, essential not only to Peruvian freedom but also to the success of patriots throughout the continent, his vice president had seen it mainly as a necessary evil—a costly diversion of the nation's scarce resources.

Santander thus had supported Bolívar's Andean Campaign with a certain ambivalence and reluctance. He also feared the implications of Bolívar's ever-unfolding ambitions and projects. While he had had rather little to say about the proposed Andean Federation, he was, at best, wary of the Bolivian Constitution. Although avoiding direct criticism of the latter, Santander had expressed reservations—about its provision for a lifetime presidency, in particular—in some of his private letters to its author. After 1825, he also began quietly endorsing the local newspaper campaign against it led by his friends Francisco Soto and Vicente Azuero.[23] Like these men (founders of the future Liberal Party), the vice president was disturbed by Bolívar's deepening reliance on the military and increasingly open drift toward dictatorship.

Above all, Santander resented Bolívar's effort to undermine him. Bolívar in recent years had grown sharply critical of his vice president, including his handling of the controversial 1824 British loan and support for reforms the Liberator disagreed with. He also had weakened Santander's (as well as Congress's) authority. As noted earlier, his unorthodox response to the Páez rebellion included a barely disguised appeasement of the rebel leader—a tactic designed to win over the latter and, as Salvador de Madariaga has suggested, turn him into an ally against the "republic of lawyers."[24]

The appeasement stung Santander personally, bruising his pride and sense of vice-presidential dignity. He reacted to it by doing nothing to restrain his allies' vociferous criticism of the Páez amnesty; indeed, he had joined in the criticism through anonymous newspaper editorials. Santander also began to work against Bolívar openly. In March 1827, for example (while the Liberator was still in Venezuela), he and his supporters publicly celebrated the news of the Third Division's mutiny in Lima. He then authorized Bustamante's promotion to the rank of colonel.

Angered by this clear sign of support for his opponents, Bolívar broke off all personal correspondence with the vice president. By 1828, he had ceased communicating with the latter and had begun to view him as an enemy and archrival.[25]

The two leaders' growing mutual antagonism contributed, in turn, to an escalating and increasingly bitter partisan rivalry: a contest between Santanderistas and Bolivarians. This contest was sharpened by the effect of the elections for deputies to the Ocaña Convention in late 1827. In addition to formally pitting the two factions against each other for the first time, the elections gave the Santanderistas a significant political lead—their candidates won more votes than those of the Bolivarians, with Santander himself being elected as a deputy for six provinces (Bogotá, Antioquia, Tunja, Pamplona, Casanare, and Neiva).[26] Partisan rivalry also manifested itself in the editorials of local newspapers and resulted in the so-called paper war, including exchanges between rival periodicals such as the Bolivarians' *El Amigo del País* and the Santanderistas' *El Conductor.*

It had begun to manifest itself, too, in occasional street violence. In an incident that occurred the first week of March 1828, infuriated by continued press attacks on Bolívar and the military, one Colonel Ignacio Luque took it on himself to teach opposition journalists a "lesson" by seizing and publicly burning all available issues of *El Zurriago*, a local anti-Bolivarian newspaper. *El Zurriago*'s editors rebounded quickly and, by March 9, were triumphantly brandishing a replacement newspaper (*El Incombustible*—The Unburnable). Luque and other officers would continue to harass members of the Santanderista press, whose writings they perceived as scurrilous and intolerable.[27] Both factions also turned their attention to the Ocaña Convention, an event that was to become the focus of intense partisan jockeying.

Manuela Sáenz, for her part, found it hard to ignore this rivalry. She had had precious little time to spend with her lover since her arrival. In mid-March, Bolívar again left Bogotá while his mistress stayed behind at his private residence: a country home (*quinta*) on the city's outskirts. Preoccupied with the start of the Ocaña Convention's proceedings and wishing to be in close touch with his supporters among the Convention delegates, he settled in early April in the northern Santanderean city of Bucaramanga. Sáenz wrote regularly, doing her best to empathize with his situation. In late March, for example, she congratulated him on the collapse of the uprising in Cartagena, led earlier that month by Admiral José Padilla, one of the Colombian military's few mulatto officers and a known Santander sympathizer. She also ground her teeth over the growing influence of Bolívar's archrival, whom she suspected of being behind the uprising and for whom she shared her lover's antagonism and suspicion. "Santander has done it again, as if what he already has done were not enough to warrant our shooting him," she wrote the Liberator, no doubt echoing his own feelings.[28]

Indeed, Sáenz made no effort to hide her hostility toward Bolívar's opponents. In the same letter, she characterized Páez, Padilla, and the vice president in one breath as "wicked men." "God grant that [they] . . . die," she added. She then hinted at her approval of Bolívar's recent decision to deal firmly with them. This decision was reflected in a February 20 decree calling for all persons accused of treason or conspiracy to be arrested and tried summarily—and, if found guilty, to be put to death immediately. It would be "a great day for Colombia" the day the aforementioned "vile" men should die, Sáenz told Bolívar, apparently with the February decree in mind. Such deaths, she continued, would be of benefit to—and, indeed, a "humane" act toward— "millions" of Colombian citizens.[29]

She also sought to advise her lover. This included offering her opinion of individuals whom she thought likely to support him and his followers. One such individual was a Señor Torres, whom Sáenz apparently met soon after her arrival in Bogotá. "I believe it my duty to tell you that this Sr. Torres is very worthy [honrado] and a good friend of ours," she told her lover.[30] While it is unclear to what extent Bolívar was influenced by such statements, it is clear that he listened to them; as will be seen, he sometimes acted on them as well.[31] By the time of the Ocaña Convention, in short, Sáenz had become one of the Liberator's advisors and confidantes.

She also acted as a link between him and various scattered friends and supporters. These included old friends in Lima such as Cayetano Freyre. Freyre had kept Bolívar informed of political developments in Peru since the Liberator's 1826 departure from that city. He had kept in touch with Sáenz as well and occasionally sent her newspaper clippings so that she could share these with her lover. Another friend with whom she stayed in contact was a rather mysterious "Aguirre"—most likely Colonel Vicente Aguirre of Quito, on whom Bolívar seems to have relied as both an ally and an informant.[32]

Sáenz, likewise, continued her habit of interceding on behalf of individuals who approached her with requests for assistance or favors. She was careful about endorsing such requests, however. In the case of a petition she apparently received from the aforementioned Señor Torres and forwarded to Bolívar (the exact nature of which remains uncertain), she was almost apologetic—reminding her lover that she had "never [before] spoken to him about anything more than [army] deserters or those condemned to death." "If you have pardoned them, I have thanked you quietly within my heart [and] if you have not pardoned them,

I have not held it against you," she told him in alluding to past seekers of his clemency. "I know full well what I can do for a friend and that, certainly, is not compromise the man I most idolize," she added.³³ Sáenz's allusion to having enclosed "two letters from Quito" in her March 28 missive to Bolívar suggests that she also routinely forwarded correspondence from residents of her native city. Among these residents was General Juan José Flores, Bolívar's ambitious young Venezuelan-born point man in the region and a man with whom the Libertadora corresponded regularly.³⁴

More important, Sáenz came to know—and ultimately collaborate with— her lover's main followers: the Bolivarians. These included civilian natives of New Granada, many of them well-to-do landowners or representatives of some of the country's oldest, wealthiest, and most respectable families—the aristocratic Mosqueras, Arboledas, and Arroyos of Popayán, for instance, as well as leading clans of Bogotá (e.g., the París family), Cartagena, and the gold-rich western New Granadan province of Antioquia (home of wealthy merchant-capitalists such as Manuel Vélez and Juan de Dios Aranzazu). Such families and individuals had supported Bolívar during the war for independence and now looked to him to reestablish postindependence peace and stability. They were joined by members of New Granada's clergy, especially the influential religious orders (the Franciscans, Dominicans, and Augustinians), long responsible for education. These orders had deeply resented the mild anticlerical and secularizing reforms enacted under the auspices of Santander and been cheered by Bolívar's recent inclination to overturn them. In March, Bolívar had catered to them by prohibiting the controversial writings of English liberal philosopher (and father of utilitarianism) Jeremy Bentham in the nation's secondary schools and universities.

The Bolivarians also included members of the Colombian army. Indeed, it was here that the Liberator found his most fervent followers. Crucial among these were a number of intensely loyal officers of Venezuelan origin, including Generals Juan José Flores, Carlos Soublette, Mariano Montilla, Rafael Urdaneta, and Antonio José de Sucre. Also crucial was the small cluster of British- and Irish-born officers who, like Lieutenant Colonels William Ferguson and Belford H. Wilson and the ubiquitous and indispensable Colonel Daniel Florencio O'Leary, had been incorporated into Bolívar's personal staff and stood out for their zeal and efficiency.³⁵

In June, the Bolivarians seized the momentum in the partisan rivalry. The Ocaña Convention had gone poorly for them, partly because of the superior oratorical and political skills of the Santanderista deputies (including Santander himself) and, also, because of the stalemate that, by May, had developed between the two sets of rivals. Indeed, the two had failed to agree on the crucial issue of constitutional reform; all cooperation between them had broken down when the bipartisan commission appointed to draft a revised constitution had ceased to function. Bolivarian and Santanderista deputies then had resorted to presenting their own constitutional reform projects. When the Santanderista project looked likely to win the day, however, the Bolivarian deputies (José María del Castillo y Rada and others) began boycotting the meetings—a reflection of their leader's growing impatience and disillusionment. On June 9, with Bolívar's endorsement, they abandoned the convention altogether, leaving it without a quorum and thus forcing it to dissolve.

The convention's dissolution allowed Bolívar's military followers to declare the nation "in crisis" and to call on the Liberator to "save" it. Colonel Pedro Alcántara Herrán, intendant of Cundinamarca Province, led the way. On June 13, Herrán called a public meeting in Bogotá's customshouse. He presented a formal resolution (*acta*) rejecting the actions of the convention and calling on Bolívar to assume "emergency" dictatorial powers. The resolution passed easily—thanks, in part, to the soldiers Herrán had standing nearby—and was later approved by Bolívar's cabinet, the Council of Ministers. Similar meetings occurred in cities throughout the country and similar resolutions were passed. Although most were orchestrated by local Bolivarians, the Liberator saw them as a genuine sign of popular support for his dictatorship. On June 24, having returned from Bucaramanga, he formally accepted the call to assume dictatorial power, explaining that he sought only to save the nation from dismemberment at the hands of Liberals and separatists. Moderate-minded observers tended to agree. Indeed, many went along, viewing dictatorship as a practical measure or as, in the words of interior minister José Manuel Restrepo, a "necessary evil."[36]

The Libertadora contributed in her own way to the Bolivarians' efforts to rally public support for the new government. On July 28, she hosted a lavish reception in honor of Bolívar's birthday. Held on the rolling grounds of the *quinta,* the party was open to the general public and featured free food and drink: grilled meat (*novilla a la llanera*) accompanied by great baskets of bread and large barrels of chicha. It included entertainment provided by a military band and the Grenadiers Battalion, the latter assigned to perform drill maneuvers. Indeed, with the *quinta* decked out in numerous small Colombian flags and other cheery decorations and the surrounding slopes dotted with pup tents (*tiendas de campaña*)—these apparently serving to commemorate the army's patriotic achievements while, perhaps, also shielding guests from anticipated afternoon showers—it resembled an independence day celebration.[37]

The reception also featured some private festivities. Inside the *quinta,* a select group of guests had gathered to toast the Liberator and his recent victory over his rivals. Wine and champagne flowed freely, and, as various accounts confirm, the toasts grew louder and more frequent. When someone mentioned the hated name of Santander, the toasting culminated with a proposal that the latter be tried and executed in effigy. Enthused by this idea, the guests proceeded to improvise a dummy from a sack of grain, several long black silk stockings (for arms and legs), and a tricorn hat. They propped it up on a bench at the entrance to the *quinta* and above it hung a sign that read: "F.[rancisco] de P.[aula] S.[antander] dies for treason." As a few witnesses would recall later, one of the guests, local cathedral dean Francisco Javier Guerra, performed "last rites" for the dummy. Members of the Grenadiers, headed by Colonel Richard Crofton, formed a voluntary firing squad. When Crofton ordered the squad to shoot, spectators laughed and applauded. Father Guerra then capped the charade by delivering an impromptu "sermon" over the effigy's dead "body."[38]

The effigy incident spawned a scandal. Sáenz, some said, had instigated it. This was the view of one of Bolívar's officers, General José María Córdova, who, in a private letter of complaint to his superior, characterized the incident as "an assault" on the government and the Liberator himself as well as on the country's laws, society, and "the army's sense of discipline." Córdova also cast blame on Sáenz. "It has been said that Señora Sáenz was the one who promoted the scandal and directed it," his letter informs Bolívar bluntly.[39]

Anticipating her lover's annoyance, Sáenz denied responsibility. "I know you will be angry with me, but I'm not to blame," she told him in alluding to the recent charade. She then explained that, while attending to a chore inside the *quinta*, she had "encountered" a nearby group of guests—the perpetrators of the mock execution, apparently—whose conduct had embarrassed her; such was her "embarrassment," she added, that it had kept her from sleeping.[40]

To what extent was Sáenz being candid? Given her previously expressed dislike of Santander, love of pranks, and general irreverence, she certainly was capable of having orchestrated the episode. Her note to Bolívar concluded with the suggestion that she not return to the *quinta* without his specific approval or invitation. "The best thing, sir, is that I not go to your house except when you can or want to see me," the letter states—a hint, perhaps, of a guilty conscience.[41]

More important, the mock execution of Santander associated Sáenz with the most extreme Bolivarians. It confirmed the public's perception of her behind-the-scenes political influence, a perception alluded to in Córdova's complaint to Bolívar: "It is generally alleged [by critics] that [Sáenz] meddles in the affairs of government and that she is listened to." Córdova's letter also mentions hearsay that, it claims, had arisen in the wake of a recent grenadiers' riot in Honda. When leaders of the riot were pardoned and transferred to a different garrison

Miniature portrait of Manuela Sáenz, ca. 1828, signed by José María Espinosa. Museo de Antioquia, Medellín. Photograph by author.

rather than punished for their insubordination, it notes (apparently referring to Bolívar's February decree against subversives), local critics had attributed the pardon to a "favor" the Liberator had granted his mistress—or "la presidenta," as, according to Córdova, they now referred to her. Such reactions and above all the perception that underlay them were bound to weaken the authority of the government and of the Liberator, the letter concludes.[42]

That the perception was not without substance is suggested in Bolívar's reply to his worried general. Bolívar at first tried to downplay the significance of the incident. In a letter to Córdova, he explained it away by characterizing it simply as an example of his friends' "excesses." He also downplayed Sáenz's role as the alleged ringleader, referring to her rather dismissively as "the amiable madwoman." "What would you have me tell her?" he wrote, implying that there was little he could say or do to control his mistress's behavior. He then promised his subordinate that he would "make the most determined effort" to persuade his mistress to "return to her country or wherever she wishes."[43]

Bolívar then denied that Sáenz had ever "meddled" in government or that she had ever "been listened to." His denial, however, was contradicted by his simultaneous admission of certain exceptions. Even as he claimed that Sáenz had "never" interfered in official matters, Bolívar acknowledged her activity as an intercessor—activity he tried to minimize by referring to it merely as an inclination "to beg [on behalf of army deserters, etc.]." While asserting that Sáenz's views fell on deaf ears, he qualified the assertion by noting that her judgment had been "right" in the case of one "Alvarado" and by promising someday to tell Córdova about it.[44] It was in this rather backhanded manner that the Liberator, zealous guardian of his authority and reputation, confirmed his mistress's informal influence in certain matters—an influence that hinted at her political role more generally and that violated traditional Hispanic prohibitions against women in government.

Sáenz's role and influence both would expand in the wake of an assassination attempt against her lover. The attempt had been long in coming. Its origin lay among extremist elements of the Santanderista opposition, including various semisecret political clubs, or *círculos*, that, since the time of the Ocaña Convention, had begun uniting Bolívar's provincial opponents with the Santanderistas and Santander's Bogotá-based allies (i.e., Francisco Soto and Vicente Azuero). Composed mainly of idealistic young lawyers and university students, these clubs had long portrayed the Liberator as nothing more than a ruthless tyrant. They argued openly for "tyrannicide"—the only way, in their view, to "save" the republic from Bolívar's and the army's perceived abuses. They were not alone in their extremist rhetoric. As the Ocaña Convention drew to a close, Liberal deputies there called openly for armed resistance to the "odious tyranny" they believed Bolívar sought to establish.[45]

The so-called tyranny had proved relatively mild, however. An August 27 Organic Decree authorized the Liberator to reorganize the nation's government and preside over a new constitutional convention to be held in January 1830. The Bolivarian dictatorship, furthermore, limited political persecution to its most obvious and implacable enemies. A few prominent Santanderistas, for example, lost their jobs or were forced into exile; their leader, in turn, was forced to give up the vice presidency, a loss mitigated somewhat by the government's offer of a new job in the United States as Colombia's minister plenipotentiary.[46] Santanderista hostility to the dictator nevertheless continued to brew unabated.

Antigovernment plots began hatching in August. One of these erupted on August 10, 1828, the anniversary of the Battle of Boyacá and of the Liberator's arrival in Bogotá nine years earlier. The plotters apparently planned to seize Bolívar while he mingled with guests at a masked ball in the city's theatre (El Coliseo) and to stab him to death with daggers that some of them had hidden beneath their costumes.

The Liberator foiled their plans. He attended the ball only briefly and left before his enemies could spring into action. Sáenz may have had something to do with this. Having apparently learned of the plot, she showed up suddenly at the theatre in an effort to warn Bolívar. Although prevented from delivering her warning in person, she became involved in a quarrel with the theatre's guard; the quarrel distracted Bolívar and induced him to leave early.[47]

A more serious plot ripened subsequently among members of the Sociedad Filológica. Formed sometime in May 1828, the Sociedad was a Liberal political club composed primarily of young lawyers, professors, and students, some with ties to the Colegio de San Bartolomé—Santander's alma mater and a hub of anti-Bolívar sentiment. Its members embraced an extreme republicanism. Indeed, inspired by the examples of the French Revolution and ancient Greek and Roman republics, they proclaimed themselves willing to die in defense of republican liberties. Such liberties, they believed, were threatened by Bolívar's dictatorship and growing reliance on the military, including an army whose numbers recently had expanded to forty thousand.[48] They were threatened by Bolívar's seeming desire to establish a monarchy. Led by President Ezequiel Rojas, the Sociedad therefore decided to strike a direct blow against Bolívar, the "tyrant."

On the evening of September 25, conspirators sprang into action. Spurred by the news that their plot had been exposed earlier that morning, they met at the home of Luis Vargas Tejada to concoct a new plan. This plan called for the conspirators to divide themselves into three groups, one of which was assigned the task of attacking the presidential palace. Led by twenty-six-year-old renegade Venezuelan officer Pedro Carujo, this group included sixteen artillery soldiers and ten civilians who, armed with knives, pistols, and swords, launched their attack toward midnight. Under a bright moon and a light drizzle, they approached the palace and subdued its guards; they then stormed in and began to make their way toward Bolívar's bedroom.[49]

Bolívar had been forewarned. Indeed, thanks to a local female informant, he had learned of the conspiracy several days earlier. He had scoffed at the news, however, and even after asking Sáenz to listen to the informant's story, apparently had dismissed it as just another one of the conspiracy rumors that were then rampant. Bolívar also had neglected to make any special security arrangements. On the night of the attack, beyond the pistol and sword he always kept beside him, he had gone to bed with nothing more than his usual outdoor guards on duty. He was virtually alone, moreover; among the officers who comprised his retinue, most—for example, aides-de-camp William Ferguson and Andrés Ibarra as well as his nephew Fernando Bolívar—were either ill or at home.[50] Only Sáenz happened to be with him. She had a separate residence by then and, despite apparently suffering from a head cold, had acceded to her lover's request that she stay with him in the Palace that evening. On arriving, she had found Bolívar taking his nightly bath and, on hearing his bland prediction of a "revolution," had responded rather crankily; considering the "fine reception" he gave to warnings of revolutionary conspiracy, there could be "not just one but up to ten [revolutions]" she had told him. Bolívar had then asked her to read to him in bed and, as Sáenz would recall later, had fallen deeply asleep just before midnight.[51]

Sáenz had dozed off when she was suddenly jolted awake by the frantic barking of Bolívar's dogs and the ruckus of the invaders. She woke Bolívar, who, startled, reacted by rushing toward the bedroom door, wearing little more than his trusty pistol and sword. Sáenz stopped him and, as she later recalled, persuaded him to dress before opening the door. She then kept him from a second attempt to leave the bedroom by redirecting his attention toward a nearby window and reminding him of his earlier remark about its usefulness as a means of escape. Bolívar acted on this reminder and, just as the attackers were trying to force their way in through the locked door, leaped out the window and onto the street below.

Sáenz, meanwhile, turned to meet the attackers. When she opened the door, the men grabbed her and demanded to know Bolívar's whereabouts. Hoping to buy time for her lover, Sáenz replied that the Liberator was in the Council Room. Some of the more observant attackers then inquired about the warm bed and open window. Sáenz had a ready response for these queries as well, explaining that the warm bed was the result of her lying on it while waiting for Bolívar to finish his meeting; she had opened the window, she added, in order to check on the reason for the barking and noise.[52]

Although Sáenz continued to delay the attackers, things went less smoothly for her afterward. Indeed, the attackers grew angry when, after at first agreeing to lead them to the Council Room, she suddenly stopped and claimed ignorance of the room's exact location. They grew even angrier when she paused in a hallway to attend to the wounded Andrés Ibarra (whose hand had been nearly severed during his earlier attempt to defend the palace); when Sáenz then refused to respond to their further questioning, including queries from a rough-mannered twenty-four-year-old named Wenceslao Zulaibar, the men's tempers exploded. As Fernando Bolívar was to recall, the attackers began insulting her and thrashing her with the sides of their swords. Sáenz developed a fever and would still feel the effects of the thrashing some twelve days later. She nevertheless continued trying to help others around her. These included Colonel Ferguson who, despite her shouts of warning, was shot dead in a belated attempt to enter and defend the palace.[53]

Finally realizing that their plot had been foiled, the attackers fled. Sáenz then ran for a doctor to minister to Ibarra and began checking on the remaining occupants of the palace, including José Palacios, Bolívar's faithful (if then severely ill) manservant. When Herrán, Urdaneta, and other senior officers arrived in the wee hours of the morning to inquire of the whereabouts of their leader, she reported his escape. She subsequently rode out to the main plaza and, to her relief, found the Liberator there—safe and surrounded by cheering soldiers, albeit exhausted and in a state of shock from his experience.[54]

The aborted assassination attempt had several consequences. One of these, of course, was Bolívar's survival. Yet another was his recognition of the special debt he owed his mistress, whose courage and quick thinking (combined with the conspirators' bungling) had ensured his escape from his would-be assassins. This recognition showed itself when, having returned home the morning after the incident, Bolívar turned to Sáenz and—apparently for the first time—told her that she was, indeed, "the Libertadora del Libertador."[55]

The Liberator was deeply disturbed by the assassination conspiracy. The conspirators' claims to stand for the very principles of liberty and justice that he had always fought for confounded him. "[It is] because of you and others like you who raise your sons poorly that these things happen," Bolívar later exclaimed angrily to a local gentleman, one Don Tomás Barriga, who had come to congratulate him on his successful escape; "as a result of being imbeciles, [these sons] confuse liberty with license," he added in a statement that reflected not only his anger but his growing sense of betrayal at the hands of the city's residents.[56] Bolívar also became increasingly indecisive. The day after the aborted attempt, for example, his first thought was to pardon the conspirators, resign the presidency, and go into exile—a plan from which his senior officers soon dissuaded him. Indeed, General Urdaneta and others convinced him to stay in power and stand firm against his enemies; they recommended, above all, that he deal sternly with the conspirators.[57]

The assassination attempt also led to a noticeable hardening of the dictatorship. This could be seen in Bolívar's decision to prohibit all secret societies, cancellation of the degrees or teaching licenses of real or suspected conspirators, and imposition of a new passport requirement for individuals crossing provincial or municipal boundaries, a measure clearly designed to restrict the movement of Bolívar's enemies and their friends or sympathizers.[58] It especially could be seen in his regime's effort to mete out justice to the September 25 conspirators. This effort began with the immediate appointment of a special tribunal—a nine-man body composed of both military officers and civilians—charged with addressing the crime in accordance with the anticonspiracy decree Bolívar had issued in February. The tribunal launched a formal investigation that, over the next five weeks, led to the arrest and interrogation of almost sixty suspects. At least seven were released after having been "absolved" by their interrogators; the rest received summary trials, most of which resulted in either imprisonment or exile. Fourteen men ultimately were found guilty of participating in the conspiracy, including the attack on the Presidential Palace, and were sentenced to death by firing squad. On September 30, five of them (Agustín Horment, Wenceslao Zulaibar, Rudesindo Silva, Cayetano Galindo, and J. Ignacio López) were executed in the main plaza.[59]

Dissatisfied with some of the sentences, however, Bolívar later dissolved the tribunal and replaced it with a smaller panel of military judges headed by the trusted Rafael Urdaneta, Cundinamarca Province's new commander-general. Urdaneta became Bolívar's hatchet man. Besides overseeing the remaining executions—one of whose victims, the hapless Admiral Padilla of Cartagena, had had nothing to do with the conspiracy—he deliberately went after Bolívar's chief opponent, Santander. Believing, like most Bolivarians, that the latter had masterminded the September 25 attack, he worked hard to blame him for it. Beyond the fact of Santander's friendship with the conspirators and general awareness of their activities, however, there was no direct proof of his involvement. Urdaneta and his fellow military judges also had to contend with local public opinion, most of which was in sympathy with the former vice president and was outraged at the news of the death sentence that had been decreed for him. Aware of this public sentiment, the Council of Ministers advised Bolívar to commute the sentence to exile, and in early November, Bolívar, rather grudgingly, agreed.[60]

Sáenz, meanwhile, had begun cooperating with the government's investigation of the conspiracy and, in particular, with its effort to interrogate suspects. Despite Bolívar's objections (and the fact that she was still in bed recovering from her injuries), she agreed to have two suspects, Ezequiel Rojas and Florentino González—both leading conspirators—brought to her home for questioning. Rojas and González both had denied their involvement; Sáenz, it seems, was expected to confirm that involvement and thus assist the judges in reaching a guilty verdict.

Yet, in the case of Rojas, who was immediately recognized by one of her maids (most likely Jonathás, who had witnessed the conspirators entering the palace), she contradicted the allegations of guilt that had been made against him. Indeed, she denied ever having seen him in the palace, apparently doing so out of pity for his mother and other female relatives who, as she later explained, had approached her to ask that she spare his life. Rojas's death sentence was commuted to exile. Sáenz proceeded similarly in the case of González, whose death sentence was commuted to imprisonment after she lied about his role in the attack, claiming that he had saved her from an assault by some of his fellow conspirators. She later hid several suspects inside her house, doing so, as she would afterward claim, with Bolívar's tacit approval.[61]

Sáenz's attitude toward these two conspirators involved more than compassion. Years later, in recalling their interviews with her, Rojas and González each would note that the Libertadora also had tried to learn more about the origin of the conspiracy, especially, Santander's alleged role in it.[62]

Sáenz cooperated with the regime in other ways. By mid-November 1828, she was in touch with one of its spies, a Gerardo Montebrune. Montebrune, a lieutenant colonel, had been assigned to escort Santander (a prisoner since his arrest some six weeks earlier) to Cartagena from where the former vice president was to go into foreign exile. He apparently also had been instructed by his superiors to record his observations and report anything interesting or unusual to Sáenz. While en route to his destination, he informed the latter of the Liberal leader's low spirits and recent illness and announced his intention to record everything he heard. He alerted her to a special folder that, he said, he had sent her, and noted that the folder contained letters he had intercepted from both Santander and his brother-in-law (who had accompanied the former).[63]

There seems no reason to doubt that the Libertadora read these letters and shared their content either with Bolívar or his dutiful minister of war, Rafael Urdaneta. She suspected Santander's involvement in the assassination attempt against her lover. The intercepting of private correspondence, moreover, was an age-old method for dealing with the threat of a political opponent. It apparently formed part of the Bolivarians' larger effort to identify Santander's remaining friends and associates, individuals presumed to form part of the Liberal opposition. Sáenz's involvement in such an effort suggests the trust authorities had deposited in her—a trust reflected in Montebrune's own assurances to her of his affection and devotion as well as his personal loyalty.[64]

Sáenz continued to cooperate with Bolivarian authorities through the end of 1828 and during 1829. The period was marked by escalating discontent with Bolívar's government. There were uprisings in September and October 1828 in New Granada's troubled southwestern region, Cauca and Pasto provinces, in particular. Led by local caudillos Colonels José María Obando and José Hilario López, both Santanderista sympathizers, the rebels had overthrown local government and threatened to interfere with travel to Quito. Bolívar's first response had been to send General José María Córdova with a force of fifteen hundred men to stop them. Toward the end of December 1828, he left for Popayán in person.[65]

In late January 1829, Bolivar consolidated Córdova's military victory by extracting a promise of the rebels' cooperation and loyalty in exchange for a general pardon. Yet, his main concern was the nation's recently erupted war with Peru. The war had various causes: ill will between the two national governments since the 1827 Third Division uprising; conflict over territorial boundaries; disagreement over the amount of the debt Peru owed Colombia for the latter's assistance in the war against the Spanish; and, not least, Peru's wish to reassert its former control over Guayaquil—a desire that had led to its army's seizure of the latter and invasion of the southernmost tip of Gran Colombia. The Liberator responded aggressively to the invasion. Before leaving Bogotá, he had eschewed diplomacy and ordered General Sucre to repel the invaders. Sucre fulfilled the order with his usual skill and savvy, and on February 27, 1829, at the Battle of Tarqui, led the Colombian army to victory. On receiving word of this, Bolívar, eager to oversee the final details of the Peruvian conflict, proceeded to Guayaquil. He remained in the Ecuadorian region until November.[66] Although she stayed in touch with him during this time, Sáenz would not see her lover again until January 1830.

She nevertheless kept busy and, indeed, became partly embroiled in what ultimately would become the year's most controversial project: a plan to convert the republic of Gran Colombia into a monarchy. The plan took shape in April 1829. In response to Bolívar's earlier suggestion, the Council of Ministers began exploring the possibility of a special arrangement or alliance between the young nation and a major European power (e.g., France or England). The idea was to establish a kind of protectorate that would guarantee peace and security. For this to work, however, council members believed that Gran Colombia needed to align itself ideologically with its future "protector" and thus abandon its republican form of government.

This idea already enjoyed a certain favor. Since the Páez rebellion, a few of Bolívar's closest followers (mostly military officers) had been suggesting that the Liberator crown himself king or at least rule like one. After the shock of the September 25 incident, moreover, some prominent Bogotá residents had begun to believe that a constitutional monarchy was the only government that could restore their country's former peace and political stability.[67]

Council members were sympathetic. Like minister of the interior Restrepo, they were disillusioned with republicanism, which they blamed for the chronic political turmoil plaguing not only Gran Colombia but most of Spanish America. "Monarchy was the [form of] government best suited to our ancient habits and under which true public tranquillity and genuine guarantees . . . may be enjoyed [while freeing us from] the oscillations of republics and their perpetual mutations," Restrepo noted.[68] A monarchy also seemed the form of government most likely to stave off Gran Colombia's political disintegration—which, in the eyes of Restrepo and his colleagues, only Bolívar, so far, had prevented.

In addition, with Bolívar's declining health increasingly apparent, in the council's eyes, special steps now needed to be taken. The monarchist project thus called for the Liberator-President to continue ruling the country until at least the time of the constitutional convention scheduled for the following January; arrangements subsequently would be made for his replacement by an heir of one of the royal houses of Europe, preferably the French Orleans dynasty. In the meantime, the ministers began testing public opinion on the matter and pursuing negotiations with diplomatic representatives of France and Great Britain. Although he had given his tacit consent to all this, Bolívar avoided any direct involvement in or endorsement of the project. In November 1829, furthermore—and in the face of mounting denunciations of his apparent monarchist leanings—he publicly disassociated himself from it.[69]

Sáenz must have known something of the council's proceedings. Beyond the fact that the latter were hardly a secret, she was friends with at least one key council member, General Rafael Urdaneta, Bolívar's minister of war and head of a group of senior army officers (the "faithful friends," as they called themselves) who backed the council's monarchist project and who had spearheaded the monarchist movement.[70] She also must have been sympathetic. Although her views on the monarchy plan per se are unknown, she believed Bolívar to be a great man—one incapable of abuse or wrongdoing—and thus, undoubtedly, favored the idea of preserving and extending his power. Like most creole elites of her generation, moreover, the Libertadora was a fan of French language and culture, a factor that may well have inclined her to embrace the idea of a special alliance between France and Gran Colombia. She, in any case, would have found it hard to refuse a chance to play hostess to the city's prestigious official French delegation. Indeed, in early May, shortly after the delegation's arrival, Sáenz hosted a special reception—including guest of honor M. Charles de Bresson, King Charles X's personal envoy and a central figure in the subsequent monarchy-related negotiations. With the noticeable exception of U.S. representative William Henry Harrison and a few others opposed to the council's initiative (including the monarchist idea and alliance with France or England), virtually all members of the city's diplomatic community attended the soirée.[71]

Sáenz also, no doubt, sought to win supporters for the monarchist project before Bolívar's decision to part ways with it. In a brief note addressed to an anonymous Bogotá acquaintance, for example, she referred to her lover as the "Liberator of Three Republics" and suggested the near-providential nature of his escape from assassination. She trumpeted his fame and achievements, including his "liberation of a continent." She then offered her correspondent a token of her personal friendship—a lock of hair she had enclosed with the letter—and concluded by referring to herself as "[one] who is always concerned for the happiness of General Bolívar and his faithful friends."[72] Whatever the precise reason behind it, this note reflected Sáenz's continuing tendency to identify closely with Bolívar and his projects. It suggests, too, that she had begun to see herself as a kind of Bolivarian mediator.

Through 1829, Sáenz continued to strengthen her ties to her lover's various friends and followers. These included personal friends of his, such as the respectable José Ignacio París, a wealthy emerald mine owner, and Juan Illingworth, a successful businessman and mine operator as well as spokesman for the small local British community (most of whom were solidly behind the Liberator and his dictatorship). Such individuals often gathered at Sáenz's home for parties a highlight of which were the performances of her maid, Jonathás. In addition to her talent as a mimic, Jonathás was known for appearing in traditional "ñapanga" costume and for regaling guests with what one described as "lascivious dances," these probably of Afro-Peruvian origin.[73]

The Libertadora also drew various young foreigners around her. Her coterie included French scientist Jean-Baptiste Boussingault, an acquaintance of Alexander Von Humboldt who had come to Bogotá several years earlier on Bolívar's invitation. It counted among its members Nimian Richard Cheyne, a Scottish-born physician, and his brother Geoffrey, both of whom became Sáenz's friends as well as beneficiaries of her hospitality. Drawn by her charm, beauty, and personal generosity—a quality one of them described as "unlimited"—the young foreigners also became admirers. "We [all] adored her," Boussingault would confess years later. Sáenz's friends called on her regularly, usually at late morning, when she welcomed visitors. As Boussingault was to recall, their hostess received them informally, usually in a simple dress or morning gown. Hands busy with a cigarette and piece of embroidery, a favorite hobby of hers, she spent most of the time listening quietly to their conversation, ears pricked for news and gossip.[74]

Sáenz also strengthened her ties to the city's pious residents. In September 1829, for example, she joined the *cofradía* (Catholic lay fraternity) of Jesús, María y José de la Peña. Her membership obliged her to pay annual dues for support of the *cofradía*'s mountaintop chapel, to visit the sick and engage in other good works, and to observe the holy days dedicated to Saints Joseph, Anne, Lawrence, and Michael, the latter being the chapel's spiritual patron.[75]

Such activities surely contributed to the Bolivarians' efforts to present themselves as defenders of the church and traditional religion. They, no doubt, also boosted Sáenz's local standing as well, which already had been enhanced by news of her role in thwarting the murderous aims of the September 25 conspirators. "I congratulate my friend Manuela because in saving her life, she also saved the Liberator and in doing so, [saved] my beloved country," one Rafael Gaytán had told her in a note sent shortly after the attack on the Presidential Palace. "What horrors might have been the result of this assassination attempt [had it succeeded] . . . long live Bolívar and by his side, my friend!" he had added.[76] Sáenz also won an admirer in one Rafael de Paul. "Allow me, dear lady, to congratulate you on this day for the great part you played in preserving such an important life, a life . . . of interest to all the American Continent," De Paul wrote her, on the occasion of the incident's first anniversary, adding, "destiny has shown you, Madame, that you are to serve as [Bolívar's] guardian angel."[77] Given the pride she took in her status not only as a member of Bolívar's personal staff but as his friend, confidante, ally, and mistress, Sáenz must have reveled in such words of praise and admiration. As events were to show, she also took her "guardian angel" role seriously.

Indeed, during the following year (1830), Manuela Sáenz became her lover's most visible defender. This trend coincided with the rapid decline in Bolívar's health and political fortunes. By the time of his January 15 return to Bogotá, the Liberator was no longer the vigorous man he had been. His struggle with tuberculosis had drained him. As a friend observed sadly on the day of his formal entrance into the city, he had grown "pale [and] emaciated"; the fire in his eyes, once so brilliant and expressive, the friend added, was now "extinguished."[78] Bolívar also was heartsick over Páez's and other former allies' most recent public attacks against him—including criticism of the ill-fated monarchist project—and had grown anguished over the tarnishing of his reputation and glory. He was increasingly depressed, distracted, and indecisive, a situation that led him to rely more and more on the assistance of faithful, if often inept, subordinates.[79]

Yet, Bolívar's declining fortunes stemmed, above all, from the crisis that had come to grip all of Gran Colombia. It had started with his government's monarchist project, news of which had ignited a storm of protest in Venezuela (where many came to believe that Bolívar truly wished to be king) and, toward the end of 1829, a revival of the potent separatist movement. The revival of Venezuelan separatism, in turn, encouraged the rise of opposition and separatist forces elsewhere, for example, Ecuador and New Granada; before the end of the year, it would lead to the unraveling of the Gran Colombian union.

Frustrated by these developments and increasingly helpless to stop them, Bolívar announced his plan to retire and appointed Don Domingo Caicedo as interim president. He resigned the presidency officially on March 1, 1830, then announced his intention to leave the country. On May 8, amid rising tensions between his friends and followers, on the one hand, and his Liberal opponents, on the other, he and a small entourage left Bogotá and began the journey to the Caribbean coastal city of Cartagena. From Cartagena, he was to board a ship and go into exile.[80]

Sáenz stayed in the capital. Although unhappy about her lover's departure, she apparently saw it as only temporary—a concession made to his opponents under difficult circumstances that, however difficult, were ultimately reversible. In this belief, Bolívar, no doubt, had encouraged her. In private statements to his friends and followers—and in sharp contrast to his public declarations— he had hinted at his desire to stay in the country and eventually return to power. He also continued to correspond regularly with leading Bolivarians and, after his June arrival in Cartagena, postponed his departure from Colombian soil. As some biographers have suggested, he was loath to give up power and inclined to listen to those who, since March (and at least in part out of fear of Santanderista reprisals) had tried to persuade him to return to it.[81] Sáenz probably was among the latter.

She, no doubt, also was encouraged by her lover's recent words to her. In a brief note penned a few days after his abandonment of the Colombian capital, the Liberator not only expressed sadness over the couple's recent separation but announced that he was "doing well." He urged her to exercise caution. "My love, [while] I love you much, I will love you more if, now more than ever, you show good sense," he stated. "Be careful with what you do, for otherwise you will lose both of us," he added cryptically.[82] Sáenz likely interpreted these words as a reason for hope—and as proof that her lover intended to return. Such hope seemed warranted by Bolívar's continuing show of concern for her. From the coastal town of Turbaco, for example, the Liberator wrote a friend in Bogotá to ask that the latter do him a favor—give Sáenz the proceeds from the sale of a mule Bolívar had left behind and that was to have been sold for him by a local acquaintance, a Señor Umaña.[83]

Sáenz also refused to accept the growing influence of Bolívar's old rivals, the Santanderistas, or Liberals. These had achieved an impressive political comeback. In the months before Bolívar's departure, they had come to dominate the proceedings of the "Congreso Admirable," the constitutional convention that had begun meeting in January 1830. They had shaped the election of a new government in April. Headed by political moderates President Joaquín Mosquera and Vice President Domingo Caicedo, this government subsequently allowed Liberal politicians to occupy key cabinet positions such as the Ministry of the Interior, awarded first to Alejandro Osorio and, later, to the formidable Vicente Azuero.

Liberals at the same time began to dominate the local press and the public sphere. This became evident in the aggressive campaign they launched against the Bolivarians. Led by the editors of newspapers such as *La Aurora* and *El Demócrata* and spurred by fears of a plot to restore Bolívar to power—these fanned by rumors that Bolívar did not really intend to go into exile—the campaign openly vilified the former dictator and his followers. Liberal partisans began trying to intimidate the latter by, among other things, issuing death threats against those they believed to be conspiring against the government.[84]

The Libertadora, not surprisingly, became one of the Liberals' main targets. Like Bolívar himself, she became an object of mockery and derision. An example of this appeared on the eve of Corpus Christi—a holiday known as much for its tradition of political satire as for its rites of religious worship. Corpus festivities generally included the lampooning of authorities and public figures; the lampoons typically consisted of crude drawings or caricatures placed strategically on or alongside the outdoor altars, arches, and other decorations set up along the path of the main religious procession.[85] On June 9, as Bogotanos prepared for the city's annual Corpus celebration, caricatures of both Bolívar and his mistress appeared in the middle of the main plaza. They were attached to the sides of a tall, linen-draped pillar, or "castle," holding the fireworks that were to be lit later by municipal authorities. One of the caricatures was a figure wearing a crown, presumably mocking Bolívar's desire for a monarchy; it was accompanied by the phrase "Down with Despotism!" The other mocked Sáenz as a would-be royal consort, the caricature accompanied by the phrase, "Down with Tyranny!" The caricatures were no ordinary Corpus prank, however. As some local residents would soon discover, they were the work of Isidoro Carrizoza, one of the city's alcaldes (a local sheriff or ward captain) and friend of the newly empowered Liberals. It was Carrizoza, no doubt, who also ensured that both the castle and the caricatures were guarded by members of the local militia.[86]

Sáenz may well have suspected Carrizoza's involvement. Her reaction to the caricatures, in any case, was immediate and furious. As witnesses would recall later, she arrived at the plaza on horseback, dressed in her colonel-style uniform and accompanied by one or two of her black female servants (also in military uniform) and two soldiers or bodyguards—these armed with knives and bayonets. She approached the fireworks castle and began circling it, all the while brandishing a pistol. On spying the offending drawings, she and her servants moved to destroy them. According to witnesses, Sáenz tried to get past the sentinels by charging at them while ordering her servants and bodyguards to knock them out of the way; she also tried to scare them by threatening to fire her two pistols. The sentinels counterattacked, using their bayonets against Sáenz's horses. The mêlée ended only after the arrival of several more militiamen, who subdued her servants and bodyguards and whisked them away to a local prison.[87] Sáenz finally went home. Her outrage over the caricatures was only partially assuaged by the knowledge that, as she later told a friend, she had done her "duty" in trying to remove them. She must have felt vindicated when, soon after the incident, authorities arranged for their removal.[88]

Sáenz resented her antagonists' tendency to flaunt their contempt for Bolívar and to trample publicly on his honor and reputation. Her temper again flared when, on June 12, some of the government's local supporters began gathering to celebrate the arrival of President Mosquera. A crowd formed on the street below Sáenz's balcony. From the balcony, where she often did her sewing, Sáenz could hear their cheering and shouting of phrases such as "Down with despotism and tyranny"—a clear allusion to Bolívar's recent government. She also could hear the crowd's celebratory fireworks. A few firecrackers apparently veered off in her direction, startling her and provoking her to unleash her pent-up frustration. After the passage of Mosquera and his entourage, Sáenz rebuked the crowd sharply, reminding them, as one witness paraphrased it, that "he [Mosquera] was not the [real] president, that the real one was Bolívar, the Liberator of three republics."[89]

Her rebuke must have aroused the anger of several ardent Mosquera supporters, including, perhaps, one or two hecklers. The infuriated woman, in any case, soon found herself embroiled in a hostile exchange with the people on the street below her. The exchange turned violent when, in an apparent attempt to scare off their mistress's antagonists, Sáenz's servants began throwing firecrackers. A few people on the street reciprocated by throwing rocks at the servants. A battle ensued, escalating when a male servant ran out and began threatening the crowd with a musket or rifle; a twenty-three-year-old witness named Agustín Zuzuarregui managed to pry it away from him. Sáenz herself joined the fray and, with Jonathás standing beside her, began trying to disperse the crowd with her own rifle. According to witnesses, she was pointing the rifle out at the street when a friend, General Mariano París, appeared suddenly and put an end to the skirmish. París then sought to soothe her ruffled feathers.[90] There would be little time for a now-hurt and resentful Sáenz to feel soothed, however.

The Libertadora soon faced a fresh attack from local antagonists. Among these was the anonymous editor of the Liberal and pro-government La Aurora.

On June 13 (the day after the balcony incident), the editor offered his readers a withering report of Sáenz's Corpus Christi–day skirmish. The report pelted Sáenz with insults, characterizing her attempt to destroy the caricatures of her and Bolívar as proof that she was "unhinged," "scatterbrained," and full of "insolence and effrontery." After reminding readers of Sáenz's alleged role in the 1828 execution of Santander in effigy, it also classified her as a symbol of the "evils" of the Bolivarian dictatorship—and of the "impunity" of members of Bolívar's "family." It went on to accuse her of the "enormous crime" of "sedition" and concluded with a call for her immediate arrest and "exemplary punishment."[91]

Sáenz's response appeared one week later in a printed broadside that included her signature. Entitled "To the Public," the broadside offered a measured reply to *La Aurora*'s allegations along with a direct appeal to public opinion. "The respect owed to public opinion obliges me to take this step . . . my silence [otherwise] would be criminal," Sáenz stated. "I have strong reasons to believe that the sensible portion of Bogotá's citizenry does not accuse me [of any crime]," she added. Her sole wish, Sáenz went on, was to be judged by the nation's laws and, thus, to demonstrate that, despite her recent follies, she had done nothing criminal or illegal. She had been "one thousand times provoked" to commit those follies, she asserted. "Everyone knows that I have been insulted, calumniated, and attacked," the broadside stated.[92]

Sáenz then noted that she had no quarrel with her recent press critic, that is, the editor of *La Aurora;* this, she suggested, explained why the editor "does not even have the backbone to reveal his identity, much less sue me." While admitting to her stridency and "hotheadedness," she also characterized herself as "long-suffering." Above all, her broadside addressed her Liberal antagonists— "my enemies" and "the enemies of His Excellency the Liberator." "You may call my hotheadedness a crime; you may insult me; [you may] thus satisfy your thirst [for vengeance]; but you have not succeeded in making me despair," it informed them. "You can do whatever you want to me personally, except make me retreat even a little in [my] respect and friendship for as well as gratitude to General Bolívar," it added, going on to state in a tone of defiance that "[in that regard] you will never make me fear or waver."[93]

The Libertadora then took the moral high ground. "Hate and vengeance are not my weapons," she announced in reference to her antagonists' behavior, including the insults directed at her by *La Aurora*'s editor. "Indeed," she continued, "I dare any member of the public anywhere to say whether I have ever acted out of spite or meanness." "[As the public can confirm], I have done all the good that has been within my power," she continued.[94]

Sáenz's patience was wearing thin, however. By late June, the Liberals' anti-Bolivarian campaign included unabashed calls for the assassination of General Urdaneta and other Bolivarian leaders as well as death threats against some of the city's foreign residents, Bolívar's British friends, in particular.[95] It included efforts to sway the sentiments of the army. In July, Liberal partisans mobilized the Boyacá Battalion, a pro-Liberal faction within the local garrison. The Bolivarians responded in kind, reaching out to the Callao Battalion. The two army factions were soon confronting each other on the streets, with Boyacá sporting red ribbons containing the phrase "Liberty or Death!" and Callao sporting green ribbons that read "For Religion!" Their mutual antagonism was to erupt in quarrels and fistfights, a factor that, on August 9, would induce the government to order Callao's soldiers out of the city.[96]

Manuela Sáenz, meanwhile, became embroiled in a separate conflict with national authorities. Toward the end of June, reflecting the growing influence of a small clique of Liberal politicians, these authorities had demanded that she relinquish Bolívar's archive. Sáenz rejected the demand outright. The archive, after all, had been entrusted to her, not the government—much less to any of the individuals now in charge of it. "I believe no one has the right to demand it [the archive] of me, at least as long as there is not a law permitting confiscation of private property," she dryly informed minister of the interior Alejandro Osorio.[97] When alcalde Juan José Gómez came to her home to insist on the government's right to the archive (which included many of Bolívar's letters and official papers), Sáenz rebuffed him; the government had no such right, she told him.[98] Her frustration with the Mosquera regime could only have deepened with the subsequent news of Osorio's replacement, in early July, by Vicente Azuero—perhaps the fiercest and most relentless of Bolívar's opponents.

Sáenz's response was to begin working actively for Bolívar's comeback. She began rallying local Bolivarian sentiment. On the night of July 8, for example, she sent one of her servants to post homemade flyers and broadsides around town, these reading "Biba Bolibar, Fundador de la Republica[!]" Witnesses would later recall seeing the servant—a tall black man wearing a white flannel cloak and black hat—posting the flyers on some of the homes near the cathedral as well as other places in the central part of the city.[99]

Sáenz also began cultivating the sympathy of (that is, "seducing") the Callao Battalion, a unit of largely Venezuelan soldiers some of whom had been assigned to guard the Presidential Palace. That same week, she sent one of her female servants—a *zambita* (mixed-race woman), as the men later referred to her—to the palace. Sporting red pants, the young woman plied the guards with gifts including a silver peso, a large bottle of beer, some pastries, cigars, and a plate of spiced peppers, this last treat intended to liven their bland meal rations. She also passed on several messages from her mistress, including a request that the guards acknowledge the gifts—and thus their sympathy for the cause of Bolívar—by sending back a bowl of their rations. Sáenz also sent some Bolivarian literature along with a request that the soldiers distribute it. The literature included reprints of a May 31 speech by General Juan José Flores, one of Bolívar's staunchest supporters, and of a poem published recently in Cartagena. Entitled "Farewell to the Liberator of Colombia, Peru, and Bolivia," the poem laments Bolívar's imminent abandonment of the country—a lament that reflected his admirers' sentiments—and, like the speech, pays homage to him and his accomplishments.[100]

Use of such propaganda showed Sáenz's desire to revive the soldiers' sense of loyalty to their old leader while weakening their support for the Mosquera government. It also suggests she had begun collaborating with the government's opponents, including individuals who, like her, were eager to oust the Liberals from power.

Indeed, Sáenz formed part of an opposition that was apparent by the middle of August. This movement, in effect, a budding rebellion, had originated with the *orejones,* local conservative-minded gentry who deeply regretted Bolívar's departure and who sought to resist the growing influence of his opponents by raising militias in the surrounding towns of Funza, Facatativá, and Serrezuela. It had the support of the Callao Battalion. Shortly after its official expulsion from the city, Callao joined forces with the *orejones* and their militias. The united rebels then demanded several personnel changes in Mosquera's cabinet. They demanded General Urdaneta's reappointment to the War Ministry as well as the resignation of several cabinet ministers, among them minister of the interior Azuero and two others—all Liberals.[101]

Sáenz apparently endorsed these demands. Along with various military officers and members of the local clergy, she surely sympathized with the *orejones'* opposition. While details of her involvement in the growing rebellion remain uncertain, the extent of that involvement may be gleaned from a friend's comments. In a letter written to her just before the rebellion's climax (near the end of August), Nimian R. Cheyne suggested teasingly that Sáenz needed to be watched "more closely than Don Quijote when he was behind bars." He gently chided her: "You should live like other women and avoid further mischief." He then promised to write Bolívar and report on "all the crazy things" she had engaged in.[102] In addition, Sáenz's support for the rebels' cause may have been critical. According to one observer, the Libertadora, thanks to her charitable giving and generosity, enjoyed "great influence in and around Bogotá."[103]

Sáenz's influence and activities, of course, had not escaped her enemies' no-tice. On July 9, minister of the interior Azuero ordered a formal investigation into reports that, as he put it, Sáenz had been "disturbing the peace" and engag-ing in "repeated scandalous acts" and "outrages."[104] The investigation (involv-ing interviews with at least sixteen witnesses) led to a July 17 criminal indict-ment. A key aspect of the indictment was its charge of subversion—a charge the district attorney supported by citing Sáenz's earlier attempt to bribe or "se-duce" the palace guards and distribute "seditious papers."[105] There were other, lesser charges as well. In apparent reference to Sáenz's June reactions to her an-tagonists (i.e., the June 9 Corpus episode and the June 12 clash with the crowd below her balcony), for example, the attorney accused her of "insulting the public" and "menacing" them with firearms as well as of "acting brusquely, in a way alien to her sex." Sáenz also was deemed guilty of "dressing like a man" and of breaking "the rules of modesty . . . [and] morality." For these reasons, the attorney concluded, she and her "accomplices" (i.e., her servants) were to be imprisoned, forced to "confess" to the charges, and punished to the full extent of the law.[106]

Sáenz managed to evade arrest for several weeks. This may have been the result, in part, of public concern over the news of her indictment—concern expressed in broadsides whose anonymous authors defended her behavior while questioning the justice of the allegations.[107] It probably was also the result of Sáenz's own resistance. Nothing came of Alcalde Carrizoza's two July 19 orders for her imprisonment, for example. In the case of at least one of these orders, Sáenz apparently convinced the arresting officer that she was too ill to leave her home.[108] She likely hoped to buy time. As late as August 11, she was still trying to appeal some of the government's criminal charges.[109] Soon after this, however, Sáenz apparently agreed to turn herself in and cooperate with an official order for her exile from the city. She must have become nervous about the assassina-tion threats made against her by local Liberal extremists as well as by the larger partisan-related violence that had begun escalating in and around Bogotá. Local friends may have persuaded her to leave town for her own safety. Toward mid-August, in any case, Sáenz left Bogotá en route to the small westerly lowland town of Guaduas, some three days away on horseback.[110]

She received good news not long afterward. Indeed, she must have rejoiced on learning of the Bolivarian rebels' victory over government forces at the Au-gust 27 Battle of Santuario (near the town of Funza) and of the subsequent resig-nation of President Mosquera.[111] In response to this, a wave of enthusiasm swept the Bolivarians and their supporters in Bogotá. On September 2, an assembly of notables—members of the city council, the church hierarchy, and various heads of household—met to call for the return of Bolívar from exile and for Urdaneta, in the meantime, to head a provisional government. The city then erupted in celebration; church bells rang and the streets filled with music and fireworks. Merrymakers paraded with Bolívar's portrait.[112]

At around the same time, Sáenz began receiving messages of congratulations from her and Bolívar's friends and supporters. Writing her in mid-October, one R. Posada of Bogotá expressed the hope that "very soon we will again have [the Liberator] among us." He also voiced a wish to see Sáenz herself return soon to Bogotá.[113]

Like her friends, Sáenz anticipated Bolívar's return in December. She began preparing to welcome him. Having learned that her lover wished her to remain a bit longer in Guaduas, she ordered dishware, crystal glasses, and other items to be sent to her home there.[114] She, nevertheless, felt weary. "Ah, my friend! Everything, everything, everything has been trouble for me since January 1830," Sáenz confided in a November 24 letter to British merchant Dundas Logan. She was "anxious" to return to her friends in the capital, she added. Her sense of loneliness and hunger for a return to her former life may be gauged by her suggestion that she and Logan dance "the Aguinaldo" the first night of her return to Bogotá. Sáenz also refused to believe the recent rumors that Bolívar was now hopelessly ill—rumors that, as she told Logan, she regarded as mere Liberal propaganda. "It is true that he [Bolívar] has suffered some from [the return of] his old biliousness," she noted, going on to observe confidently that the Liberals should know by now "that the Liberator is immortal."[115] Her lover was to die less than one month later.

FOUR

The Liberals' Revenge, 1831–1835

NEWS OF BOLÍVAR's death—on December 17, 1830, at a friend's house just outside the small Caribbean city of Santa Marta—traveled slowly. It likely did not reach Sáenz in Guaduas until just after the start of the new year, 1831. Sáenz had been waiting for some word of her lover and no doubt had been expecting to hear from friends who had gone to see him. At least one of these was a member of the special government commission that, in early December, had been appointed to visit Bolívar and personally invite him to return to power.[1]

On January 6, R. S. Illingworth wrote to inform her of the situation. Sure that Sáenz had not yet received the reports that, he said, he and Bolívar's doctor had sent earlier, he announced the "terrible news . . . that the Liberator is dying!" Bolívar's friends in Bogotá were still waiting for the news to be confirmed, he stated in his letter, adding, "I hope to God it is mistaken."[2] Around this time, Sáenz also heard from one of Bolívar's faithful friends, General Luis Perú de Lacroix, in Cartagena. In his December 18 letter to her, de Lacroix eloquently described his most recent visit with Bolívar. He had last seen the Liberator on December 16 and, he reported, had left him "in the arms of death [and] in a peaceful agony . . . that cannot last much longer." "I am waiting for the fatal news at any moment," he added. In words heavy with sadness, the Frenchman then confessed that he already had begun "weeping over the [imminent] death of the Father of the Nation, of the unhappy and great Bolívar, killed by the perversity and ingratitude of those who owed everything to him, [and] who had received everything [thanks to] his generosity."[3]

Although Sáenz at first was inclined to receive such reports with skepticism, her skepticism soon faded. On January 10, interim president Rafael Urdaneta formally announced Bolívar's death in a speech to the public. The bad news was now official; Sáenz could no longer resist or deny it. Urdaneta also declared a monthlong period of official mourning. All church bells in the city were to toll three times a day (morning, noon, and evening) for the next nine days; for the rest of the month, there were to be no public celebrations or other entertainment. On February 10, Bogotá's residents were to turn out for a special funeral mass in the city's cathedral.[4]

Sáenz postponed her plans to return to the capital. She may have done so in part for health reasons; various sources suggest she had begun to suffer from bouts of rheumatism, an illness destined to plague her in later years and whose symptoms must have been soothed by Guaduas's warm climate. She likely also preferred to postpone facing the painful reminders of her old life with Bolívar. Indeed, she may have wished to mourn her lover's death in relative privacy—away from the pitying (and, in some cases, perhaps, triumphant) gaze of Bogotá friends and neighbors. She began smoking cigars regularly, a habit that must have tranquilized her and dulled the edges of her grief and sadness.[5]

Although extant letters and documents are largely silent on the matter, Sáenz no doubt felt her personal loss keenly. One hint of her grief is the story or legend according to which she tried to commit suicide by exposing herself to a poisonous snakebite. The main source of this legend is French scientist Jean-Baptiste Boussingault. After visiting the Libertadora one day during her recovery from the snakebite—which, she told him, had been part of a "scientific experiment"—Boussingault speculated that she had been trying to imitate Cleopatra.[6]

Sáenz's apparent suicidal tendencies sprang from more than grief over the death of her lover, however. They likely also arose from guilt over having failed to recognize the seriousness of his illness and to accompany him to the bitter end. Sáenz was no doubt devastated by the loss of her hard-won status as his mistress (and as the Libertadora), as well. Her generally erratic behavior, moreover, had begun to worry friends and acquaintances. In a letter addressed to her in early March, several of these mentioned her recent "craziness" and, in their words, her "refusal to avoid dangers." "Your life is important and you should cherish it [just] as we, out of gratitude and respect for your virtues, cherish you," they chided her.[7] Such expressions of concern may have helped her to emerge from the worst of her doldrums.

Around late March, Sáenz returned to Bogotá. She had become preoccupied with practical matters, her growing shortage of money in particular. Such a problem was new to her. Sáenz, after all, had always been provided for, first by her father and husband, later by Bolívar. She also had grown accustomed to a relatively lavish lifestyle. As in the case of most of her upper-class contemporaries, this lifestyle depended heavily on the presence of servants—including the nine household maids and one male servant who had accompanied her during her exile in Guaduas and on whom she seems to have doted.[8] It involved a habit of largesse as well. Such a habit may be gleaned from the impression Sáenz left on contemporary observers, at least one of whom described her as being "possessed of great property which she distributes liberally in charity."[9] Much like Bolívar, the Libertadora had grown used to spending freely; she had lived large, spending on charitable and political causes as well as on friends and parties.

By the time of Bolívar's death, however, her income had dwindled, and she had come to depend increasingly on credit. One source of credit was her friend Dundas Logan, a merchant and, like other members of Bogotá's small British community, a longtime Bolívar friend and supporter. In late November 1830, Sáenz had asked Logan to send her fabric that, as she explained at the time, was desperately needed to clothe her "near-naked" female servants; she also requested that its cost be added to what she already owed him (one thousand pesos).[10]

Sáenz also sought to remedy her increasingly precarious financial situation. Her first thought was to sell some of her personal property, including the Hacienda Cataguango, a 575-acre farm located some fifteen kilometers south of Quito. A producer of corn, wheat, barley, potatoes, and cattle, Cataguango had belonged to the estate of the Aizpuru family. Sáenz had acquired it after Ignacia Aizpuru had failed to honor her part of their 1823 agreement—a failure that had prompted local Colombian authorities to intervene. In 1826, authorities under General Juan José Flores had seized the hacienda and auctioned it in order to raise the sum Aizpuru owed her niece. The highest bidder had been Flores himself, who subsequently had ceded Cataguango to the Libertadora after apparently having persuaded her of its usefulness as a financial asset and potential source of rental income.[11]

Yet, ownership of Cataguango proved to be more of a headache than an asset. Although Sáenz had found an administrator willing to oversee the property as well as a tenant farmer who had agreed to pay her six hundred pesos a month in rent, she had yet to receive any rental payments or income. Disappointed and desperate, she now hoped to sell the hacienda for a respectable sum, one that would give her the money she needed to live on and to pay off her growing debt. She sought the help of influential Quito acquaintances. In September 1831, for example, Sáenz asked José Modesto Larrea, scion of one of her country's wealthiest and most prestigious landowning families, to assist her in auctioning off the hacienda. Larrea's November response must have been deeply disappointing. Cataguango would not sell at the price she wanted (eighty-five hundred pesos), he told her.[12] He later would advise against selling it.

Despite this, Sáenz persisted in trying to have the property auctioned. Her efforts were to be complicated both by distance and the influence of a less-than-trustworthy administrator. She finally would sell the property, albeit at a loss, some six years later.[13] For the moment, she continued to borrow and live on credit, making the most of her friendship with some of the country's wealthy merchant-bankers.

One of these was Manuel Vélez of Medellín, who, after learning of Sáenz's financial problems, wrote to inform her of his and his business partner's desire to help her or, in his words, "alleviate her in her misfortunes." Vélez, at the same time, advised that, should she ever be bothered by a creditor, Sáenz should recur "immediately" to his firm's office (i.e., the merchant house of Vélez y Aranzazu) in Bogotá.[14] It was in this way that, over the next few years, she managed to survive and keep up appearances.

The Libertadora also kept an eye on political developments. Among these was the final collapse of Gran Colombia, mortally wounded by Venezuela's (and, later, Ecuador's) decision to separate and establish itself as an independent republic. Gran Colombia's spirit, nevertheless, lingered in Bogotá. In his aforementioned January 10 speech, for example, President Urdaneta urged his fellow citizens to work together for peace and restoration of the political union Bolívar had founded. His call fell on deaf ears, however. While most people were eager for peace, few were eager to restore the old union. They were tired of war and turmoil and, in the wake of Bolívar's death especially, saw increasingly little reason to rally around the Bolivarians.

This was the case particularly of the Bolivarians' old rivals, including General José María Obando and Colonel José Hilario López. By late March 1831, Obando and López had begun leading a series of uprisings in Cauca Department and the upper Magdalena River region of Neiva. They both saw Urdaneta as a usurper—the man responsible for the overthrow of the legitimately elected government of Joaquín Mosquera. They resented him for his tendency to favor the interests of his fellow Venezuelan-born officers over those of native New Granadans, many of whom, like themselves, recently had been passed over for government appointments. Indeed, the two caudillos and their respective followers resented the Venezuelans' continuing political dominance, a dominance of which Urdaneta was a symbol and that grated against their country's growing nationalist sensibility. They had sympathizers among Urdaneta's old enemies (the Liberals) in and around Bogotá, many of whom now, also, actively opposed the Urdaneta government.

The president responded harshly to this opposition, ordering the arrest of numerous individuals, the seizure of their homes, and their political exile. Such measures only inflamed public feeling against him. Recognizing this, the embattled executive entered into negotiations with his challengers and agreed to resign. On April 28, the belligerent parties signed the Juntas de Apulo agreement—a treaty that, in addition to bringing an end to the fighting, also provided for a new constitutional convention (the Convención Granadina), to begin in October. The treaty also provided for the creation of an interim government to be headed by the widely respected General Domingo Caicedo. Above all, it paved the way for an important political transition, one destined to bode ill for the Bolivarians.[15]

This transition essentially involved the return to power of Bolívar's old Liberal-Santanderista opponents, their more radical faction, the so-called *exaltados,* in particular. Sáenz must have looked on in frustration as, from May onward, the *exaltados* began to hold sway over the interim Caicedo administration. *Exaltado* dominance stemmed in good part from the group's ability to win appointments to key government offices, including positions in the president's cabinet. General Obando, for example, became Caicedo's minister of war, a position that ensured him considerable influence over the army. Vicente Azuero became one of the cabinet's legal advisors.[16]

The *exaltados,* thereafter, pressured the government to punish those who had collaborated with the "usurper" and, above all, purge all civil and military officials identified as Bolivarians. In May 1831, minister of war Obando threw hundreds of Bolivarian officers (of Venezuelan and British origin especially) out of the army; many of these were subsequently forced to leave the country. Obando also disbanded the Callao Battalion, a pillar of the previous Urdaneta administration.[17] Backed by a powerful clique of former Santanderistas (a group that revolved around the Azuero brothers), he and his colleagues then looked for new targets. These came into public view when, on June 4, several of the *exaltados'* military allies formally petitioned Caicedo to fire all ministers associated with the Bolívar and Urdaneta governments, prosecute the leaders of the Bolivarians' August 1830 uprising, remove certain parish priests from their posts, and undertake several lesser administrative changes.[18]

The *exaltados'* growing political strength became most evident when, on June 19, the Caicedo administration issued a decree inviting Santander to return from exile. It, at the same time, offered to restore the former vice president's military rank and citizenship. This decree reflected a triumphalist Santanderista version of history by describing Santander as a victim of Bolivarian despotism and, above all, as a hero who had suffered for the cause of republican liberty.

Not all observers, of course, agreed with this interpretation. In the eyes of José Manuel Restrepo, for instance, the decree represented a shameful endorsement of the September 25 assassination attempt against Bolívar and of Santander's own, albeit indirect, involvement in it. Restrepo and others, nevertheless, glumly looked on as, four months later, the *exaltados* obtained the decree's ratification.[19] They also watched as the Liberator's enemies rejoiced in their political triumphs. On September 25, for example, *exaltado* leaders and Bogotá's municipal authorities commemorated the third anniversary of the notorious assassination attempt against Bolívar—an event they sought to portray as an act of patriotic resistance to despotism and that they and their followers celebrated in the main plaza with music and fireworks.[20]

Sáenz no doubt was horrified by these developments. By September, she had moved out of the house she had been living in since her return to Bogotá and begun renting a *quinta* on the city's outskirts.[21] This move may have been motivated by financial circumstances and a desire to avoid unpleasant and potentially troublesome encounters with her opponents. Indeed, in the wake of the Bolivarians' recent military and political defeats, Sáenz likely was all too aware of her new vulnerability.

She closely followed the activities of the Convención Granadina. Inaugurated in mid-October and involving some sixty delegates from various provinces, this gathering embodied the first real attempt to reorganize the country since Bolívar's exile and the collapse of Gran Colombia. One order of business involved selecting a name for the territory that remained after the 1830 separation of Venezuela and Ecuador and that corresponded, in essence, to the colonial Kingdom of New Granada. The matter led to heated debate, reflecting some of the difficulties inherent in defining a nation whose primary founder was the controversial and now largely reviled Bolívar. While Bolivarian and *moderado* delegates called for keeping the country's original 1821 moniker—Republic of Colombia—their *exaltado* rivals, harkening to older (pre-1821) precedents, argued for changing it. The *exaltados* won the debate by a narrow margin. They thus succeeded in renaming their country, henceforth to be known as the Republic of New Granada—a victory of no small symbolic significance.[22]

They subsequently devoted themselves to more concrete matters, including forcing the mild-mannered Caicedo to resign in favor of their new favorite, Obando. With Obando at their head, the *exaltados* proceeded to realize the rest of their agenda. This meant exiling most of the remaining Bolivarians, especially those responsible for the August 1830 revolt against Mosquera, a move that Sáenz could not have been happy to learn about.[23] The Libertadora nevertheless must have been heartened by news of the convention's decision to issue an amnesty to individuals who had been convicted of political crimes before May 5, 1831. As one of her letters shows, she expected this amnesty to apply to her.[24]

Sáenz still had to reckon with the consequences of Santander's return to power, however. The exiled statesman had remained popular, a situation that, in March 1832, led to his nomination (in absentia) as a presidential candidate and March 9 election to the presidency by a wide margin.[25]

Yet, while his return to Bogotá seven months later met with general rejoicing, his new government would do little to break away from the previous pattern of partisan retribution. An example was the government's treatment of its Bolivarian opponents, in particular, participants in the so-called Sardá conspiracy. This conspiracy was led by a forty-five-year-old Spanish-born army veteran, José María Sardá. After a string of adventures ranging from fighting with Napoleon's forces in Russia to involvement in the cause of Mexican independence, Sardá had arrived in Colombia and offered his services to Bolívar. He had then joined the Colombian army and, starting in the 1820s, had served as military commander of Santa Marta and intendant of Panama, achievements that had helped him win promotion to the rank of brigadier general. He also had become an enthusiastic Bolivarian. The collapse of Urdaneta's government and the subsequent rise of the *exaltados*, however, had dealt a blow to his fortunes. Like other Bolivarian officers of the time, Sardá had been summarily expelled from the army. He later was charged with treason and ordered to leave the country.

The unhappy man fled to Bogotá instead. Once there, in the hope that Santander's return from exile meant the start of a new era of political reconciliation, he applied for reinstatement into the army. In January 1833, however, his application was rejected. Along with other disgruntled military colleagues, the embittered Sardá began plotting against the authorities. On July 23, the date set for the uprising, he and his colleagues planned to overthrow Santander (and replace him with General José Miguel Pey, an old Bolivarian), seize (or kill) Generals Obando and López, and champion the rights of clergy and artisans.[26]

The alert new president got wind of their plans, however. In early August 1833, his men caught Sardá and several colleagues on the run and began arresting the plot's alleged participants. By October, forty-six men had been arrested and sentenced to death. Although twenty-eight of these ultimately had their death sentences commuted to eight to ten years in prison at hard labor, the remaining eighteen were executed in the city's main plaza—much in the manner of the executions carried out earlier against Bolívar's would-be assassins. Sardá would have been among the latter had he not escaped from prison. The government launched a manhunt for him and placed a one thousand–peso bounty on his head; its agents eventually found and killed him, leading observers to consider Sardá a victim of assassination.[27]

Manuela Sáenz was implicated in the conspiracy. At least one witness at Sardá's trial claimed she was an accessory and that she had recruited some two hundred men, including deserters, for the anticipated uprising.[28] Sáenz's personal correspondence is silent on the matter—her extant letters make no mention either of the conspiracy or of her alleged involvement in it. The same letters do tend to corroborate claims that her home served as a meeting place for the opponents of the president. Sáenz, in short, quite likely had been aware of the conspirators and their activities.[29]

The Santander government, in any case, saw her as an enemy. On August 7, 1833, just two weeks after the aborted Sardá uprising, secretary of interior José Rafael Mosquera revived the order for her exile. This order apparently originated with Sáenz's criminal indictment three years earlier and, according to Mosquera, due to difficult political circumstances, had been mistakenly suspended.[30] Old allies of Santander warmly endorsed it. One such ally was Lorenzo María Lleras, a fervent former Santanderista who had left the country in the wake of the September 25 assassination attempt and who, from his self-imposed exile in the United States, had devoted himself to denouncing Bolívar's dictatorship. Even after his return to Bogotá in 1832, Lleras found himself, in the words of one historian, "unable to forgive or forget what he saw as the sins [Bolívar and his followers] had committed against the state, liberty, and justice." He also became an "unrelenting prosecutor of old Bolivarians," using his role as the anonymous editor of *El Cachaco* (a progovernment newspaper he cofounded secretly with Florentino González) to review their past actions and condemn their support for the former dictator.[31] It was no surprise that Sáenz, at some point, would fall under his scrutiny.

This scrutiny became evident when, in September 1833, *El Cachaco* published a copy of the original (July 17, 1830) indictment against her. Two months later, it urged local officials to expel the Libertadora promptly. Indeed, in December, in light of the fact that Sáenz was still in Bogotá, it practically accused them of ignoring the government's order. "Is Doña Manuela Sáenz leaving or no, Mr. Police Chief?" the paper asked pointedly.[32] It then exhorted the chief to fulfill his "duty" while reminding him and other readers of Sáenz's past "mockery" of the government and recent use of her home as a meeting place for "troublemakers." "We are now tired of waiting for the execution of the order [for Sáenz's exile]," its anonymous editor (i.e., Lleras) stated, adding somewhat ominously that, unless police saw to Sáenz's departure by next Sunday, *El Cachaco* would publicly "denounce" them for failing in their responsibilities.[33]

Sáenz chose to ignore a press campaign that must have felt familiar— resembling the provocations the Liberals had launched against her three years earlier. She apparently had decided to cooperate with the government's decision. With Bolívar gone, after all, life in Bogotá no longer had much meaning for her. She probably also had decided that it was time to return to her native Quito, where she still had relatives and, above all, important personal matters to attend to; not the least of these was the matter of the Hacienda Cataguango, the sale of which had become increasingly crucial to remedying her financial situation.

Sáenz needed time to prepare for her journey, however. She thus requested that authorities extend the August deadline for her departure. They obliged her by extending the deadline to mid-December. Although in December the Libertadora still had not left Bogotá, she signaled her travel intentions by requesting a passport for travel to Cartagena and Panama; from Panama, she apparently planned to sail to Guayaquil and, from there, return home, traveling overland.[34]

She continued to put off leaving. One reason for this may have been her bitterness over some of the accusations or allegations made against her since her criminal indictment in 1830. These allegations included the rumor or legend that she had taken part in the notorious Battle of Santuario—a legend Sáenz herself would later characterize as "pure calumny."[35] Given her pride and sense of honor and her awareness of the general amnesty granted recently by the Convención Granadina, Sáenz quite likely hoped to clear her name; an attempt to do so may well have moved her to request another extension of her departure deadline. Her delay in complying with the exile order also may well have resulted, in part, from her lack of money and need to make special arrangements for her journey. She likely anticipated traveling at least part of the way with a friend or acquaintance, perhaps a merchant with business to attend to in Cartagena and Panama. As was then common among members of the upper classes, she probably expected to defray the cost of her travel through the sale of merchandise or by acting as a friend's business agent. Given the challenging and cumbersome nature of travel in Spanish South America in the first half of the nineteenth century (especially in remote, mountainous New Granada), arranging such a trip could take several weeks or even months.

The Santander government ran out of patience. On January 1, 1834, its agent, the governor of Cundinamarca Province, duly informed the Libertadora that she would have to leave town no later than the thirteenth of January; the alternative, he told her, was to be forced out by soldiers. Sáenz's response has not survived. It is likely she tried to appeal the governor's ultimatum and, confident in her right to do so, may not have taken his warning seriously. She was to receive a harsh surprise, however. On January 13 (a Monday), at around three in the afternoon, a posse appeared at her doorstep; there stood Bogotá's police chief accompanied by ten soldiers and eight convicts, all under the command of Lieutenant Dionisio Obando and all ready to carry her off by force, if necessary. At the head of the posse was none other than Lorenzo María Lleras, recently appointed as sheriff. Lleras, it seems, had accepted a special commission from the president—the job of ensuring that Sáenz left the city forthwith and hit the road to Cartagena.[36]

Sáenz was in her bedroom; some of her allies would later allege that she was recovering from a recent illness. Apparently unnerved by the sight of the posse, she demanded that the men leave. According to several accounts, she also shouted angrily at them and, along with her servants, threw out an insult or two. The men refused to leave, however. Lleras, meanwhile, had entered the house to knock at Sáenz's bedroom door. He asked her to dress and prepare for the trip, warning that, if need be, he was willing to use force against her. The indignant Libertadora responded by grabbing her two pistols and warning, in turn, that if the sheriff used force, she would not hesitate to shoot him; indeed, she would "kill" the first man who came near her. According to one eyewitness, she also announced that she was "tired" of living and "couldn't care less about sending a few men to the next world ahead of her."[37]

Lleras at first seems to have been surprised by Sáenz's resistance. A brief standoff ensued. During this time, the sheriff sent for confirmation of his original instructions from the governor; he also used the time to gather his wits. On receiving the governor's confirmation, he ordered his soldiers to seize the Libertadora. The latter, at the last minute, tried to ward her attackers off with a dagger, a gesture cut short when one of the soldiers pried the weapon out of her hands. Lleras then ordered that she—her hands bound by then and the rest of her, at the sheriff's insistence, "decently covered"—be taken to the local *divorcio*, or women's prison. He also ordered the arrest and confinement of her two remaining personal servants. As some eyewitnesses would later report, the latter tried to defend their mistress and lashed out at her attackers "like two furies."[38]

At 5:30 the next morning, soldiers briskly led Sáenz and her servants out of the New Granadan capital. After stopping to pick up supplies in the neighboring town of Funza, the group eventually made its way to Honda and, from there, completed its journey by river to Cartagena. Available sources suggest that, on arriving on the coast (most likely in early February), the Libertadora continued to be supervised by government agents. In or around early April, she was ordered to board the first ship to Jamaica.[39]

Sáenz's unceremonious expulsion did not go unnoticed. Just six days after her departure from Bogotá, for example, U.S. minister Robert McAfee noted with a certain awe that it had taken "a guard of twenty soldiers a whole day to arrest [Sáenz] without killing her." Remarking that "Bolívar's favorite mistress" had been "as brave as Caesar," he also interpreted that departure as a sign of the Colombian government's "uneasiness."[40] British minister William Turner saw the expulsion as an example of the Santander regime's general intolerance of its opponents and habit of "moving quickly" against them—a habit that apparently included denying them their day in court. "General Santander dragged from a sickbed and sent to Cartagena with a military escort and without any judicial process a lady (former mistress of Bolívar) who was adverse and obnoxious to his government," he reported in a hasty March despatch to his London superiors.[41]

Sáenz's ouster, in addition, sparked a minor flap between the government and local critics. The latter accused the government of going overboard and deplored the abrupt and violent manner in which Sáenz was forced out of the city. As one of them reminded the general public, she had not even had a chance to say good-bye to friends or to receive the "consolation" of a priest; "that is not something done among Christians."[42]

El Cachaco shot back by reminding its readers of Sáenz's past behavior. It specifically reminded them of the various allegations against her, including some of those contained in her 1830 criminal indictment. It emphasized her past sympathy and support for the government's enemies. Above all, perhaps, it praised the actions taken by New Granadan authorities (i.e., Lleras and Obando), highlighting their "sensitivity" and "tolerance" and going on to assert, rather threateningly, that, "if special consideration had not been given her because of her sex, [Sáenz] would have received the treatment warranted by her insolence and arrogant conduct."[43]

From Kingston, meanwhile, Sáenz continued trying to shake off her antagonists' allegations. In an early May letter to General Juan José Flores, for example, she denied that her home had served as a meeting place for the "discontented"—an apparent reference to the Sardá conspirators. The home's small size and location would have made this impossible, she told him. Although she certainly had received friends and visitors there, she had not bothered to ask whether they were "contented or discontented," she went on rather sheepishly.[44]

Sáenz also dismissed the allegation of her participation in the Battle of Santuario (August 27, 1830). The battle had occurred near the town of Funza, some three days' ride from her home in Guaduas, she told Flores, adding that it also coincided with a time in which she had been recuperating from the ill effects of a snakebite. She made light of the idea that she had participated in the fighting. "Had I been feeling well, who knows if I would have mounted my horse and taken off in a flash [toward the battle]," she remarked teasingly.[45]

Perhaps more important, Sáenz denied her involvement in New Granada's recent partisan skirmishes. "What do I have to do with politics?" her letter asked Flores disingenuously. "I loved the Liberator and venerate his memory and for this, I have been banished [from the country] by Santander," it continued. Its author then scoffed at the Santander government's effort to portray her as a dangerous subversive. The New Granadan president had assigned her an "imaginary bravery," she asserted, adding, "he [Santander] says I am capable of anything but is deceiving himself miserably." "Nothing can be done by a poor woman like me," she assured him.[46]

Sáenz's denial of her partisan involvement—and of the Santander regime's allegations against her—was offset somewhat by her simultaneous admission of her role in the June 9, 1830, Corpus Christi incident, particularly her efforts to, in her words, remove "Bolívar's portrait from the [fireworks] castle." "Seeing that no one else was going to do it, I thought it my duty [to do so]," she told Flores. "I don't regret it," she added. Sáenz then wondered aloud why her action had not been forgiven her under the terms of the March 1832 amnesty. "Supposing [removal of the portrait] to be a crime, was there not an amnesty law passed by the Convención [Granadina]?" she queried; "was I placed outside the bounds of this law?" The Libertadora went on to remind her old friend that, while she was not as terrible as her enemies had painted her, she was, nevertheless, "a formidable character, friend of my friends and enemy of my enemies." Among the latter, she admitted, was Santander, "that ungrateful man," as she referred to him. Santander's personal correspondence with Bolívar happened to be in her possession, she continued; she was "making good use of it," she went on rather cryptically.[47]

Yet, Sáenz, perhaps for the first time in her adult life, had begun to feel helpless and lonely. She sought to assuage such feelings, in part, through letters to Flores, a native of Puerto Cabello (Venezuela), whom she had met some twelve years earlier in Quito. Thanks to his battlefield accomplishments, Flores's mili-

tary and political career had blossomed. By 1826, he had become the top commander in the large, strategically vital District of the South (the future Ecuador),
a position of considerable power and influence.

Sáenz became Flores's admirer. She was grateful for the role the up-and-
coming young officer had played in ensuring her receipt of her inheritance, for
example. "I owe what little I have from my mother to the interest you took in
[seeing to] its payment," she told him.[48] She also recognized Flores's past loyalty
to the Liberator and had written him often since even before Ecuador's formal
separation from Gran Colombia—a separation that, with the backing of Quito's
upper classes, Flores had helped orchestrate and that, in May 1830, had led to his
election as Ecuador's first president.

She now needed a personal favor. She had not seen a dime of income from
her hacienda since her last departure from Quito (in 1827), she told him; nor,
her letter added, had she received a response to the many letters she had written
Pedro Sanz, the hacienda's less-than-reliable administrator. "No one writes me,"
she went on plaintively. In apologetic tones, Sáenz then suggested that Flores
"commission" someone to look into the problem. She appealed to their "old
friendship" and his compassion, noting that she had been "abandoned" by her
family and was "all alone on this island."[49]

Flores responded to Sáenz's appeal and, indeed, assisted her with her return
to Ecuador. When Sáenz arrived at the port of Guayaquil around early October
1835, he was there to greet her and provide her with the permit (*salvoconducto*)
and recommendation letters needed to proceed to Quito. He was no longer
president. He had resigned from office the previous year and, in September, had
ceded the presidency to his erstwhile opponent: Vicente Rocafuerte.

Son of a wealthy Guayaquil family, Rocafuerte was Ecuador's leading statesman. He had begun his career in 1812 as a delegate to Spain's Cortes of Cádiz
and served in the 1820s as a diplomatic representative of Gran Colombia and
Mexico, respectively, in various courts of Europe. He also was a staunch advocate of republican-style government and, through his various writings, by the
time of his 1833 return to Ecuador, had emerged as the country's most prominent political thinker.[50] Rocafuerte, in addition, had been Flores's greatest rival.
In the early months of 1834, for example, he had become the head of a popular
Guayaquil-based movement known as the Revolution of the Chihuahuas. This
movement had forced Flores to enter into negotiations with its leader. Under
a formal agreement in April, the caudillo had agreed to cede the presidency to
Rocafuerte in exchange for retaining command of the country's army; he had
agreed, too, to his and Rocafuerte's alternation in power. In addition, thanks to
the army's resounding defeat of Rocafuerte's remaining opponents, members of

the Sociedad del Quiteño Libre, at the January 1835 Battle of Miñarica, Flores had become the new president's indispensable ally. Rocafuerte subsequently rewarded him richly, giving him a lifetime appointment as chief of the army while also flattering him and consulting often with him on government matters.[51] The two men—the first brilliant and irascible, the second shrewd and charming—nevertheless would continue to have differences. Sáenz, unfortunately, would be one of them.

Indeed, on the evening of October 18, having arrived at the small highland town of Guaranda (roughly halfway to Quito), the Libertadora learned that she would not be allowed to continue her journey. According to the official memo forwarded to her by Guaranda's mayor, or corregidor, Antonio Robelli, she was to be detained and, by order of President Rocafuerte, made to return to Guayaquil. Ultimately, she was to be sent out of the country. Among the stated reasons for this order was the allegation that Sáenz had returned to Ecuador to avenge her half-brother, General José María Sáenz, who had been killed the year before (on April 21, 1834) while militating on behalf of the Sociedad del Quiteño Libre. In the words of the memo's author, minister of interior José Miguel González, the Libertadora had come to "embrace her brother's cause" and seek "vengeance" for him; she was to be turned away, therefore, "for the sake of [preserving] public tranquillity."[52]

González offered several other reasons for the president's decision to send the Libertadora into exile. These included the threat that continued to be posed by the government's enemies, especially members of the Sociedad del Quiteño Libre. Despite their defeat in battle some ten months earlier, the latter had regrouped and, according to González, begun "invading" the provinces of Guayaquil and Quito with the help of foreign allies. The minister also cited the government's knowledge of Sáenz's "character" and of "the good result she obtained on behalf of the revolutionaries of [New Granada]"—an apparent reference to her support for the Bolivarians' 1830 rebellion against the Mosquera regime in Bogotá. Not least, González referred to the "extremely active role unfortunately taken by several ladies in the recent turmoil," an allusion to the wives (and other female relatives) of some of the government's chief opponents—opponents with whom, González seemed to imply, Sáenz might be allied.[53]

Sáenz's response was outrage. She waved Robelli away and, in a letter fired off to Flores afterward, characterized González's memo as having been "dictated by a drunkard and written by an imbecile." Referring to the president and his minister as mere "riffraff," she also questioned the exile order's basis. Why, she asked, had authorities seen fit to bring up the issue of her past conduct in Bogotá?[54] With regard to the allegation involving José María, she remarked only that her brothers had made her "suffer much"—a statement that hinted at her political differences with them and at her disapproval of José María's past opposition to the Flores government. Above all, Sáenz insisted on her "innocence" and, in adamant tones, informed Flores that "only force" could make her reverse her journey. There was one exception, she added, and that was if the caudillo himself ordered her out of the country: "You have only to say, 'Manuela, you committed the great crime of loving the L—[Liberator]. Abandon your country; leave behind what little you have; forget country, friends and family'; [and] you will see me obey [the order] (albeit with sadness)," she asserted. Sáenz, nevertheless, implored her old friend to stand up for her. In the letter's postscript, she asked that he enforce the passport he had given her and thus spare her the shame of "being seen as a criminal."[55]

Flores responded six days later. In his October 25 letter to Sáenz, he expressed shock over the Rocafuerte regime's failure to accept the "recommendation and supplications" that, he said, he had made in order to secure the official authorization she needed for travel to Quito. "My dear friend . . . you can imagine my surprise and astonishment at the [government's] unwillingness to concede me such a small favor," he told her in alluding to Rocafuerte's apparent decision to ignore the recommendation. Yet, there was little that could be done about it, he added. Given his apparent lack of influence and prestige within the current administration, he continued, hinting at his wounded pride, his only alternative was to be henceforth "cautious and circumspect in all my actions." The consequences, otherwise, would be grave ones, he insisted. "Were I, at this time, to resist the government's order . . . my reputation would be compromised," he told her, adding somewhat disingenuously that "unhappy peoples [would be unnecessarily] exposed to great suffering for the sake of avenging a personal slight." "Prudence counsels [that you] cede to the circumstances . . . [only] God knows my sorrow and deep regret," he then concluded.[56]

Ever savvy and self-interested, Flores, in short, was unwilling to stick his neck out. He nevertheless suggested that the Libertadora not give up hope entirely. "Come now," he told her brightly, "maybe a letter I wrote subsequently to Mr. Rocafuerte will make him retract his original order." He also appeared apologetic, explaining that if Rocafuerte chose not to retract the order, "we will be patient; and I will remain ashamed and sorry." Flores then suggested in a postscript that Sáenz appeal personally to the government so that she, at least, might be allowed to stay in Ambato, a city south of Quito, for as long as might be needed.[57]

The Libertadora had anticipated him. On October 20, after her anger had subsided, she sent a politely worded letter to Minister González. The letter assured González of her peaceful intentions and addressed the official reasons behind the order for her exile. It began by rejecting the idea that Sáenz had embraced any side in the conflict between the government and members of the Sociedad del Quiteño Libre and, indeed, insisted on her neutrality. "[While] some may see me as an enemy, others as a friend, I swear before the world that I am neither one nor the other," the Libertadora assured Rocafuerte's top cabinet official. "I am a friend of my friends on both sides [and] regret the misfortunes they share," she added.[58]

In the letter, she also questioned the Ecuadorian government's attempt to condemn her for her past conduct (i.e., support for the Bolivarians) in Bogotá—conduct that, she suggested, proved her devotion to peace and order and for which, in any case, she already had been convicted. "It is not right that I [should] suffer at the hands of both parties," she told González, highlighting the fact that she was about to be punished twice for the same alleged crime and, this time, without any legal proceeding. Sáenz then complained of her recent treatment by officials in Guayaquil. Although, on her arrival at the port, she reported, she had presented her passport to the port's authority, the governor had accused her of being without one and demanded that she leave town within twenty-four hours. "Suckling babes know that [a passport] may be gotten for [only] four pesos," she reminded the minister, still smarting from her mistreatment. In the hope of directing González's attention to the matter, she also enclosed the two passports she had been carrying (including the one used for her entry into Guayaquil and the other authorizing her travel to Quito), along with a copy of Flores's safe-conduct (*salvoconducto*).[59]

The Libertadora went on to address a more substantive matter: the government's claim that she had returned to Ecuador to avenge the death of her brother José María—a claim that, in her eyes, had no legitimate basis. "A legal government is nothing more than an agent of the Constitution," she lectured, adding, "I, in the name of the law, request the [evidence of my] supposed vow to avenge my brother; or any other proof [of that vow]." It was under this "pretext," she told González stiffly, that, while she had been en route to Riobamba, local authorities had detained her.[60]

Sáenz also sought to awaken González's sense of compassion. In the same October 20 letter to him, she described herself as "a poor, unfortunate woman [who was] on her way back to her native soil to visit friends and relatives and to bid these farewell, perhaps for the last time." She was on her way to claim the "few possessions" she had left behind in Quito, to sell the hacienda inherited from her mother, and to "withdraw [in order] to die in peace in a foreign country," she added. "Can it be that even this is to be denied me?"[61]

In a bid for González's mercy, Sáenz minced no words about the hardships that faced her. "Sir: I live by my own miserable labor; I have part of my luggage there [in Quito] and the rest spread all over; I have creditors to pay," she told him plainly. "It is not possible [for me] to travel back and forth so many times," she added, going on to suggest that "a just government should avoid the [economic] ruin of individuals." The Libertadora then gathered herself. She expressed confidence that, on reflection, the president would recognize the wisdom of her observation and rescind the order. She promised, in turn, her "good behavior." "I do not believe this [rescindment] would stain [the president's] record of conduct as a gentleman or fame as a magistrate," she continued in a further attempt to move González and his superior. She concluded by noting that it would be "indecorous" for her to propose anything that might impinge on that record and fame; she was, after all, as she reminded González, both a "patriot" and "friend of order."[62]

Sáenz's appeal fell on deaf ears. One apparent reason for this was the chronic political turmoil that had plagued the young nation for the past year and that continued to threaten the Rocafuerte government's claim to authority. Even after the government's victory over its enemies at the January 20 Battle of Miñarica (near Ambato), for example, those enemies—led by wealthy aristocrat José Félix Valdivieso, leader of the Sociedad del Quiteño Libre—had continued to plot and agitate, aided by allies such as New Granada's notorious General Obando.[63] Their activities had brought out the worst in Rocafuerte who, for all his vaunted liberalism, had little patience or tolerance for his opponents.

Indeed, since January, the president had dealt harshly with the remaining elements of the Sociedad del Quiteño Libre, arresting and executing or deporting their activists; shutting down their newspapers; and, as in the case of Valdivieso and his wife, imposing ruinous fines on their chief supporters. He harbored few doubts about the need for such measures. "Rest assured that a rigor that borders on cruelty is what is needed to choke the anarchic spirit that afflicts this society," he once told a colleague, adding "for desperate times, desperate remedies . . . only by showing a firmness that inspires terror will I achieve [my] important goal [of restoring public tranquillity]." As Sáenz herself would soon learn, neither did Rocafuerte worry much about civil rights or legal procedures. "Tribunals and legal strategies delay the rebels' punishment," he remarked to the same colleague.[64] While extreme, his attitude was, of course, far from unique in early republican Spanish America, many of whose leaders (Santander in New Granada included) treated opponents similarly—a by-product of the years of war and of elite desires to restore some semblance of postindependence order and stability.

Rocafuerte also feared Manuela Sáenz's formidable reputation—a result both of the informal political influence she had wielded as Bolívar's mistress in Bogotá and of her highly visible partisan activism, including her support for the 1830 uprising hatched by the Bolivarians. It had been magnified and distorted by her New Granadan antagonists, the *exaltados*, who had accompanied their public campaign for her expulsion with allegations that she was "masculine" and a "new Amazon."[65] A negative image of her, no doubt, also had been propagated by Santander, who, as Sáenz had noted in the letter to Flores, had claimed she was "capable of anything."[66]

Little wonder, then, that Rocafuerte (who had been in touch with his New Granadan counterpart) should view the Libertadora with wariness. In an October 14 note to Flores, he justified his decision to exile her in terms of his "practical knowledge" of her "character, talents, vices, ambition and prostitution."[67] He described her afterward as "very proud, very insubordinate, [and] very brazen" and as possessing "shrewdness and audacity."[68]

What he and his cabinet ministers feared even more, however, was the possibility that Sáenz might join forces with their political opposition: members of the still-active Sociedad del Quiteño Libre. "These need only a hand to guide them and give them momentum," the president informed his main military ally. Sáenz was that hand, he added, stating, "she is the one [who has been] called to revive the revolutionary flame."[69] Keen to persuade Flores of the truth of his statements, Rocafuerte wrote a bit over a week later to report on his opponents' reaction to the news that Sáenz had been turned back to Guayaquil. "The wake carried out by Señora Valdivieso and company [in response to the news] confirms the suspicions we had," he told the caudillo in reference to that reaction and to the apparent disappointment of José Félix's wife in particular.[70]

González seconded his superior. Word of Sáenz's planned return to Quito had sparked general excitement throughout the city and motivated the Sociedad to renew its conspiring against the government, he alleged in a missive to Flores. "No sooner was Manuela Sáenz's coming announced in this capital than the so-called Quiteños Libres, rejoicing among themselves, began to hope of subverting the garrison with her assistance," he added.[71] The Libertadora had revealed her pro-opposition political leanings, he asserted. "On reaching the towns of the interior, Manuela Sáenz began to spread the word that she was coming to avenge the death of her brother José María and was ready to commit herself to this objective," González continued. He claimed that the Libertadora's influence already had begun to make itself felt among the rebels. All of these, put together, "had neither the courage nor the coolheadedness [of] this lady," he stated, adding that Sáenz was "the only one who in the present circumstances . . . could

have done something [to] mobilize . . . [them]." Rocafuerte's minister then announced that "the so-called Quiteños Libres have been in mourning since learning that the brave Amazon, on whom they had pinned their highest hopes, has
been ordered to turn back." After confessing that "it truly seems ridiculous to
fear anything from a woman," he went on to remind Flores of the role of women
in the Sociedad's most recent rebellion (in 1834). "Weren't women the ones who
promoted the last revolution?" he queried.[72]

Such comments constituted more than a simple complaint about the activities of the government's female opponents.[73] They reflected a broader elite male
reaction to the seeming breakdown of traditional gender boundaries and, above
all, perceived female encroachment on the public sphere and traditionally male
realm of politics and governance.[74] A result of women's post-1810 mobilization—
their participation in the wars for independence (and assumption of new roles
as "patriots" and "loyalists"), especially—this encroachment subtly threatened
patriarchy and the ideal of female gender subordination. As Rebecca Earle has
hypothesized, it inspired a certain male anxiety or uneasiness, a sentiment that
may be inferred from early republican leaders' scant praise of female wartime
accomplishments and insistence on portraying women mainly as victims.[75]

It also inspired a certain male hostility. Various scholars have alluded to this
hostility in explaining how, in the wake of independence, republican spokesmen,
as Elizabeth Dore has put it, "urged women to return home . . . and sought to
marginalize [them] from the public sphere."[76] Sylvia Arrom has shown how, in
the case of early republican Mexico, such spokesmen increasingly criticized—
and vilified—women whose behavior or activities failed to conform to the new
ideology of female domesticity.[77]

Sáenz's own experience reflects an extreme version of the same trend. In
Bogotá, her involvement in competitive politics (i.e., the rivalry between Liberals and Bolivarians) not only spawned private criticism of her but, after Bolívar's
departure, led to her public pillorying. It contributed to opponents' criminal
indictment of her, including accusations that she had acted "in a way alien to her
sex" and violated "the rules of [feminine] modesty . . . [and] morality."[78]

A similar reaction appears in the semihysterical misogynist rhetoric of President Rocafuerte. Much like his counterparts in revolutionary (and Napoleonic-
era) France, Rocafuerte condemned female political activism generally, characterizing it both as improper and as a source of confusion and chaos, a virtual
perversion of nature. In an October 14 note to Flores, for example, he described
his female opponents not only as the country's "leading ladies" but as "declared
enemies of all order." He portrayed them as virtual dominatrices and thus as
threats to "natural" patriarchal arrangements; they "have much influence over

the weak souls of their brothers, husbands and [other male] relatives," he added worriedly.[79] Rocafuerte then claimed in another letter that women in general were to blame for his country's chronic turmoil and instability. "Women are the ones who [do the] most [to] stir up the spirit of anarchy in these countries," he told Flores. It was because of "this truth," he added, that his cabinet had taken the "precaution" of expelling Sáenz from Ecuadorian territory.[80]

The president reserved special criticism for members of the opposite sex who formed part of elite circles of power and whose positions, however informal, allowed them to wield political influence. The Libertadora, in his view, was one of these. Rocafuerte thus compared her to two of the recent era's most famous female figures: the Parisian salon hostess, author, and cultural arbiter Germaine Necker (Madame de Staël) and Mexican socialite and proindependence propagandist María Ignacia Rodríguez de Velasco y Osorio (La Güera Rodríguez, who once had been grilled by the Inquisition for her patriot sympathies).[81]

Like Sáenz, both women had been of privileged, upper-class background. Both had stood out not only for their looks, charm, and wit but for their boldness, influence over public opinion, and skill at backroom politics. Both also had been punished by being sent into exile for criticizing or defying their governments' authorities—Napoleon Bonaparte in the first case, the Mexican viceregal government in the second. For Rocafuerte, such women represented a dangerous example, being, as he put it, "women of loose morals renowned for their beauty and habituated to cabinet intrigues." They were "more pernicious than an [entire] army of conspirators," he added in frustration.[82]

Absorbing the lesson, Sáenz would tread more carefully.

FIVE

Exile and Vindication, 1835–1845

THE ECUADORIAN GOVERNMENT'S refusal to rescind its order left Manuela Sáenz with no alternative. She retraced her steps to Guayaquil and, toward the middle of November 1835, boarded a ship for Peru and exile. Although she probably had Lima in mind as her ultimate destination, she disembarked at the ship's first main stop: the northern Peruvian port of Paita. The sight of Paita at first must have been less than inspiring. While set against a dramatic backdrop— at the edge of a bay bordered by a 150-foot-high bluff and beyond it a desert plain—the town itself was small and gray. It sat on the protected southern side of the bay, dwarfed by a great promontory, the Silla de Paita. One contemporary visitor described it as "without exception the most uninviting desolate spot that human beings ever selected for a habitation."[1]

The hot, dusty port nevertheless had its allure. Thanks to the impact of the growing New England–based whaling industry, it was relatively prosperous, having become the center of a bustling service economy and brisk import-export trade that attracted enterprising individuals. It harbored an interesting mix of foreign and native-born residents, including a number of Sáenz's compatriots. It offered refuge. Here Sáenz would form a new circle of friends. She would rebuild her life, injecting it with new meaning and purpose. Above all,

Lithograph of nineteenth-century Paita, from A. de la Salle, *Voyage autor du monde ... ,*
Album historique (Paris: Bertrand, 1840–1866). Courtesy of Special Collections and
Archives, The Sheridan Libraries, Johns Hopkins University, Baltimore, Maryland.

she would seek to overcome the isolation and ignominy to which her exile seemingly had consigned her.

Sáenz's arrival in Paita coincided with the start of a dynamic new phase in the
small town's history. Although it long had been an important stop for ships sailing between Lima and Panama (as well as a center of contraband trade for much
of the Spanish colonial period), Paita by the mid-1830s had become an outpost
of what William Lofstrom has called an "incipient North Atlantic economic empire."[2] Its deep, sheltered bay, the best in northern Peru, had helped transform
it into a vital port of call for New England whalers—ships that roamed Pacific
waters in search of the valuable sperm whale. The year 1835 alone witnessed the
arrival of eighty-eight whalers, an unprecedented number, along with twenty-
one American merchant ships, most of them from Nantucket and New Bedford,
Massachusetts.[3] The town catered to the various needs of these vessels, supply-
ing them with fresh water, firewood, food (meat and produce brought in from
farms of the nearby Chira Valley), liquor, and provisions such as soap, salt,
sugar, and tobacco. It provided them with a variety of naval stores, including
rope, tar, pitch, and locally made sailcloth. It also catered to its Yankee visitors'
need for rest and entertainment. Beyond the old marketplace and parish church
of San Francisco on the eastern side of town, for instance, was the Maintope

district, a neighborhood known for its numerous bars (*pulperías*), billiard halls, and brothels frequented by sailors.

The general growth of trade and business had produced new signs of prosperity. One indication lay in the new, fancier homes that were increasingly visible. Although most houses in Paita still were simple huts with dirt floors and walls built of mud and split bamboo (*bajareque*), a small but growing number boasted two stories and included amenities such as plaster façades, balconies, and barred windows.[4]

Paita's growth and prosperity also had enlarged the number and variety of its permanent residents. By 1836, the year after Sáenz's arrival, its population had grown to about four thousand. It included some fifty to sixty Americans and Europeans, most of them merchants who had come to participate in the port's brisk import-export trade, a few of them officials attached to the local British, U.S., Portuguese, Spanish, and French consulates.[5] It incorporated an indeterminate number of Ecuadorians, many of them transients.

The Ecuadorian presence in Paita was not unusual. Due both to its proximity and desert environment, the port long had been a haven for well-to-do Guayaquil residents fleeing the yellow fever epidemics that periodically assailed their tropical city. It occasionally drew those intent on traveling some fifty kilometers (eighty miles) inland to Piura, capital of the Department of Piura and at the time a town of around ten thousand, for the "cure" offered by the Piura River's sarsaparilla- and palo santo–impregnated waters.[6] Thanks to its status as a regular stop for ships and, starting in 1840, British Pacific Steam Navigation Company packet boats sailing along the coast between Panama and Chile (with stops in Guayaquil, Lima, and Valparaíso), it also served frequently as a way station for traveling merchants and other individuals. By the mid-1830s, moreover, it was becoming a haven for refugees and exiles, like Sáenz, victims of war and of Ecuador's increasingly strife-ridden national politics.[7]

From all appearances, Sáenz made friends easily in Paita. One such friend was Alexander Ruden, a merchant of New York origin who arrived in town around the same time (the mid-1830s) and who was destined to emerge as one of Paita's wealthiest and most respectable personages, a fact signaled by his 1839 appointment to the position of U.S. consul.[8] Sáenz took special pride in her relationship with Ruden and, in 1840, for example, referred to him (perhaps somewhat boastfully) as "an intimate friend of mine."[9] She also came to know a number of local families, including the family of one Don José Lamas, probably a prominent local merchant or businessman. Indeed, Sáenz grew close to Lamas's wife, Luisa Godos; sister-in-law Paula Godos; and eldest daughter, Josefa (Chepita) Lamas y Godos. She came to exchange personal confidences and favors with all three and, as her extant letters suggest, regarded them as quasi-relatives. "They're a good family, I care for them, and they esteem me," she once remarked of them.[10]

She befriended various local officials and was soon enjoying daily conversations with Paita's port captain, conversations that inevitably involved politics and that, as her letters hint, at times escalated into arguments. She came to receive visits from the governor of the Department of Piura. In 1842, for example, in reference to her cordial relationship with then-governor Joaquín Torrico, she rather proudly informed a correspondent that "whenever he [Torrico] comes to this port, he visits me."[11] Such statements suggest the extent to which, during her first decade in Paita, Sáenz both made friends and garnered the respect of local notables. They also hint at her ability to cope with some of the challenges of her exile.

Perhaps the most immediate challenge was economic. Sáenz's peremptory expulsion from Ecuador—where, by her own admission, she had not intended to settle permanently—had left her without the resources she had hoped to bring with her, that is, the money and income due from the rental of her hacienda as well as other personal property left behind in Quito.[12] She soon resolved this dilemma, in part, through her early access to loans and credit. An apparent result of her ability to parlay her elite connections and credentials as a property owner, such access must have allowed her to rent or start payment on a house and perhaps start up a small retail business—possibly a shop like the one from which, according to legend, she came to sell candy and tobacco as well as English translations.[13] Although its proceeds turned out to be far less than originally expected, the sale of Cataguango in 1837 also must have given Sáenz the means to establish herself by, at the very least, ensuring her continued creditworthiness.[14] For reasons to be explained ahead, however, she was to remain in chronic debt and, like many an exiled person before her—including some of early republican Spanish America's most famous leaders—ever vulnerable to the effects of impoverishment.

Like most émigrés and displaced persons, Sáenz was no stranger to feelings of sadness, loneliness, and isolation, these often accompanied by intense longing for her native soil, Quito especially.[15] Many of these feelings may be discerned in the letters she wrote during her early years in Paita, including those addressed to General Juan José Flores. Loneliness, for example, is evident in her tendency to lament the apparent infrequency of Flores's letters to her. "You don't even remember me," she told the general at one point in 1837, adding in near desperation, "why do you not wish to write me?"[16] She then asked that her friend "console" her by writing at least occasionally. Craving news and information from home, she also asked that he send her something to read. "Send me some publications you don't need," she requested; "this [port] is an abandoned place," she added, revealing her sense of isolation.[17]

Sáenz sounded an occasional note of self-pity. Some four and a half years after her arrival in Paita, or "this miserable port," as she once called it dismissively, she did not hesitate to describe herself as "alone and unfortunate." She later would compare herself to an orphan or person who had been abandoned. "I am from Quito and have relatives there; I [also] had friends; and [yet], it is as if I had never had them," she told Flores in a letter in 1844 lamenting the difficulty she had had in finding someone to serve as her personal agent and attend to the business matters she still had in her native city.[18]

Sáenz, nevertheless, resisted the temptation to wallow in feeling sorry for herself. She maintained contact with members of her family such as half-brother Ignacio, who resided in New Granada. She stayed in touch with friends and acquaintances in Guayaquil, Quito, and Lima. Above all, perhaps, she renewed contact with old followers of Bolívar such as Juan José Flores.[19]

Indeed, Sáenz regarded Flores as a personal friend. Her view of friendship likely resembled that of most Spanish Americans of her generation, especially elites (both men and women) who had come of age during the wars for independence. According to Sarah Chambers, among political actors of similar social status, the term "friendship" generally implied "a relationship in which loyalty and mutual favors were assumed but without the negative connotations of clientage." Chambers also sees the term as connoting "a relationship of mutual respect and affection" between peers, if not equals.[20]

Sáenz's tie to the caudillo seems to have fit both of these descriptions. This tie had begun to take shape in the mid-1820s, when Flores, then prefect of the District of the South, ensured justice for Sáenz in the matter of her inheritance. It had grown with Flores's demonstration of his talents and firm allegiance to Bolívar, both of which she appreciated. By 1829, Sáenz had begun cultivating the young officer, partly by flattering him in letters filled with words of praise and admiration. One letter, for example, had extolled Flores's many "useful" qualities, citing the "love" and respect he evidently had come to inspire among Ecuadorians. It had suggested his indispensability; "how, without hurting you, might we split you into three parts?" Sáenz had queried in a phrase that, at the time, likely echoed Bolívar's own sentiments. After sending greetings to Flores's "lovable family," moreover, it had expressed its author's readiness to "be useful" to him and concluded with a reference to her as his "most affectionate friend."[21] Such words, no doubt, had reflected not only Sáenz's personal feelings of appreciation for the caudillo but a desire to ensure the latter's continued devotion to the cause of the Liberator.

Sáenz continued to view the caudillo as both friend and ally. He became a lifeline as well. Sáenz's exile to Paita, after all, had compounded the effects of a series of staggering personal losses for her, ranging from the deaths of Bolívar and her brother José María, on the one hand, to violent separation from home, country, friends, family, and material fortune, on the other. Her ongoing friendship with Flores (some of whose personal qualities, his charm and dapperness for example, must have reminded her of the Liberator), thus, likely helped compensate for, or at least soften the blow of, such losses. One hint of this may be found in the warm tone of her letters to him. These invariably address the caudillo in affectionate fashion, referring to him as "old friend," "special friend," and the like while referring to their author as his "invariable friend," "true friend," "loving friend," and so on. Indeed, they brim with professions of love and affection. "It would be hard for me to stop caring for you," Sáenz admitted in a November 1837 missive after having reminded the caudillo of her friendship; "I truly cherish you [and] could never hate you," she added.[22] "I truly want for you all the good that I crave for myself, since I love you and regard you with admiration and respect," she declared in another letter dated Christmas Day of that same year. Yet another letter, written six years later, professes Sáenz's "rare personal affection" for the caudillo.[23]

Sáenz's fondness for and attachment to Flores found expression not only in words but also in actions, including her habit of sending small gifts, usually items she had made for him. In November 1837, for example, she sent him a "Paita-style" table runner she had crocheted or embroidered (suggesting that it be used at Flores's Hacienda La Elvira) and began work on a "delicate white poncho" she hoped he would wear at La Elvira for "protection against the mosquitoes."[24] Sáenz also continued to send greetings regularly to Flores's family, along with the occasional gift for his wife, Mercedes Jijón, and his daughters. Determined to preserve a friendship that, among other things, served as a reminder of more glorious days beside Bolívar, she eventually would ask Flores to send her a small portrait of himself.[25]

She also felt that friendship should be reciprocal. During the final months of her second year in Paita, for example, Sáenz chided Flores for his apparent lapse in correspondence. "Have I committed some sin of lèse-amitié?" she asked him only half-jokingly. "No," she answered herself, going on to remark that, where friends were concerned, she would rather be "dead" than indifferent or, in her words, "inconsequent [to them]." She then reminded Flores of the kind of friend she had been. She stressed her steadfastness: "I always have been a true friend of yours and [always] will be [for] as long as I live." Such was the case even when "you may not [always] be [a true friend of] mine," she added.[26] In her view, moreover, "fifteen years of friendship" had given her the "right" to complain of Flores's epistolary neglect. Sáenz thus brushed off the admonition Flores had included in a recent, if belated, reply to her recent letters in which he had told her to "'not be querulous.'" "Let me complain!" she retorted, adding teasingly, "why overturn the natural order?" and "of whom [else] should I complain but you?" "You don't think of me," she alleged subsequently, adding that she wanted him to think of her "constantly."²⁷

Like most exiles, Sáenz clearly feared being forgotten. She also hated to be taken for granted. "Can't you see that fine things are delicate?" she asked Flores in reference to their relationship. "The [feelings of] friendship I have for you could not be finer," she continued. She then acknowledged the caudillo's "[feelings of] friendship" for her while adding that, on this point, there was "room for improvement."²⁸

Sáenz's repeated and insistent references to friendship signaled a subtle relative drop in status, a result both of her political exile and her straitened economic circumstances. Such a drop was not unusual among émigrés. Nor was it unusual for someone in a position of relative weakness or dependence to refer to someone more powerful (e.g., a political patron) as a friend. In reference to people of the borderlands of nineteenth-century Brazil and Uruguay, for example, John Chasteen has noted that "the idiom of friendship applied to equal and unequal alliances alike."²⁹ María Theresa Calderón and Clement Thibaud have observed that, in the early Colombian republic, "a [claim of] friendship that is reiterated over and over" almost always connotes "subordination and [willingness to perform] service."³⁰

In Sáenz's case, such a claim connoted, at least in part, her emergence as Flores's dependent or client. Sáenz's dependence on the powerful caudillo had been evident since the time of her temporary exile in Kingston, Jamaica. There, broke and far from old friends and family (who apparently had failed to receive or answer her letters), she had looked to him for help in ensuring her financial survival, a survival that depended on her ability to secure her rights as a property owner. Sáenz's anxious request for Flores to check on the status of her hacienda—about which, as she told him, she still had heard nothing or received any money—had included an appeal both to their "old friendship" and his "compassion." It had stressed her relative powerlessness. "Sir, you may commission anyone and be served; as for me [on the other hand], nobody even writes me," she had stated.³¹ Flores had responded to this appeal for help. He had tried to smooth her return to Ecuador and, no doubt aware of her financial hardships, had lent her three hundred pesos on the eve of her voyage to Paita. He apparently also had offered to help her collect some of the monies still owed her—including overdue rent payments and a two thousand–peso balance from her hacienda's recent sale.[32]

For all this Sáenz was grateful. "I have not forgotten what I [still] need to pay you," she told him near the end of her second year in Paita, adding in an apparent reference to the three hundred pesos she had received from him that, as soon as she could get her "head above water," she would repay what he had "so generously" lent her.[33] Two and a half years later, in explaining her decision to send him a power of attorney, she also reminded him of her status as a solitary and virtually destitute exile. "Sir, you must do two things: first, forgive me [for] the liberties I take, considering that I am alone and unfortunate; second, do what seems best to you," she stated somewhat apologetically. "A thousand and one thanks for the interest you take in my [financial] affairs . . . my gratitude will be eternal," she added in a subsequent (July 1840) missive.[34]

Sáenz thus viewed Flores as a protector. As Calderón and Thibaud have noted for Gran Colombia (and early republican Spanish America generally), individuals who called each other "friends" ultimately viewed friendship as a form of security or "protection against exclusion from circles of power."[35] While such protection had special meaning for men competing with each other for control of government or public office, it was important in general. It certainly was important for women seeking to safeguard themselves and their families as well as their homes and property against the effects of endemic civil war and violence. As Alonso Valencia has shown for the southwestern region of New Granada (Colombia) at this time, it was not unusual for women—many of them heads of household who had been widowed or otherwise left on their own—to enter into a clientelistic relationship-cum friendship with a powerful caudillo.[36]

Sáenz thus appreciated the protection Flores had offered her when, in the early months of 1837, he had used his influence in the Ecuadorian Senate to obtain the official permission she needed to return to her country. Although she ultimately chose not to return, citing her continued wariness of President Rocafuerte (who would remain in power until 1839), she duly acknowledged this sign of the caudillo's personal and political favor. She thanked Flores for what she called "this latest proof of kindness and friendship" and assured him that "wherever [I may happen to live], I will always be your grateful and admiring friend; time will show you."[37] She would reiterate her gratitude and appreciation. "You are the only one who has not denied me protection and who has tolerated my petulance . . . know that my gratitude will be eternal," she would remind him years later.[38]

Sáenz also wished to reciprocate Flores's favors. Indeed, she longed for a chance to, in her words, "serve" him—a longing made plain in some of her earliest extant letters from Paita. "Of what use to you is my friendship?" she asked Flores rhetorically in October 1837, right after her earlier complaint that he did not "even remember" her.[39] "What might you need of me or of Paita?" she later queried, adding, "although you may make fun of my offer, I tell you with all my heart that I wish to serve you and to have the pleasure of doing something [for you]." "I would gladly make any kind of sacrifice for you and call it my duty," she continued.[40] "When will you give me something to do?" she again asked the caudillo in the postscript of her Christmas Day letter to him that year, going on impatiently, "Is there [truly] nothing, nothing you need from Paita?"[41]

Sáenz finally got her answer some two and a half years later. In early June 1840, after having regained control of the Ecuadorian presidency, Flores wrote to suggest the possibility of her collaborating with him, including sending him information. Sáenz rejoiced over this and over the idea that she might have the chance to assist her powerful friend. "It is hard for me to express the delight I received in [reading] your June 3 letter," she wrote in her July 12 response, noting that Flores had "flattered" her by offering "the hope that one day I will be useful to you." "Would that I could serve you even with my own life, Sir," she added. In what may have been a veiled reference to a recent (and ultimately crippling) hip injury, she then expressed doubt over her ability to serve Flores to the full extent that she wished or that the caudillo himself "merited." "I won't try to prove this [wish to serve you] with words," she continued, adding, "I'm convinced that nothing that I could say would be enough to do so." "You've known me 18 years [and] you know that I love you," she went on; "that [should be] enough."[42]

Sáenz's desire to collaborate with or, in her words, "be useful" to Flores sprang from more than mere gratitude or a desire to please him. She still burned with the memory of the expulsion she had suffered at the hands of Ecuadorian authorities. She nursed a grudge against Vicente Rocafuerte, in particular. In explaining her reluctance to return to Ecuador despite the safe-conduct with which Flores had provided her, she cited the former president's "past injustice" and continuing "opposition" toward her; because of this, she added, she preferred to wait until his departure or removal from power.[43] She also had little good to say about him, at one point characterizing her country's most prominent Liberal statesman as both "malevolent" and an untrustworthy ally. "When you least expect it, he [Rocafuerte] pulls a trick on you," she wrote the caudillo, adding, "You should be well aware that he is scheming, cowardly, and traitorous." "Don't rely on him," she exhorted.[44] Six years later, she would still burn with the memory of Rocafuerte's order for her exile, referring to it as "a terrible anathema from hell."[45]

Sáenz also nursed a grudge against Guayaquil's governor, Vicente Ramón Roca. Besides having played a key role in her expulsion from the country, Roca,

she told Flores, had tried to associate her with a notorious group of antigovernment rebels: the Chihuahuas. He tried to "make me appear [as a member] of
that [political] faction," she resentfully noted.⁴⁶

Above all, perhaps, Sáenz sought vindication. This meant, in part, evening
the score against those who had exiled her. "General, why not allow a revolution
to be made against Rocafuerte?" she asked Flores roughly two years after settling
in Paita.⁴⁷ Forgiving and forgetting had never been one of her strong points.
"Believe me, my friend, that I have a capital defect, [and that defect is] vengeful-
ness," she would admit to the caudillo in 1843, while recalling the notorious assassination of General Antonio José de Sucre, Bolívar's best friend, in June 1830.
Yet, in her view, her vengeful sentiments also were a testimony to her loyalty to
"dear friends, both living and dead"—a reference, no doubt, to men like Sucre
and Flores, who had been among the Liberator's staunchest followers.⁴⁸

Vindication also meant redeeming her reputation as a "friend of order" and a
"patriot," a reputation that, in her eyes, had been damaged less by the fact of her
expulsion from Ecuador than by the allegations used to justify it. At least one
of these, the allegation that she was an ally of the Chihuahuas, apparently still
dogged her. Sáenz was determined to shake it. "I could never be a supporter of
a faction that opposed you," she assured the caudillo. Time, she continued, will
give her a chance to prove it.⁴⁹

Other circumstances also contributed to Sáenz's emerging alliance with the
Ecuadorian president. One of these was President Flores's own disillusionment
with government, a tendency exacerbated by his recent domestic policy failures.
In January 1841, Flores failed to win legislative approval for what biographer
Mark Van Aken has described as an "ambitious and controversial" package of
reform proposals, including a proposal to modify the nation's tax structure and
thus lessen the burden on its large Indian population. He thereafter lost interest
in domestic matters and, restless and eager for glory, began to focus instead on
foreign adventures—including efforts to reclaim territory Ecuador had lost to
its neighbors after the wars for independence.⁵⁰ Indeed, as Van Aken has noted,
he found it hard to "resist the temptation" to exploit opportunities for both rec-
lamation and aggrandizement. One example was Flores's response to the rebellion that, in 1840–1841, erupted next door, in the ever-volatile region of Pasto.
Although he answered New Granadan authorities' appeal for help in ending the
rebellion (sending fifteen hundred troops in July 1840, for example), the caudillo
also tried to turn the situation to his advantage, demanding territorial conces-
sions as a reward for his assistance and reasserting Ecuadorian claims to Pasto.⁵¹

Sáenz, meanwhile, applauded her friend's aid to the New Granadans. Possibly unaware of his ulterior motives—or of his failed bid for New Granadan

territory—she hailed his military victories, congratulating him on fulfillment of a "mission" that had proved, in her words, "useful" to both republics. She viewed those victories as a harbinger of Flores's success in future endeavors. "Let us agree on one thing, General, and that is that fortune [victory] smiles upon you," she told him in a letter, adding, in an apparent bid to flatter and encourage him, "I am certain that you [will] succeed at whatever you put your mind to."[52]

Sáenz also supported Flores's revival of Ecuadorian claims to northern Peruvian territory. These claims were based on the 1829 Treaty of Guayaquil (signed between Peru and the now-defunct Gran Colombia), which, according to authorities in Quito, stipulated the boundary between the two countries along with Ecuador's sovereignty over Maynas and Jaén provinces. Peru disagreed with this interpretation and declared its right to the two provinces on the basis of continuous occupation (i.e., the principle of *uti possidetis*) since the time of its independence from Spain. During a December 1841 interview with Peruvian diplomat Matías León, the Flores government, nevertheless, publicly demanded the "return" of the disputed real estate. It then threatened to seize the latter by force if necessary. The Peruvians responded the following January by breaking off negotiations.[53]

Eager to prove her patriotism and loyalty to the Flores government, Sáenz, not surprisingly, took Flores's side on the boundary quarrel. Indeed, she already had written to inform him of the purpose behind León's diplomatic mission. She knew "for certain" that León had been sent to "distract" the Ecuadorians until his own government (by then at war with Bolivia) was "better situated," she had told the president in December in a statement apparently based on information she had received from sources in Lima. She also urged him to use the occasion of the diplomat's visit to advance strategic Ecuadorian interests. "You must know better than I or anyone . . . that this is the most brilliant opportunity for [discussing] this matter of boundaries, etc.," she stated.[54]

Sáenz's subsequent missives reported on Peruvian political developments. They sought to warn Flores of what their author saw as Peru's aggressive, expansionist tendency—including its perennial effort to reclaim territory that, like the port of Guayaquil, had once belonged to it. "Believe me, my dear general, that if the Peruvians have not [yet] gone to Guayaquil, it is only because of the thing [conflict] with Bolivia; otherwise, they would have taken advantage of the time you were [away] in Pasto," she told Flores in late January 1842, recalling a key factor behind the war that had erupted between Peru and her country (at the time, part of Gran Colombia) some thirteen years earlier.[55] She went on to allege that, while most Peruvians were too "indolent" to care about either side of the boundary controversy, a significant number of them dreamed of controlling Ecuadorian territory; these, she stated, "aspired" to control "as far as the Juanambú [River]."[56]

Sáenz became involved in the so-called Grand Project. This was a semisecret plan to restore the Peru-Bolivia Confederation, a union that had been founded in 1836 by Bolivian-born General Andrés de Santa Cruz (1792–1865), another former follower of the Liberator. Although this union had collapsed in January 1839 in the face of combined Peruvian and Chilean pressure—along with a successful invasion by the Chilean army—the smooth-talking Santa Cruz hoped to resurrect it with the help of his old colleague Flores.[57] Indeed, since going into exile and settling in Ecuador in 1840 at Flores's invitation, he had persuaded the Ecuadorian president to support the project by promising him rich dividends in prestige and territory. The idea was for Flores to lead an expanded confederation, one that would include his country and that would contribute to the project's stated goal of promoting "civilization" and "saving" the Andean peoples from anarchy. Such an idea appealed to Flores's ambition and vanity. The proposed entity, after all, harkened back to the Liberator's old (and unrealized) Andean Federation and was to enjoy a reach as vast as that of the ancient Inca Empire.[58] Commitment to it helps explain the Ecuadorian president's aggressive approach toward the Peruvian boundary controversy. It also clarifies his support for Santa Cruz's various filibustering expeditions. Launched from Guayaquil (two in 1841, one in 1843), these expeditions were meant both to intimidate the Peruvians and to rally Santa Cruz's old followers; ultimately, it seems, they were to pave the way for an Ecuadorian invasion—a key step in fulfilling the aims of the Grand Project.[59]

Sáenz knew of the Grand Project through both Santa Cruz and Flores. She probably had learned of it first from the former, with whom she seems to have been in touch since around the time of her arrival in Paita and whom she considered an old friend. Her feelings of closeness to Santa Cruz may be gleaned from her reaction to the news of his failed filibustering expedition and capture by enemy forces less than two years later. "I should not have friends, given how much their misfortunes affect me; I'm worried sick over General Santa Cruz," she would lament to Flores after learning of the general's late October 1843 arrest and imprisonment by soldiers under the command of Peruvian general Ramón Castilla. "[Santa Cruz's imprisonment and transfer to Cuzco] has me beside myself; I don't know what to think . . . poor thing! What a terrible misfortune!" she would add later, despite feeling relief that her friend's life was to be spared.[60] Sáenz also acknowledged her "intimate friendship" with the former Protector, recalling that this friendship had begun with their 1821 meeting in Lima and admitting that she felt deeply "all that happens to him."[61]

Sáenz's extant letters to Flores also reveal her cooperation with the main ar-
chitects of the Grand Project. They allude to her correspondence with Santa
Cruz, correspondence through which she no doubt kept the former Protector
informed of the latest twists and turns of Peruvian politics. They suggest, too,
that she assisted Santa Cruz with various logistical matters. In one April 22, 1843,
missive, for example, Sáenz relayed her greetings to the exiled general while in-
forming him that a safe-conduct pass was on its way to his old ally and fellow
exile, General Luis José de Orbegoso. The letters thus reveal that Sáenz acted as
an intermediary as well as an informant for the Grand Project's leaders.[62]

The same sources show Sáenz's efforts to supply Flores with news and information she thought useful to him. They include reports on the filibustering
expeditions Santa Cruz had launched from Guayaquil with Flores's blessing. In
a February 1842 letter, for instance, Sáenz informed the Ecuadorian president
of the fate of the 120-man expeditionary force that, led by one Justo Hercelles
(a Santa Cruz ally), had landed in northern Peru the previous December and
been intercepted by Peruvian authorities in January. The government in Lima
had ordered the filibusters' imprisonment and was determined to have them
executed by firing squad, she told him, referring to news she apparently had
received from friends in Lima as well as recent steamship arrivals in Paita. The
Peruvian authorities were planning to retaliate against Ecuador for this, she then
suggested, claiming the government planned to send two thousand Peruvian
troops to Piura; after this, she added breathlessly, the "whole [Peruvian] army"
was to be sent across the border and into Ecuador. Peruvians already had begun
mobilizing for war, she continued, noting that a call for the drafting of men between the ages of twenty-five and fifty-five had recently been issued.[63]

Sáenz portrayed the surrounding region (and, by extension, northern Peru
generally) as being ripe for an Ecuadorian invasion. A February 1841 missive
of hers to Flores offers an upbeat assessment of local political sentiment, portraying Piura Province as a virtual bastion of Santa Cruz support (Santacru-
cismo). "Every Piurano [citizen of Piura] . . . is a soldier of Santa Cruz," the letter notes.[64] A subsequent letter assures the caudillo that a significant proportion
of Peruvians are "friends of Flores." These, Sáenz asserted in a brief analysis of
public opinion, disliked their own government and hoped for a "breakdown" in
Peru-Ecuador relations so that, she went on, they might witness their favorite's
victory in the ensuing conflict.[65]

Sáenz also encouraged Flores to follow through on his and Santa Cruz's
apparent plans for an invasion. While acknowledging that, in any future war
with Ecuador, Peru held a financial advantage thanks to the recent boom in
guano exports, she opined that that advantage was "the only [one] they have

over us." She went on to portray the Ecuadorians as possessing superior military capability—something she naturally attributed to the leadership of Flores. "With you [as our leader], we should not be afraid of any rivals, much less the Peruvians," one of her letters to him stated.[66]

Sáenz cast doubt on the capability of the Peruvian army. Indeed, in addition to reporting on the Peruvians' ongoing conflict with Bolivia (through June 1842) and on their increasing factionalism, she offered a withering assessment of the country's armed forces. In a June 1842 letter to Flores, for example, she assessed one of the local army units, specifically the corps commanded by Colonel Juan José Arrieta—one that, she added, was reputed to be the best in the army's southern division. "I know it [Arrieta's corps] very well," she told him, explaining that, during the corps' stay in Paita, the men had lodged in a barracks located next to her house. This circumstance had allowed her to form an impression of the soldiers and to conclude that the latter represented poor fighting material. Sáenz described the corps as "not worth a seashell." "Only the chasseurs [cazadores] company is good; the grenadiers, average; and the rest, trash," she added, remarking that most of the men "don't even know how to throw a lasso." She stressed the soldiers' lack of experience by noting, too, that most of them were fresh conscripts from Cuzco and nearby villages. "These Peruvians have nothing but guano with which to conquer everyone," she concluded disdainfully.[67]

Sáenz then reminded Flores of his sympathizers in Paita and the surrounding region of Piura and suggested that these were prepared to support the cause of an Ecuadorian-led confederation. Every man in the region was a militia member and every Paiteño (citizen of Paita), in particular, an experienced "gunner," she assured him.[68] She clarified in mid-July that, although local Peruvian authorities were, in her words, "panicked" over the thought of a Flores invasion, ordinary citizens "wished for the arrival of the Ecuadorians." She therefore remained hopeful of eventually giving her friend "a hug" in Peru, she added, revealing a wish to see Flores and her nation covered in glory—a hint, perhaps, of a yearning for the halcyon days of Bolívar and Gran Colombia.[69]

Indeed, despite her apparent commitment to the internationalist aim of the Grand Project, Sáenz's alliance with Flores (including her efforts to serve him as an informant) also sharpened her sense of national identity. This sense of identity, no doubt, had arisen gradually since the time that Sáenz had first left her native Quito. It had been enhanced by her experience of exile—an experience that had made her keenly aware of the differences between herself and those around her as well as of her Ecuadorian origins.

An example of this was an incident that occurred during her second year in Paita and that started with a conversation she had with the local port captain.

During the conversation, the latter apparently displayed a certain xenophobia that seems to have been not uncommon at the time among Peruvians. He expressed disdain for Ecuador and, according to Saenz, referred to the small country as being nothing more than a "poor place" lacking in leaders and statesmen. Offended by the man's comments, the Libertadora crisply rebutted them, telling "the crazy imbecile [what he] deserved to hear," as she later told Flores.[70]

In the course of the subsequent Peru-Ecuador boundary controversy, moreover, she began to vent her growing feelings of national loyalty. She attempted to obtain an Ecuadorian response to a poem that had appeared around the middle of 1842 in Lima's *El Comercio*. The poem wittily mocked Peru's Bolivian and Ecuadorian neighbors, portraying them as "proletarians" who, "petty and envious," coveted valuable parts of Peruvian territory. Sáenz was eager to see it answered and hoped Flores would find a compatriot to do so; "my God, sir, don't let me die with this [unsatisfied] craving," she told him, fairly bursting with desire to see the offending verses rebutted. She enclosed a copy of the poem while suggesting that, in Quito, the caudillo would likely find someone with the wit and skill needed to meet its literary challenge—"[in Quito] they're good at satire," she noted. She expressed hope Flores would publish the results in an Ecuadorian newspaper such as *La Balanza,* the Flores government's unofficial organ.[71]

Nationalism also allowed Sáenz to justify her growing interest (and possibly more than vicarious involvement) in Peruvian politics—an interest linked in large part to her knowledge of and collaboration with the Grand Project. Since January 1842, she had been watching Peru's increasingly chaotic situation, including its struggle against the Bolivians and growing civil war as well as the shifting balance of power among its various military leaders. "If another country's politics has an interest for me it is only because of its relationship to [the politics of] my own [country] and [the interests of] my friends," she once told Flores rather defensively after remarking on some unidentified piece of news from southern Peru, this likely related to Santa Cruz's or his allies' activities.[72]

She became frustrated with Peru's seemingly endless political turmoil, blaming it on what she characterized as Peruvian "fickleness" and "lack of character." In an August 1842 letter to Flores, for example, she highlighted the ease with which the ordinary citizen changed his opinion. "Over here [in Peru], there's more [of a tendency toward] getting tied up in knots than [actual] fighting," she reported in reference to the national elections being prepared for that year. "It's amusing to live here, since today there's one thing and tomorrow, another [while] the opinions within a single person vary in accordance with circumstances," she added. "Poor country! Here there is no political creed that springs from the heart; everything is [done] out of fear or [material] interest."[73]

In contrast to an increasingly chaotic Peru, Ecuador in these years was a veritable oasis of political stability. Sáenz attributed this stability to the Flores government and thus gave her approval to her friend's plan to be reelected for a third term. "This will be the only way to avoid revolutions in the country," she told him in late March 1843, after having learned of his anticipated reelection by delegates to the constitutional convention in Quito. Flores's reelection would ensure avoidance of "Peru's example of having a [new] president every six months," she added.[74]

Sáenz also sought to defend her friend's government from attacks by its increasingly vocal domestic opposition. This opposition had risen partly in response to recent secularizing policies that had alienated conservative Catholics, members of the clergy in particular. It had grown in reaction to Flores's arrogance and errors of judgment, including his failure to consult with his main ally, Rocafuerte, about his plans for reelection and revision of the country's Constitution of Ambato (1835). Over the objections of Rocafuerte and other liberal politicians, Flores and his supporters had replaced the older charter with a new, more authoritarian one—in essence, a milder version of the charter Simon Bolívar had long ago drafted for Bolivia. Formally adopted by convention delegates in April 1843, this new Constitution sought to ensure order by boosting the powers of the executive branch while reducing civil liberties. It extended the presidential term to eight years (the first draft permitted the president's immediate reelection) and gave the president almost unlimited power to veto legislation as well as appoint and remove government officials. It also greatly reduced the power of the bicameral legislature, calling for that body to meet only once every four years and then only for a maximum of ninety days; senators were to serve for twelve years, deputies for eight. The 1843 Constitution thus called for a virtual dictatorship.[75]

Despite his willingness to support it at first, in late March, Rocafuerte (by then serving as a delegate for the Department of Guayas) roundly rejected the charter—referring to it as "a political abortion" while, at the same time, accusing Flores of "tyranny." He then abandoned the convention and returned to Guayaquil, from where in June, after an unsuccessful attempt to launch a rebellion, he went into voluntary exile in Peru. From Lima, he waged a relentless war of words against his country's president over the next eighteen months, producing a series of hard-hitting essays entitled "To the Ecuadorian Nation." Written in Rocafuerte's usual irascible style, the essays brim with personal insults. They characterize Flores as a vulgar tyrant and "political strumpet"; they also refer to him as the head of a "Negroid military aristocracy" (in an apparent slam against his rival's humble Venezuelan origin) which aspires to return Ecuador to monarchism. Above all, they galvanized other Flores opponents. Among these were Rocafuerte's numerous supporters in Guayaquil, including members of an influential merchant elite who, later that year, would throw their support to a burgeoning antigovernment conspiracy.[76]

Sáenz was quick to notice some of the early signs of this conspiracy, including the activities of Ecuadorians both in Paita and nearby Piura. At forty-six years of age, thanks to her elite background and connections (including her known friendships with President Flores and important local figures like Consul Ruden), she had achieved a certain prominence. She also had become a pillar of the region's tiny Ecuadorian émigré community, a status reflected in the words of a Piura-based compatriot who once referred to her as "an important and influential woman."[77]

Sáenz's status among her fellow exiles and émigrés seems to have stemmed, in part, from the concern she showed for them—a quality manifested, for example, in her efforts to minister to one Chana Torres, a compatriot who had fallen ill and for whom Sáenz had found a physician.[78] It also stemmed from her willingness to use her social and political connections to perform special favors. Some evidence, for example, suggests that Sáenz occasionally served as an intermediary in or facilitator of small business transactions between the émigrés and Ruden.[79] It shows, too, that she interceded with the Ecuadorian president on behalf of individuals seeking official permission to return to their country. An example of this is her June 1843 petition to Flores on behalf of an individual identified only as "poor Oyarbide." Sáenz's petition expresses pity for the latter, describing him as a "refugee" who is "dying of illness and hunger" and announces that she is enclosing his personal letter. It explains that Oyarbide is "anxiously awaiting" a safe-conduct pass in order to return to his home in Cuenca, where, it adds, he hopes to rejoin his elderly father, recuperate, and indulge his craving for "locro." It then suggests that Flores intervene in the matter. Indeed, Sáenz asked that the caudillo "take pity on [Oyarbide's] situation" and informed him that the man was "not in a condition to be anybody's enemy"; he had "[only] a few years left to live," she added.[80] Although Flores's response remains unknown, available evidence suggests the caudillo was accustomed to receiving such requests for favor and that he generally granted them.

Sáenz's peaceful relationship with her fellow émigrés soon became complicated, however, as it dawned on her that some of them were Flores's opponents. An example was the case of Pedro Moncayo who, until April 1843, was Ecuador's official consul in Piura. A native of Ibarra and former director of the now-defunct Liberal newspaper *El Quiteño Libre,* Moncayo had once been one of Flores's fiercest opponents. He had been exiled by the president in 1833 and had joined forces with the government's Chihuahua opposition. He also had been a close ally of and advisor to Vicente Rocafuerte, parting ways with the famous statesman only

after the latter's 1834 political accord with Flores. He then had settled as a voluntary exile in Paita, where he eventually had reconciled with the president and, in
1839, accepted the offer of a consular appointment.[81] It was during this time that,
encouraged by both mutual need and isolation (at one point, they may have been
virtually the only permanent Ecuadorian residents in the region), he and Sáenz
had developed a cordial and, it seems, mutually satisfactory relationship.

Sáenz approved of what she saw as Moncayo's sense of patriotism, once referring to the consul as "very Ecuadorian" (muchacho muy ecuatoriano).[82] Yet, she
also had reservations about him. In a January 1842 letter to Flores, she suggested
that the consul had not yet given up his old radical liberal ideas and biases, observing that Moncayo "thinks only of [abstract] principles when we are now at
[the point of reaching] our goals . . . [and] is a confirmed enemy of the [sierra]
oligarchy . . . [with] a head full of [ideas] from Cassius, Brutus, etc."[83] Once
convinced of his renewed (albeit secret) opposition to Flores, she occasionally
referred to him in subsequent letters as a "Jacobin."

Sáenz's suspicions of Moncayo were aroused by apparent irregularities in the
conduct of his assistant, a native of Guayaquil named Juan Otoya, whom the
consul (who resided in Piura) had left in charge of a small office in Paita. In
the same letter, she alleged Otoya had allowed unauthorized individuals to open
the consul's official despatches as well as to remit private letters via the supposedly
exclusive consular mail service. She then wondered aloud why Moncayo would
employ a man like him; as she reminded the overconfident president, the vice-
consul was an old enemy of his or, in her words, "the most anti-Ecuadorian."[84]

By January 1843, Sáenz had learned of Moncayo's secret editorship of a new
anti-Flores newspaper, La Linterna Mágica (the Magic Lantern), in Piura. She
hastened to report this news to Flores. Anxious that the consul should not learn
of her role as the president's informant (and afraid the caudillo might reveal it
to his advisors), however, she stopped short of a direct accusation. Her January
30 letter to Flores thus only hints that La Linterna Mágica was the work of a traitor. "General, you always raise crows so that they can take out your eyes," she
chided. "I very much wish to know who is the author of this newspaper," she
added; "[friends] assure me that he is a person [who has been] much favored by
you," she went on delicately. Sáenz then suggested the president might learn that
person's (i.e., Moncayo's) identity by having his consul general in Lima lodge a
formal protest with the Peruvian government, a move that, she surmised, might
prompt authorities to investigate the offending paper.[85]

Over the next several months, she continued trying to warn him of Moncayo's betrayal. This included his authorship of various antigovernment pamphlets, or "libels," that, by July, as she reported, were being published in Piura.

Given Flores's decision to replace Moncayo with a new consul later that year, her warnings must have been at least somewhat effective.[86]

Sáenz's discovery of Moncayo's and other émigrés' involvement in the underground opposition to Flores put her in a quandary. She wished to maintain good relations with compatriots who trusted her and with whom she had developed ties of friendship and interdependence. Her first warnings to Flores about Moncayo, therefore, had included a reminder to maintain confidentiality and her identity as his informant a secret. "It is vital you keep this [my comments] a complete secret from everyone, especially your [cabinet] ministers, as these are friends of his [Moncayo's]," Sáenz told him, adding, "I only wish to warn you of this [Moncayo's activity] in case it might be useful [and] hope you tear up this letter [after reading it]." She wished heartily to avoid offending the sensitive consul and thus run the risk of turning him into "an enemy."[87]

Yet, ultimately, Sáenz's desire to avoid alienating Moncayo and those around him was less important than her sense of personal loyalty and obligation to the Ecuadorian president. In the context of the growing struggle between Flores and his opponents, it was this sense of loyalty and obligation that took precedence. "A thousand and more occurrences almost, almost prepared me to be the opposite [of a steadfast friend and ally]," she told the caudillo cryptically in June 1843.[88] Sáenz, by then, had become increasingly aware of her status as one of Flores's few local adherents—one who, for years, had lived "in the middle of the club of his enemies," as she put it. She also had not forgotten Flores's past Bolivarianism. "A deep reflection and imperious voice [inside me] screamed [and persuaded me that] 'General Flores is not to blame for your misfortunes and has been and [always] will be the friend and admirer of Bolívar," she wrote the caudillo, adding that, because of this, he could count on her unflinching loyalty, "pure and without stain." In return for this loyalty, Sáenz asked only that Flores trust her and believe what she had to tell him while keeping her role as his informant a secret. Sáenz's conscious decision to serve as Flores's agent and informant also sprang from her fear that the conspirators sought to kill him. She had learned of a plot to assassinate him, she wrote the caudillo worriedly, citing an allusion to such a plot in a letter from Quito that she apparently intercepted. "I tremble at the thought of it [the alleged plot], knowing how trusting you are," she added.[89]

Having confirmed her pro-Flores allegiance, Sáenz turned to dealing with Flores's opponents. This included reporting to the president on their plan to overthrow him, a plan that she had learned about as early as March 1843 with the help of a letter she (or a friend) apparently intercepted.[90] Sáenz also gave details about the activities of local conspirators. As may be gleaned from her missives to

Flores, the conspirators consisted of a handful (in her words, a "club") of young men who had gathered around Moncayo and Otoya and who operated out of Piura, all the while staying in touch with Rocafuerte, Vicente Ramón Roca, and other opposition leaders in Lima. They occasionally met at Otoya's home in Paita—from where Sáenz and friends such as Paula Godos could keep an eye on them.[91] One of their major activities involved disseminating anti-Flores propaganda, much of it designed to be smuggled into Ecuador in defiance of Flores's censorship laws.

Beyond Moncayo, a main source of this propaganda was Manuel Cárdenas, a native of New Granada's Cauca Province as well as Liberal journalist and former personal secretary of General José María Obando. Based in Piura and with access to his own printing press, Cárdenas also had contributed many of the anti-Flores comments that had appeared recently in *El Comercio*.[92]

Alarmed by these discoveries, Sáenz sought to stop the flow of the conspirators' "vile" writings. She began alerting Flores to his enemies' efforts to smuggle such writings across the border. At one point, for example, having learned of the despatch of a series of "libels" to southern Ecuador, she advised the president to intercept all packages traveling from Piura to either Cuenca or Loja. She also suggested he order such packages to be brought to him for inspection before allowing them to proceed to their destinations.[93]

She at the same time kept him informed of the appearance of new opposition publications. Her letters often contained one or two copies of the offending document so that the latter could be rebutted in *La Gaceta del Gobierno del Ecuador* or in another government organ, *La Balanza,* both edited by Guatemalan-born publicist José Irisarri. In late July, for example, Sáenz sent Flores two copies of the third issue of *La Linterna Mágica* and promised to follow these with copies of a broadside entitled *Libertad o muerte* (Liberty or Death), apparently authored by Rocafuerte.[94]

Restless as always, she also sought to block the spread of such publications. As her letters make clear, she began gathering and burning large numbers of them. Her initial success may be explained by the continued secrecy of her role as Flores's informant (along with the fact that most of the conspirators lived roughly a day's distance away, in Piura) and by her ability to seem neutral in the growing Ecuadorian civil conflict. Her age and experience as well as her respectable upper-class status and known personal ties to the Liberator and other lofty personages no doubt contributed to this appearance of neutrality. Such factors likely contributed to her image as a patriot who stood above mere partisan factions.[95]

They also facilitated Sáenz's efforts to deceive some of the conspirators. Through 1843, the latter seem to have assumed that their amiable and high-minded countrywoman agreed with them. An example was the case of one Avendaño, a rather impressionable young man whom Sáenz had persuaded to bring her copies of the latest anti-Flores publications, apparently having convinced him that she would ensure their proper forwarding to Quito. Her true intentions, of course, were just the opposite. As she reported to Flores in July with impish glee, she had burned seventy-eight of the eighty copies of *The Magic Lantern* (third issue) Avendaño had brought her. She planned a similar fate for *Libertad o muerte,* copies of which the unwary conspirator also was supposed to bring her.[96] Yet another example of Sáenz's deception of the conspirators was the case of one Víctor Proaño who, before leaving Paita for Lima sometime in October, apparently left her in charge of forwarding his personal mail to him.[97]

The Libertadora, in addition, sought to counter the conspirators' anti-Flores propaganda. Among the latter was a broadside attributed to Manuel Cárdenas. "I become irritated when I see broadsides as vile as the one produced by Cárdenas," Sáenz wrote to the Ecuadorian president. Her irritation, moreover, led her to denounce it to her compatriots. Exploiting her reputation as a patriotic matron (someone who stood above the partisan fray), she wrote Ecuadorians in Piura in the hope, as she stated in her missive to the caudillo, of "making them see that it [the broadside] is not just against General Flores but against Ecuador as a whole." She sought to encourage the Piura émigrés to "not be complacent" in the face of insults to their nation's leader; such insults, she added, were proof that Cárdenas was "looking for trouble."[98]

Sáenz also complained about the broadside to various officials in person. She expressed her concerns to Moncayo and brought up the matter with the new Ecuadorian consul, Colonel Carlos Joaquín Monsalve (Moncayo's recent replacement), apparently asking him to respond to the offending literature. She hoped the consul, now a "good friend" of hers, might buy Cárdenas's printing press. As she told Flores, she wanted to see Cárdenas—"that sarcastic native of Cauca"—deprived of his "diversion." She would buy the press herself if only she had the money, she continued, adding impulsively that, for just this once, she wished she "could be [act as freely as] a man."[99]

Sáenz then reported on her conversations with the conspirators. By late October 1843, she had spoken with two of them: Víctor Proaño and one Maldonado, both of whom seem to have been relatively recent arrivals in Paita. She also had spoken with Juan Otoya. The three men had announced news that frightened her—including a rumor that Flores had been assassinated. "Here, the only news has been that you were assassinated at a [recent] party," Sáenz told the president worriedly. The men also filled her in on various aspects of the conspiracy. "You cannot imagine the naughty things these boys speak of," she told the caudillo, launching into a breathless listing of what she had learned from them: that people throughout Ecuador were poised to fight the Ecuadorian president; that it had been decided to lay siege to him; that Flores's own associates would betray him; that the conspiracy had won the sympathy of all the nation's important people; that one-third of Flores's troops were ready to mutiny; and that Rocafuerte—who, along with Roca, was at the head of the opposition movement—was to arrive with two ships; and on and on. "They say a thousand wonderful things," she concluded sarcastically.[100]

Confident of her skill at conversation and argument, Sáenz sought to dissuade them from their conspiracy. She already had discussed the matter with Otoya, chiding him for his apparent habit of spreading false rumors. "I have spoken [with him] at length various times," she told the president. Indeed, she apparently got the conspirators to reconsider their plan of action. As she reported to Flores (and during what must have been an intense discussion with Proaño and Maldonado), she had questioned their claim that the president had been assassinated, observing that if such a claim were true, then there would no longer be a need for a plan to overthrow him. In an effort to further deflate the conspirators' enthusiasm, she also had laid out the likely consequences of Flores's assassination. "I explained to them that [your assassination] would be the worst calamity for the country," Sáenz told Flores, adding that she had warned the men that the president's death would likely trigger a civil war and foreign invasion. She then had explained how the nation would disintegrate—or how, in her words, "we [inevitably] would bathe ourselves in blood and become the prey of neighboring republics." She had asserted, too, that anyone who wished for Flores's death "ought not to call himself a patriot."[101]

Her arguments and assertions apparently were convincing. "They [the conspirators] agreed with me and said their plan was to separate him [Flores] from office and exile him from the country," she informed her friend triumphantly. She nevertheless remained frustrated with Flores for his apparent willingness to continue employing (and trusting) officials who betrayed him. She alluded once again to Otoya, whom Flores had allowed to continue in the vice-consular position. "Otoya is the worst [of the conspirators]," she reminded him, adding, "it seems you work hard to look for bad guys to employ . . . what fits you put me in." "I wish you were my son so that I could scold you as you deserve!"[102]

Sáenz's effort to divert the conspirators from their plans came to an abrupt halt as soon as she lost the neutral image she had cultivated and, in turn, the trust of those she had hoped to influence. That image was shattered as a result of the Flores government's decision to publish a letter from Proaño to Moncayo that she had intercepted. News of the letter's publication in two major progovernment newspapers, La Gaceta del Ecuador and La Concordia, left Sáenz flabbergasted. She responded by reminding Flores that she had sent him the missive only to inform him of the conspirators' progress—so that he "might be aware of the state of these gentlemen's [the conspirators'] affairs"—and not so that he could divulge it to the public. "They know I am the only one here [in a position to intercept their letters]," she explained in reference to the conspirators, adding that the latter "will now distrust me and for [good] reason."[103]

Although conscious of the risks involved in acting as Flores's secret informant, Sáenz must have been disappointed by her friend's apparent carelessness and little regard for the danger to which, for his sake, she had exposed herself. She had long warned him to avoid the public mail system and to send his letters to her only via specially designated mail recipients (including one Señor Luzzáraga of Guayaquil, for example, who was responsible for routing the letters through the U.S. or Ecuadorian diplomatic pouch).[104] She had repeatedly reminded him of the need for confidentiality, often marking certain letters of hers or the most sensitive portions of them as "confidential" or "highly confidential." "Not even God [himself] should see my letters to you," she once told him.[105]

Sáenz also warned Flores of the possible presence of spies among the men who surrounded him, which she had heard about from certain conspirators. "You yourself don't know among whom you live," she told him. She expected the president to take additional security measures, including avoiding mention of controversial political matters (attempts to revive the Peru-Bolivia Confederation, for example) in his correspondence and of her identity as his informant.[106] Sáenz also often asked Flores to tear up her letters after reading them. She, in short, expected him to do everything possible to avoid exposing her. In the wake of her exposure, she once again urged him to be cautious. "For God's sake, tear up this letter," she reminded him in February 1844, adding, "you're [so] careless with your papers."[107]

Sáenz did not hesitate to tell Flores of the consequences of the letter incident. Among these was local conspirators' new wariness of her. Avendaño was no longer stopping by the house, Sáenz reported. He had told the other Ecuadorians in town not to share any news with her unless they wanted it passed on to Flores, she later told the caudillo.[108]

Sáenz also feared the conspirators' anger and believed they would retaliate by turning other émigrés against her. She predicted trouble with a creditor, for example. "I owe some money [here], and these gentlemen [Moncayo et al.]—

who before [the letter incident] had calmed [the concerns of] my creditor—
will [now] ensure that I suffer," she informed the president in a burst of
paranoia.[109]

She then complained to him about her troubles with Moncayo. As she revealed in an April letter, the latter blamed her for Flores's recent decision to
order him out of Piura and had begun speaking ill of her to his friends and
anyone else who would listen.[110] Although Sáenz claimed to have had nothing
to do with Moncayo's banishment—and, indeed, had even advised that Flores
leave the former consul where local friends could keep an eye on him—she
should not have been too surprised by his reaction. She had, after all, continued
to inform the president of his collaboration with antigovernment conspirators
and, in a February 7 letter, for example, had told him of specific amounts of
money the former consul apparently had received for the purpose of purchasing
rifles in Lima.[111] Sáenz, in short, was now reaping the results of her willingness
to sacrifice her cordial relations with Moncayo and other émigrés for the sake of
maintaining her cherished alliance with Flores.

These results, however bothersome, nevertheless left her unshaken. "It is
nothing to me that they [the conspirators] know who I am and who I should
be," she declared to the president in late January, having already anticipated the
fallout of the Proaño letter's publication. What exactly did she mean by this?
Sáenz herself answered the question by stating the reasons for her continued
allegiance to the Ecuadorian dictator and, above all, her deep sense of loyalty to
Bolívar's former followers. "Since 1830, I have no [political] party; I am a friend
only of the friends of the Liberator and, since you are one of them, I am a friend
of yours," she told the caudillo plainly. Yet, her loyalty to him was more than
personalist. It also sprang from Sáenz's growing feelings of attachment to (and
identification with) the Ecuadorian nation—feelings revealed in her occasional
references to herself as "a patriot" and in her oft-stated desire that her country
avoid the example of its politically unstable southern neighbor, that is, that it
"not imitate Peru."[112]

The determined woman thus continued to warn Flores of the conspiracy.
Word of growing antigovernment sentiment in Ecuador (in Guayaquil, especially) had her worried. Indeed, although Flores apparently had written to reas-
sure her of his government's readiness to avert danger, Sáenz increasingly feared
the worst. "General Flores has been writing me and says things are going well;
may God hear him, since, based on what I hear, I'm afraid [there is going to
be] an explosion [massive uprising]," she observed to her new friend Monsalve
the second week of January.[113] Several months later, she expressed approval of
Flores's assumption of "extraordinary faculties," a response to the unrest in

Guayaquil, which she characterized as an "opportune" action. Sáenz then counseled the president to keep a sharp eye on the simmering port city, explaining that, based on what she had heard from recent visitors to Paita from Guayaquil, she "feared" the outbreak of "some [sort of] riot."[114] With the help of a circle of friends who helped her keep track of the activities of local anti-Flores conspirators, she also continued to send Flores whatever news and information she could gather. In July 1844, for example, she informed him of his enemies' plan to smuggle rifles into Ecuador through the ports of Pailón and Esmeraldas, observing, at the same time, that some rifles had been smuggled into the country already. "I hear so much these days about [the opposition's activities in] Ecuador that I sometimes fear something may happen to you; there's no need to be careless," she advised him later.[115] By September, continuing news of Flores's enemies—who, in her words, had been "working diligently to hatch a revolution"—had Sáenz feeling "very worried and even . . . anguished."[116] She again warned the president to be vigilant and to keep a close watch on Guayaquil; "that [city] is where the [revolution's] focus is said to be," she reminded him. She also expressed doubt about Guayaquileño army commander General Charles Wright's efficacy. "Wright is incapable of [committing] a felony but is too trusting," she told Flores, going on to remark that, although the British-born general was a true friend of the caudillo—"one of the few," she emphasized—he had a tendency to let his emotions rule his judgment. Her warnings, she added, sprang purely from patriotic motives. "I am giving you these warnings as a patriot [and] with no object other than . . . the peace of my country," she assured him.[117]

Flores, for his part, may well not have taken Sáenz's warnings seriously. Overwhelmed by the rebellion that erupted on March 6, 1845, the so-called March Revolution, he ultimately signed a truce with his opponents and, in June, went into exile in Europe. For Sáenz, such news must have been deeply disappointing if not entirely unexpected.[118]

Sáenz's friendship and alliance with Flores, nevertheless, had fulfilled a vital purpose. It had helped assuage the loneliness, feelings of isolation, anger, and sense of grievance that had haunted her in her early years as a political exile. It had kept her from feeling powerless. Sáenz, after all, not only had served as Flores's secret informant but had emerged as his collaborator, an example being her role, however minor, in the rather quixotic Grand Project. She had thrown her energies into thwarting the efforts of his émigré opponents—an activity that had allowed her to vindicate herself against the claims of former antagonists by proving that she was, indeed, a "friend of order." Her special relationship with Flores, of course, also had allowed her to feel useful and important.

Indeed, Sáenz seems to have made much of it and to have used her proximity to the Ecuadorian president to secure the respect of those around her as well as her place among Paita's and the Piura region's leading residents. In a hierarchical society whose members were still bound together mainly by personal ties of kinship and *compadrazgo* as well as relations between patrons and clients, such behavior was, no doubt, far from unusual.

Sáenz also had had a chance to reflect on the basis of her political allegiance to Flores. By 1845, she had begun to justify that allegiance less on purely personalist grounds than on the basis of an incipient nationalist and conservative ideology. Her conservatism was evident not only in her support for a strong Flores presidency (and revived Peru-Bolivia Confederation) but in her sympathy for the movement led by Peruvian-born General Manuel Ignacio Vivanco. Vivanco (1806–1873), like Flores, was a follower of Bolívar. A blue-eyed, fair-haired Spanish merchant's son from Lima, he had joined the Colombian army as an eighteen-year-old officer and, in 1824, participated in the Battles of Junín and Ayacucho. He had forged an alliance with another former Bolivarian, the ambitious Cuzco-born General Agustín Gamarra and, in the early 1830s, had entered the fray of Peruvian politics. By the early 1840s, Vivanco had made a name for himself as a reformer and acquired a strong personal and political following, especially in Arequipa. In April 1843, moreover, he had become president—or Supreme Director—of the Peruvian republic.[119]

Sáenz's sympathy for Vivanco showed itself the following year in her characterization of herself as a "Vivanquista" (supporter of Vivanco). "I was, am, and will be [a] Vivanquista," she declared to Flores, despite the news of the director's recent defeat at the hands of his caudillo rivals, General Castilla and others. Her identification with the fallen president stemmed only partly from his past association with and support for Bolívar. It also reflected Sáenz's general preference for military leaders, who, in her eyes, were more likely to lead honestly than their civilian counterparts. Whereas civilians, in her view, tended to be men "full of sophisms and intrigues" (a phrase that, no doubt, referred to lawyers in particular), military men, by contrast, were motivated mainly by "noble and sincere" impulses.[120]

Sáenz's preference was strengthened by her observation of the recent conduct of Domingo Elías, the Lima prefect whom Vivanco had left in charge of the government and who ensured Vivanco's fall through his sudden revolt against him (in June 1844). Sáenz condemned the revolt (referring to it as an "infamous and vile rebellion") and in a letter to Flores explained the real causes behind it. These included Elías's financial self-interest. According to Sáenz, the prefect's action had been motivated less by a professed desire to stand up for Lima's war-weary citizens than by a desire to hide the corruption and scandal that, she alleged, characterized his administration. An example of such corruption was the abundant revenues that, she explained, supposedly had been sent to the Supreme Director and his army (at the time engaged in a desperate showdown with opponents) and that, in her words, had "disappeared like smoke." Sáenz then implied that Elías and his cronies had used these revenues to enrich themselves by investing in market speculations, thereby contributing to the government's bankruptcy. Indeed, under Elías's leadership, the national government had abandoned its financial obligations—"neither widows, government employees, nor soldiers have been paid," her letter noted.[121]

Sáenz's support for Vivanco and frustration over the Elías government also reflected nostalgia for an earlier era of greater order and stability. In this she had something in common with her Peruvian neighbors, a significant number of whom, according to Jorge Basadre, had seen Vivanco as the last best hope for ending the turmoil that, since independence, had ravaged the young nation. Indeed, Vivanquismo appealed to many of Peru's discontented youth and educated upper and middle classes. These had become fed up with, as Basadre states, "twenty years of fruitless mestizo and torpid caudillo leadership." Some also had begun to dream of replacing their dysfunctional republic with either a constitutional monarchy or a sturdy Bolívar-style dictatorship.[122]

That Sáenz sympathized with this dream and with her fellow creoles' larger quest for orderly, effective government may be gleaned, in part, from her strong criticism of Elías. She characterized the latter not only as a usurper and "nobody" but as "a [mere] merchant" who was out of place and who, in abandoning the cause of his noble superior, had revealed himself to be nothing more than "a lowly traitor."[123]

SIX

Finding Home, circa 1845—1856

WITH THE TRIUMPH of Ecuador's March 1845 revolution and the fall of Juan José Flores, Manuela Sáenz turned away from the world of politics, a world that, until then, had been dominated by men she knew personally. She had grown tired and disillusioned. One sign of this was her reaction the previous year to news of Vivanco's defeat by his rivals. "You must know [by now] that the Vivanco affair has ended, miserably," she wrote Flores, going on to characterize Peru's seemingly endless cycle of civil war and caudillo conflict as little more than "a [ridiculous] farce or madman's contra dance." What a wonder it was that "poor" Peru still happened to possess a few "[decent] men of character," she added with a certain disgusted weariness.[1]

The Libertadora also claimed to be unimpressed, overall, by the caliber of the region's political leaders. "No government head is loved or feared by me," she confessed to her nation's president, noting, however, that, as in his case, if a particular magistrate happened to be a friend of hers, she did, "watch out for him" and, in her "[own] small way," seek to "promote . . . his aggrandizement." Most leaders, nevertheless, seemed "unremarkable and even contemptible."[2]

Sáenz's opinions reflected, in part, disappointment over the fate of old friends and allies as well as chagrin over the return to power of antagonists like Vicente

Ramón Roca, the latter destined to become president the year after Flores's exile. They also reveal a skepticism born of observation and personal experience. Although Sáenz would continue to follow her nation's fortunes, she would abandon her former efforts to influence them through active support for one or another public figure. "No one speaks to me of politics," she would remark to a friend six years later, adding with a hint of resignation that, in that sphere of endeavor, she did not "meddle."[3]

She also had become preoccupied with more private matters. One of these was her health, including the impact of a recent leg or hip injury. Sáenz seldom spoke of the injury. Indeed, her extant correspondence makes no mention of it—a reticence that may have stemmed partly from pride and from a belief that, as she once told a friend, "frequent complaining tends to chase away compassion."[4] A January 30, 1842, letter to Flores does allude to one of the injury's main consequences as it mentions, perhaps for the first time, its author's "inability to move" herself or to get about normally. This problem was to be confirmed by close friends and acquaintances. In the course of courtroom testimony some six years later, for example, Sáenz's lawyer, Cayetano Freyre, informed the judge that his client had "dislocated" a hipbone, a circumstance that obliged her to spend most of her day in a hammock.[5]

Other evidence confirms that Sáenz had become permanently disabled. This evidence includes the recollections of the famous Italian nationalist leader Giuseppe Garibaldi, who in 1851 (having been recently exiled from his native Italy), stopped off in Paita while en route to Lima. Sáenz—not one to miss an opportunity to meet with such a dashing personage—apparently invited him to her home. Garibaldi would later recall his hostess's charm and graciousness as well as a pleasant half day spent lying on her sofa while listening to stories about the Liberator. He also would remember her as an "invalid," noting that she had lost the "use of her legs" and had been "confined to her bed for several years," a situation he attributed to "a paralytic stroke."[6] After a visit to Paita in the mid-1850s, when he was still a young man, Peruvian writer Ricardo Palma would describe Sáenz similarly. He recalled seeing her, by then in her late fifties, seated "majestically" in a large leather wheelchair and described her as "a heavyset lady [with] the liveliest of black eyes . . . round face and genteel hand" who, for many years, had been "crippled." His recollection also suggests that Sáenz's condition may have been aggravated in her later years by a tendency toward obesity.[7]

Sáenz's disability—and resulting confinement—must have caused her considerable anguish. She had long been accustomed to freedom of movement, having once been an enthusiastic horseback rider. Her injured hip also must have been a source of chronic pain and discomfort. Yet, beyond the existence

of a Bethlemite Hospital in the city of Piura, by the early 1840s, the medical facilities and treatment available to her (before the advent of modern orthopedic
medicine) were limited.[8] Medical doctors were scarce in Paita. The tiny American Consular Hospital founded there sometime in the mid- to late 1840s—and
designed to serve the needs of ill seamen, most of them U.S. citizens—may have
been the only local institution with a resident physician.[9]

Sáenz did manage to consult with at least one doctor or professional healer.
Her letters contain occasional references to a "Dr. Bonetti," identifying him as a
physician who had been recommended to her by friends in Lima.[10] While we do
not know what Bonetti prescribed her, treatment of Sáenz's injured hip (which
may have been fractured as well as dislocated) probably did not go beyond the
palliative. It seems to have included a variety of therapies, among them occasional bathing in the nearby bay. Such bathing was widely regarded as a healthful
activity, good for ailments ranging from rashes to rheumatism; it constituted
one of the main reasons visitors, especially from Guayaquil and Piura, came to
Paita.

Sáenz looked forward to the therapy. The short trek to the beach (accom-
plished, perhaps, with the help of a mule-drawn litter) offered her a rare chance
to leave the house and lay eyes once again on her neighborhood. Exposure to
the bay's gentle, salty waves must have been both soothing and bracing. Such
dips, in Sáenz's view, helped "freshen" her blood and erase the effect of "life's
[day-to-day] irritations."[11]

Like urban female heads of household in Latin America generally—a group
that, at the time and in some cities, comprised as much as 45 percent of all urban
heads of household—Sáenz also faced the challenge of making a living. Gender
and genteel birth complicated the matter. By tradition, women were barred from
most occupations, for example, the majority of the professions (law, medicine,
the military) and skilled trades, access to which was seen as an exclusive male
prerogative. Those of "white" or upper-class background faced further restrictions. More so than—and, indeed, often in stark contrast to—their darker-
skinned, working-class sisters, they were expected to stay at home and thus limit
their contact with the supposedly corrupting influences of the outside world
and public sphere. They were expected to adhere to certain standards or norms
of female respectability.

Such norms reflected the impact of the traditional Hispanic ideal of the se-
cluded or sheltered female, an ideal that presumed that women who "strayed"
much beyond the home were prone to losing their (sexual) virtue and thus
their and their family's honor, or reputation.[12] Upper-class ladies were thus seldom seen on the streets alone. During their outings—these usually confined

to attendance at church and visiting friends and relatives—they were inevitably accompanied by a chaperone or trusted servant. The notion of a lady going anywhere on her own, much less leaving her home to go to work, was scarcely considered.

Income-earning options for upper-class women, therefore, were limited. The luckiest were widows who enjoyed sufficient inherited wealth to live on, usually income from a rural estate or rents from urban property, and who, like wealthy women generally, often invested their money in commerce, mining, or other business. The less-affluent earned a living through one or another home-based activity. They might lease a domestic slave (i.e., sending him or her out to work for wages), take in sewing or boarders, tutor children, or administer a small retail business such as a tobacco stand or *pulpería*. With the help of one or two servants, an industrious woman might engage at once in several such activities.[13] Given their demographic preponderance in Paita, moreover, women probably ran or administered most of the small businesses—bars, restaurants, boardinghouses, brothels, and so on—catering to sailors and others associated with the town's vital whaling industry.[14]

In theory, Sáenz was among the lucky few whose inherited fortune allowed her to anticipate a life of relative comfort. Besides the hacienda she sold in 1837, she owned a house and retail store in Quito, both of which she apparently inherited from her father and that she must have sold at or around the time of her brief return visit to the city in 1827. She also owned various other possessions, for example, fabric and textiles left from the store as well as household furniture and other personal belongings (dishes, carpets, and paintings) she had left in the care of her estate's administrator.[15]

By the early 1840s, her fortune consisted mainly of debts that others owed her. One was the seventeen-hundred-peso balance still due on Cataguango—payment of which the hacienda's new owner, one Señora Gangotena, had postponed seemingly indefinitely. This outstanding balance served as a bitter reminder of Sáenz's diminished inheritance. It contributed to the difficulty she had had in recent years in meeting her own financial obligations, including debts she had incurred with creditors in Paita. As she once told Flores, the need to pay off some of these debts had been what had compelled her to sell her "poor little hacienda" for nearly half its original value, that is, for six thousand pesos as opposed to the ten thousand pesos it had cost her and to demand, as a condition of sale, that the hacienda's purchaser provide an immediate down payment of four thousand pesos, hard currency.[16] All in all, despite the "considerable quantities [of money]" she had invested in it over the years and that in her estimation had increased her total financial stake in the farm to "some fifteen thousand pesos," Cataguango had proven to be a boondoggle.[17]

The determined woman, nevertheless, hoped to improve her financial situation. The main obstacle to this was Don Pedro Sanz, her estate administrator. Possibly a native of Pasto, Don Pedro seems to have been less than honest—something of which friends such as José Modesto Larrea had tried to warn Sáenz years earlier. The administrator had "deceived" her with regard to Cataguango's true worth or sale value, Larrea long ago had told her.[18] Sáenz, in turn, admitted to having had doubts about him. As she told Roberto Ascásubi somewhat bitterly, Don Pedro had taken charge of her estate only after having "fooled" her old guardian, Sor Josefa del Santísimo Sacramento, the abbess of La Concepción convent, through his habit of joining the nuns for mass regularly. Impressed by this show of piety, the abbess had recommended him for the job of estate administrator. Although Sáenz had gone along with the idea at the time, she had harbored reservations: "[Don Pedro] never fooled me as I have no faith in [religious] hypocrites."[19]

After repeated, fruitless inquiries into the fate of her rental income—including the six hundred pesos a month she was supposed to have received from tenant farmer Jacobo Gómez—Sáenz's reservations escalated. Already by 1840, she suspected her administrator of financial malfeasance. Her suspicions stemmed from the realization that Don Pedro had ignored her past instructions and acted without her authorization. "[In 1827] I left the hacienda rented out through a public auction. Don Pedro took it away [canceling the rental arrangement] without my order," Sáenz explained to Flores.[20] She had learned, too, that for some six years, the administrator had quietly leased the hacienda to his brother Ignacio; neither man had informed her of the arrangement nor sent her any of the rent due her.[21]

Sáenz now demanded accountability. Among other things, she asked that Don Pedro be made to submit a report for the years 1827–1837 along with a list of all tenants who owed her money. Don Pedro "must account for [the time] . . . that he and others used the hacienda," she told Flores. He also was to submit a statement of her assets and liabilities ("cuenta de cargo y data"), crediting her account for the period he and Ignacio had operated Cataguango without her authorization and debiting it only for those expenditures she had approved in writing. Sáenz, moreover, demanded reparations. She expected both Ignacio Sanz and Jacobo Gómez to compensate her for the cattle that reportedly were missing at the time of the hacienda's sale to its new owner. She also sought payment of the interest they and other debtors still owed her.[22]

The Libertadora, in addition, expected friends to assist her. She counted on the help of Flores in particular, hoping the latter would find someone in Quito to serve as her agent. It was with this in mind that, in 1840, she had sent the Ecuadorian president her power of attorney along with the request that he transfer it to whomever he deemed appropriate.[23] Sáenz also expected Flores to intercede on her behalf with her estate administrator. In 1842, for example, she exhorted him to tell Don Pedro to "not be shameless" and to "send her something [of the money owed her]."[24] She reminded him thereafter of her debtors' failure to fulfill their obligations. "Don Ignacio Sanz owes me some 4,000 pesos; Gómez owes me, Benítez owes me, [as do] various others and [yet] nobody pays me," she once reported, adding, "Don Pedro deceives me from month to month, from year to year, without realizing what my situation must be like in a foreign country and without [financial] resources." Sensing Flores's preoccupation with other matters, she also suggested that he transfer her power of attorney to one Colonel Pareja, an Ecuadorian army officer she had met in Paita who apparently had promised to find her a good debt-claims attorney.[25]

In late July 1843, Sáenz reiterated her estate-related grievances. Don Pedro had "taken advantage" not only of Cataguango but of all the property with which she had entrusted him since her 1827 return from Lima, she told Flores. Convinced of the administrator's unscrupulousness, she then begged him to do something about it. "In the name of God, sir, see to it that they [local authorities] restrain [Don Pedro] until the account books and other [records] have been audited," her letter pleads.[26] The appeal reflected her assumption that, as in the bygone days of Bolívar, Flores would continue to use his influence in her favor—an assumption encouraged by his earlier offer of assistance. "I shall thank you greatly for ensuring that I am paid by those individuals who owe me [money] such as Señora Gangotena and Señora Benítez, Don Ignacio and Don Pedro Sanz and Don Jacobo Gómez," Sáenz wrote him afterward, adding, with a hint of impatience, that "with your intercession [in this matter] . . . I do not doubt that I will be freed of my [financial] troubles, which are not inconsiderable."[27]

Yet, in 1844, distracted by the growing rumblings of his domestic opponents, Flores decided against intervening in Sáenz's estate matters. Sáenz tried to understand the reasons. "I know full well, sir, that you cannot and should not involve yourself in this [debt-claims dispute]," she wrote him.[28] Despite this, she continued trying to appeal to his compassion, hoping to move him with statements that reveal her mounting desperation. "[Even] a stranger would not be without someone to do his errands and collect for him [on debts owed]," she remarked at one point with a twinge of self-pity. Sáenz then reported on her lack of success with Colonel Pareja. Despite having promised to help her find someone to deal with Don Pedro over a year earlier, the colonel still had not informed her of the person to whom he had transferred her power of attorney or to whom she was to address her instructions. She had grown "weary" of waiting for him to do so, she told her friend. "One cannot survive [solely] on hope for ten years," she added in an allusion to her precarious financial (indeed, penurious) situation.[29] She had tried to tell Flores before of that situation. Indeed, by late September, almost a year after she had asked him to lend her some money, she was still waiting to receive the personal loan of "thirty gold ounces" the caudillo apparently had promised to send her; anxious for the loan's arrival, she already had sent him an advance receipt (included in a letter of six months earlier) acknowledging its purpose—that of covering her "urgent necessities."[30]

Sáenz also continued trying to impress Flores with the seriousness of her debt claims. "I don't know what to do," she lamented in her August 10, 1844, letter to him, adding that, at times, she felt an urge to "make a donation to the most enterprising lawyer in Quito." As she envisioned it, this "donation" would consist of her allowing the lawyer to keep all the money he sued for, even if this meant that she were to be left with nothing or, in her words, left to "starve to death." "At least then," she stated, "my debtors would not get away with their deviousness."[31] Sáenz then asked the caudillo for two small favors: that he give Pareja a letter that she had enclosed; and that he tell the colonel to inform her of whom to contact to discuss her debt claims and related matters. She also requested that he not abandon her, reminding him that, someday, his own daughters might find themselves in a similar state of "orphanhood." She had not forgotten his past displays of kindness and favor: "Only you have not denied me [your] protection; know that my gratitude will be eternal."[32]

After Flores's exile from Ecuador, Sáenz stayed in touch with his wife and some of his followers (the Floreanos), a number of whom had fled to Paita and who included Flores's son-in-law General Leonardo Stagg. Whether she continued corresponding directly with the caudillo himself, however, remains uncertain.[33] By October 1846, in any case, she had found someone else to assist her with her estate matters and efforts to obtain justice from her debtors. She thus remained hopeful. "If only I had my money, I would pay off my debts while lending the remainder at interest and [thus] would have enough [income] to live on free from worry," she told her friend Roberto Ascásubi. She would be able to send for her belongings in Bogotá, she added. "Without money, I [can] do nothing, [while] with it, I would do much in this port," she continued, her old optimism reviving.[34]

Sáenz's effort to salvage the remains of her Quito fortune was disrupted by the news of her husband's murder in February 1847. According to the brief reports that appeared in Lima five months after the incident, Thorne—by then probably in his mid- to late sixties and referred to simply as the "owner of the Hacienda Huaito"—had been ambushed and stabbed to death by unknown assailants, these alleged to be local slaves. He apparently had been strolling the grounds of his hacienda in the company of the woman, likely his mistress, who was killed with him and who, by one account, had been drowned in a nearby irrigation or drainage ditch. The couple's death seems to have been part of a crime wave terrorizing Chancay Province.[35]

For Sáenz, the news was deeply disturbing. She and Thorne had resumed corresponding with each other in the years since her arrival in Paita; indeed, they apparently had put aside their old differences. "I'm on good terms with my husband; he writes me often [and] as a friend," Sáenz had told Flores with evident satisfaction five years earlier.[36] Although the couple's relationship may have cooled somewhat afterward—due to the "calumnies" that Moncayo and Sáenz's other antagonists apparently told Thorne during one of their trips to Lima—it had been one she had come to cherish. Thorne's death, thus, left her horrified. "I am sick with the news of the horrible assassination of my husband," she confessed to Roberto Ascásubi in August, adding, in possible reference to a migraine headache, that "this incident has left my head exploding."[37]

She also yearned for justice. "Even though I didn't live with [my husband], I cannot be indifferent to [his murder]," she continued. Indeed, as she went on, she already had asked someone in Lima to "see what could be done" about it. By November 1847, she had authorized her old friend, lawyer Cayetano Freyre, to press civil and criminal charges ("querellas") against the assassins the moment they were identified.[38]

At the same time, Sáenz sought to assert her prerogatives as a widow. She began donning a widow's traditional mourning garments, including, as her friend Freyre had suggested, a black dress, black stockings, and black scarf—items Freyre offered to have sent to her from Lima.[39] She wrote Lima's British consul-general, John Barton, to ask for guidance and, above all, help in clarifying her rights or entitlements as the widow of a British subject. She also asked that he inform her and her attorney of any laws that might apply to her situation, perhaps thinking she might be eligible for some sort of pension.[40]

More important, Sáenz appointed Freyre to represent her in the courts of Lima. The attorney was to assert her right to recover the dowry her husband had administered for her and that, under traditional Spanish law, along with various paraphernalia (clothes, jewelry, and furniture) and the *arras propter nuptias* (the groom's gift to the bride), constituted a woman's exclusive personal property. Spanish law also entitled a widow to receive half the acquest, or community property ("bienes gananciales"), that is, the wealth generated over the course of a marriage through the investment of dowry funds.[41] If she were especially penurious and lucky enough to have a compassionate probate judge, she might receive more than half that property.[42]

Yet, a widow's rights also tended to be contingent. As various scholars have observed, a woman who violated her perceived moral obligations—who abandoned her home or committed adultery, for instance—risked losing some of those rights. Christine Hunefeldt has observed that a wife who abandoned her home "could not claim an acquest for the period of time she had been absent." Sylvia Arrom has noted that "a woman's adultery, always illegal unless she was raped or deceived, might cause her to lose her dowry and share of the community property."[43] What is certain is that, in Sáenz's case, such factors would spawn considerable courtroom argument.

By the end of the year, Sáenz had learned of the estate Thorne had left behind him. Now in the hands of his old business partner and executor, Don Manuel Escobar, this estate probably was somewhat less than what she and her lawyer had anticipated. Indeed, although Thorne's assets (some 212,000 pesos in all) exceeded his liabilities (37,000 pesos), more than half their total value (some 130,000 pesos) depended on the outcome of two lawsuits still pending at the time of his murder. One lawsuit sought compensation from the Chilean government for the merchant ship, the *Columbia,* the Chileans had seized during the war for independence and whose value Thorne had estimated at 100,000 pesos. The other concerned a debt of 30,000 pesos owed by the estate of one José Escobar, possibly Don Manuel's relative.[44] Thorne's remaining assets included property—farm buildings, equipment, and other "capital goods"—he had accumulated during the years he had leased the Hacienda Huaito from his old friend Domingo Orué. They included 82,000 pesos that he had invested in Huaito for "capital improvements" and for which his estate was to be reimbursed by Huaito's new owner.[45]

For Sáenz, of course, it was the assets' disposal that was of greatest interest. She must have been surprised to learn that, according to the will executed by Escobar, the estate's single largest asset—the 100,000 or so pesos anticipated from the Chilean lawsuit—belonged to Thorne exclusively; it was to be treated separately from what constituted the estate's community property. After payment of Thorne's lawyer, a portion of it was to go to the "Aylesbury Hospital"—a reference, no doubt, to the Royal Buckinghamshire Hospital, a public or charity hospital in Aylesbury of which Thorne seems to have been a patron. The rest was to go to four designated heirs. These heirs were the children of two women who, at one time or another, apparently had been Thorne's mistresses:

Doña Rosa Alvarado y Valdivieso (second wife and widow of his old friend and patron Domingo Orué) and Doña Buenaventura Concha.[46] At least two of those children, young Jorge and Isabel Concha, were quite likely Thorne's illegitimate offspring; their mother, as Sáenz may have known by then, was the same woman who was with Thorne the day of his murder and who also was killed by his assailants.[47]

After all the estate's outstanding debts had been paid, the four designated heirs were to receive half the acquest. The other half was to go to Thorne's executor. Sáenz, meanwhile, was to receive nothing more than what Thorne, apparently, had believed he owed her: the eight-thousand-peso dowry given him by her father and that was listed in his will as a debt or liability. Nor was she to receive it anytime soon. Thorne's will stated that, until such time as the dowry funds could be gathered in full, Sáenz was to be sent only a small sum equivalent to 6 percent annual interest on the dowry principal in order to help cover her living expenses.[48] It thus denied her the benefits to which widows traditionally were entitled: the full return of their dowries and access to half the couple's community property. Thorne or his executor, it seems, had shortchanged her.

Sáenz's shocked reaction may be gleaned from the words and actions of her lawyer in Lima. In early January 1848, Cayetano Freyre appeared before Judge Manuel Julio Rospigliosi and announced his client's intention to claim her dowry along with the interest that had accrued on it, both of which she saw as her due. Freyre also announced that Sáenz expected to be compensated for the years Thorne had not provided for her as per his legal husbandly responsibility. He warned, too, that Sáenz had no intention of forfeiting "her right to make further claims" on her husband's estate. "Let it be understood that my client does not consider herself satisfied [only] with the eight thousand pesos and interest that have been assigned her," he informed the magistrate, thus hinting at Sáenz's desire for a share of the acquest that had been denied her. Freyre then asked that a witness be called to confirm the terms of the will Escobar had drafted in ostensible compliance with Thorne's instructions—a demand that revealed his and his client's distrust of the executor. He asked, too, that the judge summon testimony from some half dozen witnesses for the purpose of drafting a "poverty report"; this seems to have been a standard procedure required for an individual to be officially recognized as "insolvent" or indigent and, thus, entitled to be exempt from the usual court fees and other routine costs of litigation.[49]

Sáenz's impoverishment was real. Her letters allude to it. In one 1842 missive to Flores, for example, Sáenz admitted to being in severe financial straits or, in her words, "in [more] misery" than she had "ever imagined [she would be]." At times, she felt like "shooting" herself, she added in a phrase that reflected her growing worry and frustration.[50] In an April 1843 letter, she noted that she lacked money even to send for the belongings (including personal papers) she had left behind in Bogotá; in a subsequent missive, she described herself as "very poor" (cash strapped) and in "dire" need.[51] In late October 1843, as noted earlier, Sáenz asked Flores for a loan, promising to repay it with funds she was expecting to receive from her debtors in Quito.

The delay in receipt of those funds also prompted her to look for alternative sources of income. A few of her extant letters show, for example, that, by the mid-1840s, Sáenz was thinking of selling traditional Quito textile goods, embroidered handkerchiefs and garments especially, to friends and clients in Chile.[52] She undoubtedly earned income—or at least access to loans and credit—in other ways. The frequent references to Alexander Ruden in her 1840s correspondence with Flores and others, for instance, hint not only that she saw the consul regularly but that she collaborated with or assisted him in some manner. Sáenz, after all, had long ago learned how to make herself useful to those whose friendship she valued; she knew how to charm and curry favor with powerful and influential individuals, wealthy merchants like Ruden included. Given her literacy and knowledge of foreign languages (French and English), moreover, it is likely she served the consul as an interpreter or translator. She may have served him in other capacities as well, perhaps as a mediator in the disputes that occasionally arose between local officials, on the one hand, and foreign arrivals, often English-speaking sailors, on the other. For such services, Ruden surely compensated her.[53] Sáenz also may have earned some money by performing various small administrative-type services and favors. One letter suggests that she collected money, perhaps payments or rents due, for others, including a local friend, Paula Godos, who seems to have had a small business selling imported garments.[54]

Other sources point to Sáenz's involvement in small-scale enterprise, including the manufacture and sale of handicrafts, an industry with which she was familiar as a result of her youth among Quito's Concepcionistas. These sources include the recollections of Paula Orejuela, a native of Paita who apparently began frequenting Sáenz's home as a little girl and who, over half a century later, would recall seeing the Libertadora and her two female servants (Juana Rosa and Dominga) engaged in the manufacture of cloth flowers; after a full day of helping their mistress sew the flowers, the servants sold them, thus providing Sáenz's household with at least a modest income.[55]

Yet, by 1848, the Libertadora was barely supporting herself. According to one of the witnesses Freyre asked to testify in early February of that year, her "small means and work" were insufficient to provide for "life's most vital necessities."[56] Indeed, for all practical purposes, Sáenz was destitute. Even taking into account his evident bias (i.e., his desire to move the judge in her favor), Freyre's description of his client was, no doubt, essentially accurate. He described Sáenz as having been reduced to "living in Paita in a pitiful hut, submerged in the worst [kind of] misery, without any sort of income on which to subsist, [and] dependent for her daily bread on the charity of various friends."[57]

Seven witnesses agreed with him. In their brief courtroom testimonies, each attested to Sáenz's "impoverished state" and dependence for her subsistence on "the philanthropy of her good friends and other charitable individuals." One witness, U.S. Consul Ruden (who happened to be passing through Lima at the time of his deposition) added that "for more than five years" he had furnished Sáenz with the food on her table.[58] Others—including Eugenio Raygada, a Paita native and member of Peru's Chamber of Deputies; former Piura governor Cipriano Delgado; Gregorio Rafael Escalona, head of Paita's customshouse; Colonel Carlos Vincendón, an old Ecuadorian friend of Sáenz's; and Señora Doña Josefa Puch de Valencia of Lima, an acquaintance who had visited Sáenz recently—confirmed his portrayal of her indigence.[59]

Sáenz's poverty was far from unusual in early republican Spanish America. Poverty tended to haunt the lives of most widows while, in the wake of the destructive wars for independence, elites everywhere had suffered a decline in their material fortune and standard of living. This decline may have been especially noticeable among elite residents of cities like Lima, whose merchant establishment had been hard hit by war-induced trade disruptions, including the loss of their old monopoly privileges and arrival of new foreign (above all, British) competition. Lima's loss of its vital Chilean sugar and tobacco export markets, moreover, had diminished the value of nearby landholdings along with the rents or land-based income on which had depended many a well-to-do creole family.[60]

Post-independence economic depression, in turn, accelerated the decay of the old dowry system. Among the upper classes generally, dowries became smaller and less frequent, their value and significance less unquestioned. As Christine Hunefeldt has shown, the dowry system's erosion meant that elite women lost much of the legal and social protection (including guaranteed access to a family's resources) the system had provided. It also meant that, in their legal conflicts with men, women of all classes increasingly had to adapt their claims to the new language and logic of economic liberalism.[61]

This trend may be seen to some extent in the case of the conflict between Sáenz and Thorne's executor. In May 1848, Escobar rejected Sáenz's demand for the prompt return of her eight thousand pesos and asked the judge to dismiss her suit for payment ("auto-de-pago"). The terms of the dowry's return were conditional, he argued, reminding the judge of the will's stipulation that the amount in question be paid only after sufficient funds had been gathered.[62] Indeed, according to Escobar, the return of the dowry embodied not an obligation but a "favor" Thorne had granted. Sáenz's claim to her dowry was void and invalid, the executor continued. "Whatever recourse Doña Manuela may have had in other circumstances for the purpose of obtaining the return of [her dowry], she has lost it as a result of having broken her [marital] ties to her husband and . . . [of having engaged in] conduct of which all Peru is aware," he stated grimly. "However painful it may be to recall certain events of her [Sáenz's] past, it is vital to point out that the woman who separates from her consort . . . and launches an openly illicit affair with another person, loses . . . the right to her dowry," he continued. Escobar minced no words in summing up his argument. "The whole world knows that Doña Manuela engaged [in an illicit affair]," he asserted, adding, alluding to her well-known relationship with Bolívar, that "her proceedings in this sense were quite public [and] patent."[63] Sáenz, in short, had no legitimate claim on Thorne's estate, according to his executor, much less a right to demand immediate payment.

Freyre's response was bristling. The lawyer scolded Escobar for his "atrocious" attack on Sáenz's "honor and reputation" and accused him of unjustly "defaming" his client. He reminded him of the "great favors" Sáenz had once "bestowed" on him, in effect portraying the executor as an ungrateful and rather shameless former dependent. He also argued that Escobar had no right to judge Sáenz's conduct in a matter that, as he explained, had been strictly between her and her husband. Only Thorne himself could judge that conduct, he added. Indeed, Thorne, Freyre asserted, had never uttered a complaint against his wife. Until the end of his life, he went on, the Englishman had "respected her"; Escobar therefore ought not to cast aspersions or make "calumnious" references that "dishonored" the memory of the man he represented.[64] Freyre then denied that the eight thousand pesos (plus interest) Sáenz was asking for constituted a "dowry"—the money was, instead, a "debt" owed to her like any other.[65]

In somewhat tortured fashion, the lawyer also dismissed the allegations of sexual misconduct. These, he asserted, had been proven baseless by Thorne's own behavior. Had the "sensitive" and "extremely proud" Englishman even suspected his wife of being unfaithful, he would have requested a divorce (or legal separation) on the spot, he argued. Inspired, no doubt, by sympathy for his friend and client, Freyre also declared that Thorne himself bore most of the blame for the couple's troubled marriage and separation. "If Doña Manuela Sáenz found herself separated from her husband for some time, it was because the latter's behavior obliged her to be," he concluded. Sáenz, he informed the

judge, had found it hard to accept her husband's infidelities, including his relationship with the concubine who had shared his life at the Hacienda Huaito
(a reference, no doubt, to Buenaventura Concha). Guilt, he added, lay behind
Thorne's decision to ensure that his wife receive the eight thousand pesos he
owed her. The dearth of further documentary evidence, however, makes it difficult to gauge the effect of his arguments—or the outcome of his client's effort
to reclaim her dowry.[66]

Manuela Sáenz did eventually make headway on her claims against debtors
in Quito. Vital to this process was the help she received from Roberto Ascásubi.
A gentleman-bachelor, Ascásubi belonged to one of Quito's wealthiest and most
illustrious creole families. His mother, Mariana Matheu, had inherited the title
of Marquise of Maenza while his father, José Javier, had been a prominent city
councilman and participant in the famous August 10, 1809, autonomist conspiracy. His older brother Manuel, a major landowner, was destined to serve
as the country's vice president and, for a short while in 1849, as interim president. Don Roberto himself also had been active in public life. As a young man,
he had militated in the ranks of the country's liberals, having been (along with
Pedro Moncayo and Sáenz's half-brother José María) a founding member of
the Sociedad del Quiteño Libre and supporter of the Sociedad's failed October
1833 coup against Flores. He and José María may have been friends as well as
allies, moreover. In the wake of the failed coup, the two men had fled together
to New Granada and become, for a few months, companions in exile. Ascásubi
later had joined the opposition to Flores's second administration and, in 1844,
apparently supplied money to the conspirators operating in Piura. In the wake
of the caudillo's fall, he was elected as a national deputy for the Province of
Pichincha and established himself as a respected statesmen.[67]

It may not have been until the time of his visit to Paita in July 1844 (or, of
his return there in the first few months of 1845 as a political exile), however,
that Ascásubi renewed his acquaintance with his former colleague's sister—a
sign of the extent to which ties of family and friendship could transcend political disagreement. Don Roberto also agreed to help Sáenz with her estate and
debt-claims problems. In November 1845, Sáenz sent him her power of attorney
accompanied by several documents and a letter of instruction. She asked him to
contract the services of two lawyers: one to press her claims against Don Pedro
and his brother, another to press her claims against Señora Gangotena (who still
owed her the balance on Cataguango plus interest).[68]

She did not hesitate to fill him in thoroughly on her grievances as well, re-
lieved that, at long last, she had found someone willing to attend to them. In
one lengthy 1847 missive, Sáenz informed Ascásubi of the discrepancies she
had found between her records and a financial report that Don Pedro and his

son-in-law, José Ortiz de la Villota, finally had sent her. She wondered aloud about the fate of the furniture and dishware she long ago had left with them and that they were to have sold for her. She alleged that the administrator had improperly charged her for items she never asked for while failing to send her items, bolts of fabric, for example, that she had, in fact, requested. Sáenz also did not hide her frustration over her debtors' apparent efforts to elude their obligations—at one point, characterizing them as "shifty" and, in a flash of bitter irony, as "heirs" she had acquired inadvertently.[69]

She found Gangotena's conduct especially exasperating. By 1847, the new owner and occupant of Cataguango apparently had begun building a vacation home (*casa de recreo*) on the hacienda's property. Word of it left Sáenz indignant. "You tell Señora Gangotena [that] how dare she build a vacation home on property for which she has yet to finish paying an unhappy, exiled compatriot!" she told Ascásubi. "Either she pays me [what she owes] or I will sue for payment," she added determinedly.[70]

Over the next few years, Sáenz urged her friend to put pressure on the lady. "My dear friend [and] benefactor, do [whatever is necessary] to extract the remaining [money] from her," she instructed in November 1849, going on to say that she hoped Gangotena would not continue "to make a fool of" her for much longer.[71] As she informed Ascásubi in a subsequent missive, she had tried appealing to the debtor directly, having written her at least once to explain her need for the money in question. Her appeal had fallen on deaf ears, however. While Gangotena had renewed her promises to pay, she had not answered any of Sáenz's letters and had continued to evade her obligation.[72] By mid-July 1850, Sáenz was out of patience. "For how much longer will she continue to harm [my interests]?" she asked Ascásubi in allusion to Gangotena's seemingly endless delays. She already had contracted new debts of her own, she added, having counted on Gangotena to fulfill her latest promise of payment. She then announced that she no longer could tolerate the woman's procrastination. "My God, do not listen to her [excuses] any further," she told her friend, adding that he should "oblige" Gangotena to pay; "I cannot take any further [delays]," she continued in a tone of anguish.[73]

Ascásubi already had had some success in persuading the debtor to pay at least part of what she owed his friend. Sáenz's acknowledgment of the "thirty [gold] ounces" she had received less than a year earlier and which she attributed solely to his assistance in the claim against Gangotena suggests that he had begun to overcome the latter's resistance.[74]

Sáenz began to reap the rewards of her persistence. By the early 1850s, she was receiving both goods and money from Quito—a development suggesting that, with Ascásubi's help, her debt claims finally were being satisfied. In an August

1850 letter, for example, she acknowledged receipt of an unspecified sum, perhaps a payment from one of her debtors. She asked that Ascásubi turn the sum
over to one Señora Doña Carmen Martín of Guayaquil. She needed "[to order]
things from Guayaquil continually," she told him, adding in explanation that
Martín had agreed to receive funds "every month" in her name.[75] Sáenz also
now had the money she needed to send for her personal papers, particularly
the archive she had left behind in Bogotá and that, despite earnest appeals to
New Granadan president Tomás Cipriano de Mosquera, she had been unable to
obtain earlier.[76] With increasing frequency, she asked friends to send her various
items, these generally referred to in her letters as "encargos," and another example of her improved financial footing. In March 1851, for example, she asked
for a crèche (*nacimiento*) from La Concepción convent; it was to be procured
or commissioned by a Quito friend, one Doña Dolores Campos, and paid for
with special funds held by Ascásubi, by then apparently acting as her financial
administrator.[77]

Sáenz's extant letters suggest, furthermore, that by the early 1850s she was
developing a small business in Ecuadorian, especially Quito, handicrafts. Such
a development was not surprising. Since at least 1847 (as noted earlier), Sáenz
had hoped to earn money by selling "embroidered things," especially handkerchiefs, to clients in Chile. Her hopes seem to have become reality as, from 1851
onward, she began regularly asking Ascásubi to send her textiles from Quito. In
June 1851, for instance, Sáenz reminded him to send her some of what she had
previously ordered along with two wool scarves or wraps ("fajas de lana"). A
bit over two years later, she asked that, instead of sending her money, he "stock
up" on "basket sets, lace, and embroidered things" to be forwarded to her at his
earliest convenience.[78]

For the procurement and transport of such items, she relied on a network
of trusted intermediaries. Among these were three of Don Roberto's sisters:
Rosario, Dolores, and María Josefa Ascásubi. The three women apparently were
responsible for procuring many of the handicrafts Sáenz requested, commis-
sioning them directly from La Concepción and other convents. Sáenz's intermediaries also included one Carlos Aguirre (apparently the son of Bolívar's old
ally, General Vicente Aguirre), to whom she entrusted part of the money collected for her. They included friends and acquaintances in Guayaquil, among
them, besides the aforementioned Carmen Martín, one Señor Avellán (possibly
a merchant) and a family referred to in her letters simply as "los Martínez."[79]

The Libertadora's brightening economic prospects coincided with another
vital trend in these years: her growing closeness to members of her country's
social and political elite, especially a small group of wealthy and aristocratic

Quito families. This closeness may be gleaned from her friendship with the Ascásubis—a family linked by bonds of marriage and kinship to the prestigious Salinases, Klingers, Aguirres, and Montúfars and who, like these, formed part of a tight-knit oligarchy whose homes were located on or near their city's main plaza.[80]

It may be gauged from her relationship with Don Roberto, in particular, for whom Sáenz felt profound respect and gratitude. "You have no idea how deeply grateful I am to you," she once told her friend, going on to explain that Ascásubi so far had been "the only person to feel for [her] in [her] forsaken situation." "A friend in need is very rare [but] I have found one in you," she added earnestly.[81] Sáenz thereafter would express her appreciation repeatedly, with one 1851 letter addressing the kindly bachelor as "benefactor," "good Samaritan," and even "second providence." "Where would I be without you?" she asked him, going on to state that "God will pay you for your good offices and give you prosperity."[82] Her thankfulness had been forever "engraved" in her "ageless" heart, she later assured him.[83]

Sáenz also did her best to show her appreciation in a concrete manner. She once sent Don Roberto a pair of puppies he had asked for and that she had raised for him. One of these was a "pretty" female named Presumida, whom, as she informed her friend in March 1851, was to be sent first and be entrusted to his brother-in-law in Guayaquil, the twenty-nine-year-old Gabriel García Moreno. Then a budding young statesman about to return to his wife and home in Quito, García Moreno apparently had agreed to ensure the young canine's proper delivery.[84]

Sáenz's bond with the Ascásubi family no doubt was strengthened by the opportunity she had to welcome Roberto and two of his sisters (Rosario and María Josefa) to Paita toward the end of that same year. She arranged a house for the siblings to stay in and, for the next few days, enjoyed their visits and, no doubt, the chance to preside over long, nostalgia-filled conversations. Although the Ascásubis soon continued their journey inland, she remained in touch with them during their ten-month stay in Piura, where the two women hoped to find relief from skin rashes. Her warm feelings for them were reciprocated. In a July 1852 letter to García Moreno, for example, Don Roberto spoke of Sáenz affectionately and alluded to her familiarly as his "comadre."[85]

Sáenz's deepening ties to the Ascásubis and their relatives signaled her alignment with a nascent Ecuadorian conservatism. This conservatism was based in part on the desire of the country's wealthiest families to maintain their traditional status and influence—factors that, as in the case of the powerful landowning, or latifundista, clans of the central Ecuadorian highlands, the Montúfars and the

Larreas, for example, depended on access to and control over Indian labor.[86] It entailed identification with Juan José Flores, whose governments had provided the strong centralized authority deemed vital to landowner interests (and hierarchical principles generally) and whose followers, the Floreanos, had remained active since their leader's exile.[87] It included sympathy for the country's powerful religious orders in their resistance toward attempts at secularization. It found unity and a voice, moreover, through growing opposition to the recently established regime of General José María Urbina.

A native of the central highland city of Ambato, Urbina (1808–1891) had briefly attended Guayaquil's naval academy and risen up in the ranks of the military during the last phase of the wars for independence. Although he was once a follower and protégé of Juan José Flores (especially during Flores's second administration), he later turned against the caudillo, in 1845 joining forces with leaders of the Guayaquil-based March Revolution. He was rewarded for his role in the revolution with a promotion to brigadier general and appointment, under President Vicente Ramón Roca, as army chief of staff. By 1850, Urbina was Ecuador's new caudillo. On July 17, 1851, backed by his many followers in the army and in Guayaquil, he overthrew the government of interim president Diego Noboa and declared himself dictator (*jefe supremo*); he then oversaw the drafting of a new Constitution and won election to the presidency the following year.[88]

Urbina also embarked on a liberal reform program. Besides the abolition of slavery (and, in 1857, Indian tribute), this program included an attempt to secularize Ecuadorian society while reducing the Catholic Church's influence. More extreme in this regard than that of any of his predecessors, Urbina's church policy led ultimately to a severing of relations between Ecuador and the Vatican. It included a campaign to rid the nation of the Jesuits, the powerful and influential religious order founded in 1534 by Spaniard Ignatius Loyola. Although the order had begun to recover from the effect of its earlier expulsion from Spanish America (in 1767), it recently had found itself, once again, hounded by enemies, these inclined to see it as a threat to the nation's authority as well as to liberal political principles. In 1850, for example, thanks to the fears of radical Liberals led by President José Hilario López, the Jesuits had been expelled from the neighboring Republic of New Granada. Although they had found a haven in Ecuador, they soon lost it, thanks to Urbina's open hostility; this culminated in his government's official November 1852 order for their expulsion.[89]

The Jesuits' expulsion became a cause célèbre for Urbina's opponents. The most forceful and articulate of these was young Gabriel García Moreno. Born in 1821 in Guayaquil, García Moreno spent numerous years in the Ecuadorian capital, where he attended secondary school and earned a doctorate in law from the University of Quito. In 1846, at the age of twenty-five, he married Rosa Ascásubi Matheu, one of Don Roberto's sisters. This marriage incorporated him into the Ascásubis' elite circle and, ultimately, contributed to his identification with the church and highland latifundista interests. García Moreno also was a dynamic, up-and-coming politician. He began his political career as a Liberal and admirer of Rocafuerte as well as a colleague of Pedro Moncayo. Toward the mid-1840s, he joined the opposition to the dictatorship of then-president Flores. His views began to be known through his work as a newspaper editor, including his publication of the polemical *El Zurriago* (1845) and *El Vengador* (1846–1847), the latter shrilly opposed to Flores's attempt to return to the country via a military invasion. García Moreno had had some practical administrative experience. In 1847, he was appointed governor of Guayas Province by then-president Roca and, for a bit over a year, served effectively in that position.

By the time of his arrival in Paita as a political exile six years later (in late September 1853), however, the fiery young journalist and budding statesman was increasingly known for his antagonism toward Urbina. He also had attracted attention for his "Defense of the Jesuits"—an essay that had appeared the year before in his latest newspaper, *La Nación,* and that had condemned the government for its blatant anticlericalism. He thus had begun to develop the first strands of his future conservative ideology, one that would stress the importance of the church and Catholic religion and that, on his election to the Ecuadorian presidency eight years later, would be translated into national policies.[90]

Manuela Sáenz welcomed the young García Moreno to Paita. She had been waiting for him, having learned months earlier from Don Roberto of his troubles with the Urbina government and the official order for his exile.[91] She undoubtedly recalled the many small favors he had done for her; since the time of his Guayas governorship (a post that had required his residence in Guayaquil), García Moreno often had seen personally to the safe forwarding of letters and money sent her by Ascásubi in Quito. Sáenz had written at least once to thank him for this and ask that he continue his "good works on behalf of an unlucky Ecuadorian."[92] She had looked forward to the "honor" of making his personal acquaintance, moreover, and, as she informed Ascásubi in late October 1853, was now "gratified" to finally have done so.[93]

She also must have sensed García's unhappiness in Paita. Indeed, she almost certainly recognized his loneliness and despondency—signs, no doubt, of the same exile-related malaise she had experienced and that found expression in some of his extant letters home to relatives. In one of these, García described Paita sourly as "this dry and desolate beach squeezed in between the sea on one side and ruins and utterly barren cliffs on the other [side]; with the narrowest of streets . . . full of filth; with houses that look like huts and huts that are called houses; with no amenities whatsoever; with nothing . . . but sand, air and salt water."[94]

No doubt alert to such feelings, Sáenz strove to sweeten her new friend's stay in the small port city. She already had begun reaching out to some of his fellow exiles and to the town's recent Jesuit arrivals (those exiled earlier by Urbina), in particular. She had found a house for the priests to reside in and, pleased at the chance to play hostess, had been trying to attend to them. "We are very happy with the Jesuits here," she reported to Roberto Ascásubi in late January 1853, go- ing on to describe her new acquaintances as "exemplary" and to explain that she was striving to "serve" them to the full extent of her "limited" capacity.[95] Sáenz also began welcoming the Jesuits to her home, hosting visits from individuals such as Francisco Javier Hernáez (a future Ecuadorian provincial), young no- vitiate José Antonio Lizarzaburu, and Rafael Polit Cevallos, an Ascásubi family acquaintance and personal friend of García Moreno's.[96]

She welcomed García as well, apparently inviting him to join her and the other visitors. Indeed, before long, the young politician was a regular. "I have not wanted to make [new] friends or waste time in tedious socializing," he wrote his Ascásubi sisters-in-law, adding that, because of this, he never left his house "except to take exercise and visit the excellent compatriot, Doña Manuela." His appreciation of his hostess also may be seen in his allusion to the "daily kind- nesses" with which, it seems, she had begun to shower him.[97]

The Libertadora, for her part, must have been impressed by García. Despite his relative youth—at thirty-two, he was slightly more than half her age—her new friend was a mature, serious, and talented individual, one clearly marked for leadership. He had shown courage as well as honesty and integrity, traits that Sáenz admired and that she had found lacking in most leaders; it is quite likely that she congratulated him on his brave written defense of the persecuted Jesuits. Not unlike her old idol, Bolívar, furthermore, the incipient conservative ideo- logue and president had an intense, passionate (and combative) nature that had revealed itself in his conflict with the Urbina government as well as in his fiery journalistic rhetoric. He was politically ambitious, something the older woman must have recognized and approved of. Sáenz, in any case, came to know, trust, and grow fond of him, a development attested to in a number of García's surviv- ing letters. By late October 1853, the young statesman counted himself, as he told Roberto Ascásubi, "a wholly trusted friend" of hers.[98]

Sáenz's friendship with García Moreno also revived her interest in Ecuador- ian national politics. The two discussed subjects such as the possibility of a new Flores naval expedition. Since his exile, the seemingly indefatigable general had organized two such expeditions, both aimed at toppling Urbina and restoring himself and his allies to power. The first expedition had been organized in secret in Europe with the help of the Spanish and British governments; set to launch in 1847, it had been aborted that same year after news of its existence had leaked to the Ecuadorian press and authorities. Its successor, launched from the port of Callao in February 1852 with the blessing of the Peruvian authorities, had ended in defeat and disaster. After suffering various mishaps en route to Guayaquil—including a mutiny onboard the *Chile,* a ship whose mostly Chilean crew was lured away by Urbina's agents—Flores's much-vaunted squadron had been scattered. By August, six of the ships had retreated to Paita, leaving the small town to deal with two hundred or so hungry, bedraggled, and desperate soldiers, many of them recruits of British and U.S. origin.[99]

Despite this inglorious ending, in the latter half of 1853, talk of yet another Flores expedition had arisen. Sáenz was disinclined to believe it. "[There is] no sign at all of the [anticipated] Flores expedition," she wrote Ascásubi in late October, adding that reports of the expedition were nothing more than "rumors." These, she then implied, had been concocted by the Urbina regime as an excuse to obtain "extraordinary" or emergency powers.[100]

Manuela Sáenz may have persuaded García Moreno to think likewise. In a letter to his brother-in-law earlier that month, the young politician alluded briefly to opinions and information he had received from her. Identifying her in the letter simply as "our good friend," he added that such opinions had led to his being "convinced" that there was "absolutely nothing to [the reports of the Flores expedition]."[101]

Sáenz probably apprised García Moreno of Peruvian developments, including a reported conspiracy to overthrow Urbina's government. Mentioned in García's October 1853 letter to Ascásubi, this conspiracy involved a revolt allegedly being planned by followers of Domingo Elías with the cooperation of Flores's old allies, one Deustua in particular. On it, the young politician opined, rode the Floreanos' latest hope of restoring themselves and their leader to power.[102] Although García did not acknowledge it explicitly, his awareness of such a revolt likely stemmed from his conversations with Sáenz, whose contact with and knowledge of both Peruvians and Floreanos must have made her a font of information on the subject of Peru-Ecuador relations.

Sáenz also helped her friend avoid the dangers of involvement in Peruvian politics, including the rivalry that had emerged between local supporters of Generals Castilla (the Castillistas) and Echenique. She found herself thrust into the middle of this rivalry when, one day in early January 1854, a small group of Castillistas asked her to intercede with García on their behalf, hopeful the young firebrand would be willing to lead an uprising, or *pronunciamiento*, against their opponents in control of the provincial government in Piura. She refused to do so. "She [Sáenz] told them that I would not take charge of such a thing [uprising], since she had heard me [say] that as a foreigner [in Peru], I ought not to get involved [politically] in anything," García later explained to relatives in Quito; because of her frequent conversations with him, Sáenz "already knew" his "way of thinking," he added.[103]

While respecting her friend's desires and protecting him from the danger of local political entanglements, the Libertadora also must have had her own reasons for refusing the Castillistas. She had grown weary of politics generally and now preferred to be more of a spectator than an activist. She was content to remain García's confidante, informant, and, to some extent, advisor—roles she had assumed earlier with Bolívar and Flores—and to leave behind her former activities as an operative.

Perhaps more important, Manuela Sáenz's friendship with García, like her friendships with leaders before him, signaled the unique place that literate middle- and upper-class women had begun to occupy in early republican Spanish America. It reflected the existence of a middle ground between the public and the private (or domestic) spheres of activity as well as between worlds designated as either masculine or feminine. Indeed, as Sarah Chambers has observed regarding nineteenth-century Latin America generally, "although women were excluded from formal politics and the press, they were active in social spaces between the public and private spheres, where philosophies were discussed, plots hatched, and alliances formed."[104] Elite women's sociability, for example, their letter writing and hosting of salons or *tertulias*, Chambers continues, ultimately allowed them to be integrated into larger "imagined communities," that is, into the new Latin American nations.[105]

Such observations also suggest that further study of women's activities can yield rich insights into those spaces in which they operated and thus into the many intersections between the public and the private. They can shed light on the social networks and personal relationships that underlay political life in the early national period and that would continue to influence it after the consolidation of formal institutions and parties.[106] They hint, too, at the existence of a complex link between gender and citizenship. While, until the twentieth century, gender excluded women from the exercise of most of the formal political and civic rights enjoyed by men, it did not necessarily exclude them from being active in civil society or from realms of power and influence. Sáenz's career, at least—including her cooperation with the exiled Jesuits and García—seems to confirm this.

With age, the Libertadora drew deepening pleasure from the sociability she long had practiced and cultivated. She delighted in the small gatherings that, by the time of García Moreno's arrival in Paita, she had begun hosting at her home regularly. An October 1853 letter, for example, not only alludes to these gatherings but also praises her Jesuit guests' "agreeable company." That company had contributed in no small way to her recent "[good] health" and sense of well-being, she explained to a friend happily. "When you [can] relate to people with liking and candor, you nourish the soul," she continued, referring to her recent interactions with both García and his Jesuit friend Rafael Polit, two of her frequent visitors. She then went on to express the hope that her new Jesuit friends would linger in the region, postponing their return to Quito for as long as feasible.[107]

Sáenz also drew satisfaction from her continuing correspondence with Gabriel García who, in 1855, left Paita in order to study at the Sorbonne in Paris. "[My] peerless friend, Dr. García, still writes me from Paris," she informed Ascásubi a year later. "I am very fortunate, my friends don't forget me," she added contentedly.[108] She no doubt would have been delighted to learn of García's election to the Ecuadorian presidency just five years later.

Beyond the effects of sporadic political turmoil in the Province of Piura, Sáenz's last years were peaceful. Her health, however, became fragile. Gabriel García worried about her occasional bouts of illness (colds and fevers) and, near the end of his stay in Paita, opined that "her excessively sanguine constitution and extreme heaviness" tended to aggravate the effect of any ailment.[109] Sáenz, moreover, had come to rely increasingly on Juana Rosa, the former slave who had been incorporated into her household decades earlier (while still an infant) and who, of the many servants who had once made up that household, seems to have been the only one to follow her mistress into exile. Indeed, Juana Rosa had become an indispensable companion. Since the time of her crippling hip injury, Sáenz had depended on the younger woman for assistance in carrying out daily functions such as bathing and dressing as well as moving from her bed to the large hammock in which she wrote her letters or to the wheelchair in which she received special visitors (or strangers).

She also regarded her as a close friend or cherished relative. This may be gleaned, in part, from the recognition Juana Rosa receives in some of the letters addressed to her mistress that, besides mentioning the servant by name, include greetings to her—in one instance, referring to her as "countrywoman." Juana Rosa's standing may be seen, too, from Sáenz's practice of occasionally reading her personal letters aloud to her, as she did an 1844 missive from a friend in Piura.[110] Such a practice suggests feelings of trust and affection that may not have been unusual among older women, especially widows, who lacked children and whose main source of companionship was a faithful household servant.

Toward the end of June 1856, the Libertadora contracted a severe illness. "I am very sick of the face [sinuses and/or throat]," she informed her friend Ascásubi that month in her last known letter, explaining that, for that reason, she had not written him.[111] Although the exact nature of this illness remains uncertain, it may have been a result of the diphtheria epidemic that seems to have struck the region, including Guayaquil and the north coast of Peru, that same year. The disease itself may have arrived on a ship or packet boat whose crew or passengers were affected by the pandemic that had originated in England a year or two earlier.[112]

Diphtheria of the throat—assuming that that is what Sáenz contracted—was an acute and deadly infection. Triggered by an airborne bacillus not yet discovered during Sáenz's lifetime (and that would not be identified until 1883), its symptoms included a severe sore throat and fever, this followed by difficulty breathing due to swelling of the mucous membranes. If left unchecked, the bacillus also emits a toxin that damages the heart, kidneys, and central nervous system. Victims had little chance of survival until the development of a diphtheria antitoxin near the end of the century; mortality rates were as high as 90 percent.[113]

On November 23, at around six in the evening (two days after the death of the faithful Juana Rosa), the fifty-nine-year-old Sáenz succumbed to illness.[114] Her death would be noted by friends. Her life, in time, would be remembered.

SEVEN

Afterlife

> *En Paita preguntamos por ella, la Difunta. Tocar, tocar la tierra de la bella*
> *Enterrada. No sabían.*

AFTER HER DEATH, Manuela Sáenz's remains slipped anonymously into the dry earth on the outskirts of Paita.[1] Local tradition has it that, along with other victims of the 1856 diphtheria epidemic, the Libertadora was buried in a common grave south of town instead of in the parish cemetery, the normal burial ground for town residents. Despite a Peruvian government–sponsored investigation into the matter in the late 1980s, her exact resting place—the site of her bones—remains uncertain.[2]

Public interest in where she is buried, however, is telling. Reflected in the pilgrimages made to Paita in the many years since her death, such interest has coincided with a growing awareness of Paita's history and folk memory, including Paiteños' recollection of the close bonds Sáenz had with local families, including ties of *compadrazgo* with some of the women who worked in her home and helped her earn a living.[3]

Yet, Sáenz has transcended memory. In recent decades, thanks to the work of scores of writers, journalists, novelists, and others (including filmmakers) in Spanish America, she has become a mythic, even iconic, figure.[4] Her iconic status owes much to Alfonso Rumazo's *Manuela Sáenz: La Libertadora del Libertador.*

View of contemporary Paita. Photograph by author.

House in Paita believed to have been Sáenz's home. The brass plaque next to the doorway reads: "En esta casa vivió y murió Manuelita Sáenz, 'La Libertadora del Libertador Bolívar,' Homenaje del Rotary Club de Paita, Paita, 29 de Julio de 1970." Photograph by author.

This book was the first to offer a compelling portrait of the Libertadora; unlike most earlier writings, it shows her to have been less a stereotype or sensational character than a dynamic, complex, flesh-and-blood woman. It also dismisses the moralistic assessments of earlier authors, noting, for example, that Sáenz's "original sin [of illicit love] has been cleansed in the dew of the liberty that she herself helped uncover."[5]

As this assessment illustrates, moreover, Rumazo cast his protagonist as an epic heroine. Indeed, reflecting the nationalist (and Pan-American) sensibility among writers of his generation, he cast her as a key participant in the continentwide anticolonial war led by Bolívar. He thus highlighted Sáenz's role in the final, Peruvian, stages of that war, including, as noted earlier, the Andean Campaign and important Battle of Ayacucho. He characterized Sáenz overall as a patriot and freedom fighter—in effect, an Amazon-like "founding mother." In Rumazo's view, the Libertadora was "not only a lover worthy of the Libertador but an American soldier who battled heroically . . . for the independence of the continent."[6] The broad appeal of this portrayal may be gauged from the fact that, since 1944, Rumazo's biography has appeared in at least ten Spanish-language editions published in Spain and four Spanish American countries: the most recent edition was published in 2003 in Quito.[7]

Rumazo's dashing, freedom-fighting heroine, moreover, has captivated a wide range of readers. She has inspired authors of left-wing ideological inclination, for example. The most famous of these, no doubt, is Chilean-born poet Pablo Neruda. In his haunting and lyrical "La insepulta de Paita: Elegía dedicada a la memoria de Manuela Sáenz, amante de Simón Bolívar" (The Unburied Woman of Paita: Elegy Dedicated to the Memory of Manuela Sáenz, Lover of Simón Bolívar), Neruda celebrated the Libertadora as a passionate revolutionary, a militant in the ranks of a guerilla-style insurgency. The poem's third stanza refers to her as "the siren of rifles, the widow of nets, the tiny creole merchant of honey, doves, pineapples, and pistols [who] slept among the casks, familiar with the insurgent gunpowder." Subsequent lines recall the "lost commander" with her "turbulent eyes [and] short hands like iron." The poem later characterizes Saenz as a "pure smuggler" and "guerilla fighter" as well as a "wounded woman . . . [who] had victory in her dreams [and] a sword for a lover."[8]

Such phrases suggest that, for Neruda, Sáenz's real significance has less to do with her role in any actual historical circumstances than with her well-known commitment to the cause of revolution—and thus, in the poet's mind, to Spanish America's ongoing (anti-imperialist) struggle for freedom. The Libertadora has been "crowned not only with lemon flowers . . . [and] with great love" but also ". . . with our blood and our war."[9] In short, as he invoked her memory

amid the bare cliffs of Paita, Neruda transformed Sáenz into a progressive symbol, indeed, an icon of revolution and independence on a par with Bolívar.[10]

Novelists and other contemporary writers generally have embraced this ide-
alized image of Sáenz as revolutionary. In his well-known 1989 historical novel,
El general en su laberinto (*The General in His Labyrinth*), Gabriel García Márquez
imagines Sáenz almost in the mold of a modern *guerrillera*. He describes her
as "the bold Quiteña [who] smoked a sailor's pipe, used the verbena water favored by the military as her perfume, dressed in men's clothing, and spent time
with soldiers, [and whose] husky voice still suited the penumbra of love."[11] In
his 1990 play, *El libertador y la guerillera*, Germán Arciniegas reinforced Sáenz's
image as a member of a Bolivarian vanguard. The play assumes the form of a
classic three-part tragedy and traces the story of Bolívar's political rise and fall.
Its plot is punctuated by a chorus consisting of the region's recently freed black
slaves. It portrays Sáenz both as the Liberator's partner-in-arms and as a witness
to his unhappy fate, including the collapse of his dream of Spanish American
unity. She also appears as a kind of prophet or diviner, one who foresees that fate
yet is helpless to change or stop it.[12]

Spanish American feminists, especially, have embraced Sáenz with special
fervor. Their interest in her first blossomed in the 1980s, stimulated by the various women's rights and human rights movements of that decade as well as by
the special efforts of Ecuadorian author-activist Nela Martínez. In a pioneering
collection of essays entitled *Manuela Libertad* (1983), Martínez—a Communist
Party member and leader of the Frente Continental de Mujeres por la Paz y
Contra la Intervención—called for a fresh, more-balanced look at Sáenz and
her "many faces." In her contribution to this collection, she asked that historians recognize the Libertadora's "rightful place in history" and admit that she
had been much more than a famous mistress.[13] She later organized an event
designed to highlight that place and celebrate the Quito heroine. Known as the
Primer Encuentro con la Historia: Manuela Sáenz, the event brought together
some forty women from Ecuador, Peru, and Cuba who, in late September 1989,
met in Paita in order to honor Sáenz's memory and visit her alleged house
and tomb.[14]

The Primer Encuentro also gave its participants a unique forum. During the
opening ceremony, Martínez, the keynote speaker, articulated her view of the
Libertadora as both an emancipated woman and a feminist "precursor"—one
whose life demonstrated "woman's [leadership] capacities." She also vouched
for Sáenz's Bolivarian vision. Like her famous lover, Sáenz had recognized "the
need to create a greater Latin American homeland, erase colonial boundaries,
and lead these countries toward . . . full-fledged independence [and] solidarity."

She went on to suggest that this vision included concern for the plight of "the abused heirs of Indo-America."[15]

Martínez then declared that Sáenz's contributions to independence were on a par with those of her lover, that she was a "coparticipant" in his continental project, and that, therefore, she should be regarded less as the Libertadora (a term apparently tainted by its patriarchalist origin) than as the "Co-Liberator." She and other participants later signed a document known as the Declaración de Paita. The signers promised to "take up Sáenz's banner" and to complete the emancipation process she ostensibly had started; they above all promised to "fight for the elimination of every form of discrimination [whether] of sex, race, class, or nationality."[16]

In addition, the Primer Encuentro gave its Ecuadorian contingent (members of the Frente Continental de Mujeres por la Paz) a chance to air their policy agenda. This included plans to persuade Ecuador's Congress to recognize the Hacienda Cataguango as a "national monument" and to authorize funds for its restoration: to sponsor an essay contest on Sáenz's "political thought"; to see to the opening of a new public library in the Casa Municipal de Cultura of Quito, this recently named after her; and to develop a course on the heroine's life and thought to be included in Ecuador's public school curriculum.[17] While it is unclear to what extent these plans have been realized, their announcement at the Primer Encuentro showed the degree to which Sáenz had become not just a feminist role model and source of inspiration but a rallying point for civic and social activists.[18]

Sáenz has continued to serve as a rallying point. Above all, she has become a potent national symbol. A recent example of this was her invocation during a protest against the effects of Ecuador's neoliberal policies, held March 8, 1998 (International Women's Day), in the central historic district of Quito. The protestors, members of the self-styled "autonomous feminists," rode on horseback to the Plaza de Independencia dressed as the Libertadora. According to Amy Lind, "their performance as Manuela Sáenz was intended to reclaim the project of nation-building with which she is associated . . . [and] to engender and critique the modern practice of nation-building, for example, political corruption and the nation's debt burden." Lind adds that "inherent in their protest was the idea that women are affected in gender-specific ways by the current economic and political reforms." She concludes her analysis by observing that Sáenz has become "a modern icon for feminists remaking the nation in the context of neoliberalism."[19]

Sáenz's importance to Ecuadorian national identity generally also may be gleaned from elite Ecuadorians' reaction in 1988 to Venezuelan author Denzil

Romero's prize-winning erotic novel, *La esposa del doctor Thorne*. The novel portrays its famous protagonist as nymphomaniacal, more whore than heroine. Authors from across the ideological spectrum—from conservative nationalists of the Sociedad Bolivariana to left-leaning feminists of the Frente Continental de Mujeres to the respected Rumazo González—objected strongly to this. While one spokesman for the Sociedad Bolivariana accused Romero of "defaming the memory of the Quito heroine," other critics condemned the novel for its "abuse" of history; still others characterized it simply as "pornographic."[20]

As a widely accepted symbol of patriotism, moreover, the Libertadora has been useful to governments seeking to bolster their popularity and legitimacy. With this in mind, it seems, on May 25, 2007, the anniversary of the Battle of Pichincha, the Ecuadorian government symbolically promoted her to the rank of General of the Army.[21]

Who exactly was this woman whose memory is now celebrated, whose honor so vigorously, if posthumously, defended, and whose image leaders now place on the loftiest of pedestals? Beyond her status as a Quito native and member of Spanish America's small urban upper class, she was an exceptionally independent and strong-minded individual—a woman who, despite the constraints of gender-related social conventions (along with the stigma attached to illegitimate birth), forged a path for herself and, in turn, a unique personal and political destiny.

Sáenz's independence showed itself early. Although she bowed to her father's choice of husband, for example, she attained considerable autonomy during her marriage to James Thorne. Some of this may be attributed to the 1820 power of attorney Thorne granted her, a circumstance that accustomed his young wife to managing her own legal and business affairs including, in 1822, her claim to a maternal inheritance. Some of it stemmed from her ability to win Thorne's personal confidence; by 1822, after all, Sáenz had made herself his indispensable helper and partner.

Another example of her independent streak was her involvement in Lima's small but important patriot movement. That involvement almost certainly grated against her husband's sensibilities, these shaped by his close ties to members of the city's social and business establishment. It clashed sharply with the sentiments of her royalist father and older half-siblings, including half-sister María Josefa.[22] Indeed, Sáenz's independent spirit may have been, in part, a rebellion against Sáenz de Vergara and his patriarchal influence. Such a rebellion was not unusual in light of the intergenerational conflict that formed part of the larger Age of Revolution and that, in the case of Chile, for example, fueled the creole-peninsular tensions that lay behind the bloody fight for independence.[23]

Sáenz's strong-mindedness showed itself in her affair with her famous lover. While Bolívar may have initiated the affair, it was she who, in the face of hostile forces, for example, her husband's protests and her lover's misgivings, pursued it. The protean Liberator must have embodied her most ardent dreams and desires. Among other things and, if only at a subconscious level, he must have filled the shoes left by her once all-powerful father whose return to Spain, interestingly, occurred shortly after her and Bolívar's initial encounter. Sáenz's surviving correspondence certainly reveals her deep attachment to and admiration for him as well as her emotional neediness.

Bolívar also offered his mistress the chance to shine in public. Having something of her ambitious, social-climbing parent in her, Sáenz took full advantage of this. She reveled in her association with the victorious Colombian army, a tendency manifested in her fondness for dressing occasionally in military-style uniform. She took pride in her roles as Bolívar's personal archivist and as the Libertadora—including the functions she adopted as an intercessor or mediator. After she saved her lover's life on September 25, 1828, she basked in his supporters' praise and recognition.

Sáenz's relationship with Bolívar also gave her a unique and heady sense of belonging. Besides ensuring her status as mistress of the era's single most influential leader, it confirmed her place in Spanish America's new family of republican citizens, citizens of Gran Colombia in particular. While aware of her sex's traditional gender-based subordination, Sáenz considered herself a "fully vested" family member. She was, after all, part of the same creole elite that had spearheaded the cause of independence. Like her half-brother José María and his fellow officers as well as patriot-minded ladies in Lima, she had rallied to the call of General San Martín and been publicly recognized for her contributions. She knew of her rights under the various constitutions.

By 1828, not surprisingly, Sáenz also thought herself entitled to a voice in Gran Colombia's expanding public sphere and increasingly partisan political arena; she threw herself into the fray between Liberals and Bolivarians. On this, of course, her contemporaries—her and her lover's enemies especially—took issue with her. Above all, Sáenz's relationship with Bolívar gave her a heady sense of empowerment. This sense of empowerment, ironically, seems to have increased even as the Liberator went into decline. It helps explain the boldness with which Sáenz proceeded after her lover's final departure from Bogotá in 1830, her refusal to accept the taunting of his opponents, and, not least, her deliberate attempt to restore him and his followers to power.

Ultimately more important, however, were Sáenz's enduring ties to the Bolivarians, including powerful military men such as Andrés de Santa Cruz and

Juan José Flores. It was such ties that, in her mind and after her exile to Paita in 1835, justified her continued political activism, for example, her cooperation with the Grand Project and efforts to defend Flores from his Ecuadorian opponents. Sáenz, moreover, came to function not only as an intermediary and informant but as an operative and, above all, perhaps, power broker; she mediated between her powerful caudillo friends and their real or would-be supporters/constituents in and around Paita. She also sought to win them new allies. One striking example of this were her efforts to foster a friendship between Flores and the women of the important Godos y Lamas family. As her personal correspondence suggests, she succeeded in turning the latter (Luisa, Paula, and Josefa) into ardent Flores admirers as well as cohorts who kept her informed of the activities of his émigré opponents.[24]

This raises the question of Manuela Sáenz's place in a larger history of Spanish American women. Her life story holds clues for an understanding of women's experiences in a crucial time of transition, a time in which leaders generally looked for ways to reimpose order and stability while grappling with the complex challenges of emergent nations. It especially sheds light on female participation in early national and republican politics, a world that, for much of the nineteenth century, was dominated by caudillos. Indeed, it suggests that, like men of the period and for a variety of reasons, members of the female sex often found it expedient to ally themselves with one or another caudillo, in effect becoming the latter's followers or clients.

This pattern is corroborated by Alonso Valencia's study of women in nineteenth-century southern Colombia, the Cauca region particularly. Valencia shows that, beginning with the era of independence, Caucanas—many of them widows or wives abandoned by husbands who had gone off to war—became participants in the political life of the region by actively aligning themselves with men like General Tomás Cipriano de Mosquera and other powerful regional leaders. He also shows how they entered into cliental relationships (these evident, for example, in their letters to Mosquera) for a variety of reasons, including both personal necessity, that is, a desire to protect their families and property, and political partisanship.[25] More of such studies, of course, are needed. They are likely to show what may be inferred from Sáenz's own experiences: that, despite their exclusion from the public sphere and formal realms of government and politics, Spanish American women were far from strangers to the larger world of power and influence. Neither were they strangers to notions that, in time, would justify their inclusion in the promise of republican citizenship.

Introduction

1. Von Hagen, *The Four Seasons of Manuela*. Von Hagen was the author of at least seventeen popular books on Latin America (many of them concerning the native peoples and natural wonders of Central America and Ecuador) published in the 1930s and 1940s. His book on Sáenz has been, until now, the only English-language biography of her; it has been translated into Spanish in several Latin American editions.

2. Quotation from Ellis, "Get a Life!" See also biographies Ellis has written: *Passionate Sage* and *American Sphinx*.

3. Ellis, "Get a Life!" Although Ellis laments social historians' tendency to stigmatize "the venerable tradition of life-writing," he does not see social history itself as at all "bad" for biography but, rather, as a trend that keeps the genre vigorous and vibrant—a by-product of its "outlaw status." For perceptive comments on the challenges involved in reconstructing the lives of women—and on her own experience in the case of the famous nineteenth-century former slave, feminist, and abolitionist Sojourner Truth—see Painter, "Writing Biographies of Women."

4. Margadant, *The New Biography*, 7. According to Margadant, "the subject of biography is no longer the coherent self but rather a self that is performed in order to create an impression of coherence or an individual of multiple selves whose different manifestations reflect the passage of time, the demands and options of different settings, or the varieties of ways that others seek to represent that person." For further examples of this new theoretical approach, see Goodman, *Marie-Antoinette*.

5. Monteón, "Biography and Latin American History," 193.

6. Guy, "Biography."

7. Mogollón and Narváez, *Manuela Sáenz*, 72–75 (all translations are mine unless otherwise noted). The three national histories the authors survey are Fermín Cevallos, *Resumen;* P. Moncayo, *El Ecuador;* and Andrade, *Historia.* For further discussion of these authors' (and Calle's) portrayals of Sáenz, see Murray, "'Loca' or 'Libertadora'?"; and Conway, *The Cult of Bolívar,* 104–105.

8. See Núñez, "El Ecuador en Colombia," 251. For a more recent effort to highlight Sáenz's importance within the context of the larger history of women of her era, see Taxin, "La participación."

9. See Galvis, *Historia extensa de Colombia,* vol. 7: *La Gran Colombia,* 343; and Ocampo López, "El proceso político."

10. For a detailed survey of historical interpretations of Sáenz, see Murray, "'Loca' or 'Libertadora'?"

11. Ibid., 294.

12. Ibid., 296–297. Quotation from Palma, "La protectora y la libertadora," in *Tradiciones peruanas completas,* 962.

13. Ibid. In his memoirs, besides noting her love of pranks and occasional use of a military uniform, Boussingault suggests that Sáenz was bisexual. See *Mémoires,* vol. 3, chap. 7.

14. Miramón, *La vida ardiente,* 16. In the author's words: "La amante de Bolívar perteneció a cierta tipología erótica de mujeres que la ciencia moderna ha discriminado."

15. De Madariaga, *Bolívar,* vol. 2 (1979), 299, 370.

16. Moreno de Ángel, *José María Córdova,* 404.

17. Moreno de Ángel, *Santander,* 433.

18. Lecuna (ed.), "Papeles de Manuela Sáenz," 494: "Su [Sáenz's] serenidad y valor ahorraron a nuestra patria la vergüenza del asesinato del héroe, motivo suficiente para evocar su recuerdo con respeto y simpatía, y procurar que su historia quede limpia de leyendas inverosímiles o impropias."

19. Ibid., 498. Lecuna's statement, of course, shows that his primary interest lies less in elucidating Sáenz's life than in protecting his hero's historical reputation. For a further critique of his article, see Murray, "'Loca' or 'Libertadora'?" 300–302. In a subtle, penetrating analysis, Chris Conway shows how various literary and historical representations of Sáenz shed light on the gendered nature of the cult of Bolívar; he also classifies those representations into two basic types or models: that of the "epic (or manly woman)" and that of the "romantic (or womanly woman)." See Conway, *The Cult of Bolívar,* 99–107.

20. Chiriboga Navarro, "Los Sáenz en el Ecuador," 225. See my "'Loca' or 'Libertadora'?" for further discussion of Chiriboga and other Ecuadorian nationalist writings on Sáenz.

21. First published in Cali, Colombia, Rumazo's biography has since appeared in at least nine Spanish-language editions and, along with Von Hagen's work, has long served as the standard source on the Ecuadorian heroine. For a fuller summary and analysis of Rumazo's interpretation, see Murray, "'Loca' or 'Libertadora'?" 304–305.

22. Rumazo, *Manuela Sáenz,* 175–176. Such unsubstantiated claims are addressed both in Lecuna (ed.), "Papeles de Manuela Sáenz" and in Villalba, *Manuela Sáenz en la leyenda.* See also Chap. 2 here.

23. See, for example, Rumazo, *Manuela Sáenz,* 283–304. Entitled "Sexta parte: Trágica peregrinación y muerte," this final chapter or section of the book covers the period from 1831 through Sáenz's death in Paita twenty-five years later. It also mistakenly gives the date of her death as 1859.

24. Von Hagen's fictionalizing tendency may be seen in his occasional habit of attributing words and statements to Sáenz which no sources show her to have said, at least not literally. See, for example, *The Four Seasons of Manuela*, 265.

25. This personal correspondence comprises only about 130 letters. As will be seen, its biggest gaps concern her youth, early married life, and relationship with Bolívar in the years 1822–1830. Many of Sáenz's own letters seem to have been lost over time (some, perhaps, are still waiting to be discovered) while most of the ones she received from Bolívar and other correspondents are believed to have been burned in the fire that destroyed her personal belongings after her death in a diphtheria epidemic. An exception are the letters published in Álvarez Saá and Villacis, *Manuela,* which most scholars, including me, regard as apocryphal. For an exemplary critique of this collection, see Vargas Martínez, "Bolívar y Manuelita."

26. Sáenz's letters to Flores have been preserved in the Flores archive, which forms part of the Fondo Jacinto Jijón y Caamaño ("Quinta Serie: Documentos del General J. J. Flores"), and is available on microfilm at the Archivo Histórico del Banco Central del Ecuador in Quito (henceforth AHBC-Quito). Most have been transcribed and edited in Villalba, *Manuela Sáenz: Epistolario.* Few of Flores's letters to Sáenz have survived.

27. According to Alberto Miramón, for example, Sáenz was like a satellite who, in the wake of Bolívar's death, lost its way. She was, he states, "el satélite que, arrebatado por el esplendente meteoro, lo siguió en su ruta; brilló esplendoroso en la cohorte libertadora y cuando aquel cumplió la órbita que la Providencia le habia señalado, vagó triste y olvidada." See Miramón, *Vida ardiente,* 16. An important corrective to this view of Sáenz's later years is Sarah Chambers's study of Sáenz's friendship with Flores and effort to place her within a larger history of women. See "Republican Friendship."

28. For a good discussion of the Age of Revolution as a distinct historical period, see Uribe, *State and Society,* especially his introductory essay and the conclusion by Eric Van Young.

29. Arrom, *The Women of Mexico City,* 38. Arrom sees this process as one that started in the late eighteenth century with the impact of a new, Enlightenment-inspired view of women as potential contributors to national development—a view that underlay a modest expansion in education for women as well as reforms designed to improve female access to remunerative employment. Although her ideas stem from her study of the specific case of Mexico City, it seems reasonable to infer their relevance to the situation of women in other Spanish American capitals affected by similar efforts to improve women's status as well as by widespread female participation in the struggles for independence.

Chapter One

1. Mannareli, *Pecados públicos,* 307–308. According to Mannareli, the term "*expósito/a*" was often used to refer euphemistically to the offspring of illicit, especially adulterous, unions.

2. Ibid., 165–167. See also Twinam, *Public Lives,* 127–141.

3. Twinam, *Public Lives,* 140–141.

4. Jurado Noboa, "La familia y ascendientes de Manuelita," 209–210.

5. Twinam, "Honor," 124–128.

6. Archivo Nacional de Historia del Ecuador (eds.), "Expediente . . . sobre su filiación," 91.

7. Villalba (ed.), *Manuela Sáenz: Epistolario,* 82–85. Although she apparently died single (*soltera*) before 1804, Aizpuru's death certificate has not been found, nor has the birth certificate for her daughter, Manuela, whose surviving letters never mention her mother.

8. Jurado Noboa, "La familia y ascendientes de Manuelita," 193–196. On upper-class marriage patterns in the region at the time, see Rodríguez, "Las mujeres," vol. 2, 216 passim.

9. Ibid., 198. See also Borchart de Moreno, "La imbecilidad," 174n32. Borchart's note hints at Sáenz de Vergara's business as an importer of European textiles ("ropas de castilla").

10. Jurado Noboa, "La familia y ascendientes de Manuelita," 196–197; Flores y Caamaño, "Origen de Manuela Sáenz," 342–344. Tithe collectors generally were wealthy men, as the position required an individual to post a bond or surety (*fianza*) that could be as high as ten thousand pesos; they also could expect to earn at least a 5 percent commission on anticipated tithe revenues. For details, see Brungardt, "Tithe Production."

11. Lynch, *The Spanish American Revolutions,* 17–18; Andrien, *The Kingdom of Quito,* 194–195.

12. Jurado Noboa, "La familia y ascendientes de Manuelita," 210. Sáenz, for example, may have benefitted from the social connections of his friend and fellow peninsular Spaniard Carlos Antonio del Mazo, who was married to Ignacia Aizpuru, Joaquina's older sister.

13. Ibid., 209. Sáenz's house was No. 19; the Aizpurus' was No. 30.

14. Archivo Nacional de Historia del Ecuador (eds.), "Expediente . . . sobre su filiación," 91.

15. On the Concepcionistas generally, see Lavrin, "Female Religious"; on their convent in Quito, see González Suárez, *Historia General,* vol. 3, 161–162; Londoño, *Entre la sumisión y la resistencia,* 241–242.

16. Minchom, *The People of Quito, 1690–1810,* 22 (fig. 2.1); Jurado N., Aguilar, and Moreno, *Casas del Quito Viejo,* 16.

17. Londoño, *Entre la sumisión y la resistencia,* 242. For a lively and comprehensive description of convent life, see Martín, *Daughters of the Conquistadores,* 172–186.

18. Londoño, *Entre la sumisión y la resistencia,* 242.

19. Ibid., 222.

20. On the practice of *hijos expósitos* being made part of their father's legitimate households, see Twinam, *Public Lives,* 164–168.

21. Jurado Noboa, "La familia y ascendientes de Manuelita," 198–203. Sáenz had at least seven paternal half-siblings, six of whom survived into adulthood: Juan Antonio (b. 1785); José Camilo (b. 1786); María Josefa (b. 1788); José María (b. 1797); María Manuela (b. 1800); and Ignacio (b. 1803). The two half-sisters both would return to Spain with their husbands and father in 1822.

22. Minchom, *The People of Quito,* 133, 145 (table 6.7). In 1797, Quito had about fifty-three men for every one hundred women, the result of an overall decline in the city's male population beginning in the 1780s.

23. Perhaps the earliest reference to this legend is in Boussingault, *Mémoires,* vol. 3, chap. 7. The legend has been incorporated into the standard biographies of Sáenz, including those by Rumazo González (*Manuela Sáenz*) and Von Hagen (*The Four Seasons of Manuela*). It has been challenged by Villalba in *Manuela Sáenz en la leyenda,* which stresses the lack of evidence.

24. Socolow, "Acceptable Partners," 210–211 passim.

25. On how a woman's illegitimate birth could affect her marriage prospects, see Twinam, *Public Lives,* 199–201. Mention of Sáenz's dowry appears in Thorne's will, Testamento de Don Jayme Thornet, Oct. 25, 1847, Archivo General de la Nación, Lima (henceforth AGN-Lima), Sección Historia, Libro de Protocolos, leg. 160, ff. 248–251.

26. John Lynch notes that, by 1824, there already were about 250 British immigrants (mostly representatives of various business firms) in Lima alone. See *The Spanish American Revolutions,* 275.

27. Information on Thorne's background, wealth, and sociobusiness relationships comes largely from Testamento de Don Jayme Thornet, Oct. 25, 1847, AGN-Lima, Sección Historia, Libro de Protocolos, leg. 160, ff. 248–251; and Testamento del Sr. General Don Domingo Orué hecho en virtud de poder por su albacea Don Jayme Thorne [April 1835], AGN-Lima, Sección Historia, Libro de Protocolos, leg. 62. Orué also held the title of Count of Torre Antigua de Orué. For further information, see Leguía y Martínez, *Historia de la emancipación del Perú,* vol. 2: *El Protectorado,* 172–174nn14, 15, 25. Leguía y Martínez states that, in 1819, the Hacienda Huaito had an estimated worth of one million gold pesos.

28. For insight into Sáenz de Vergara's role in the creole-peninsular political tensions leading up to the uprising, see Zúñiga, *Juan Pío Montúfar y Larrea,* vol. 1, 365–370, 376. On the uprising and its aftermath, see Minchom, *The People of Quito,* 243–251.

29. Rumazo González, *Manuela Sáenz,* 41–56.

30. Partida de matrimonio de Don Jayme Thornet con Doña Manuela Sáenz, 27 julio 1817, Libro de casamientos de españoles, mestizos y quarterones de esta parroquia de San Sebastián, 1788–1825, Archivo Arzobispal de Lima; Von Hagen, *The Four Seasons of Manuela,* 170–171.

31. Twinam, *Public Lives,* 33. According to Twinam, the malleability or negotiability of honor arose from Spanish Americans' tendency to inhabit two different

worlds simultaneously: a private world of friends and family, and a public world consisting of everyone outside the private circle.

32. Ibid.

33. Ibid., 199–200.

34. Lavrin "Women in Spanish Colonial Society, 327–328; Mannareli, *Pecados públicos,* 220. According to Christine Hunefeldt, the average value of a dowry in Lima in 1820 was 8,787 pesos; see *Liberalism in the Bedroom,* 233, table 7.2.

35. See Martín, *Daughters of the Conquistadores,* for a good discussion of the impact of this ideal and the influence of Catholic doctrine on marriage generally.

36. Arrom, *The Women of Mexico City,* 59–62.

37. Ibid., 66–67.

38. Letter from James Thorne to Manuela Sáenz, Lima, Dec. 11, 1822, in Villalba (ed.), *Manuela Sáenz: Epistolario,* 186–188.

39. "Most beloved wife of my heart" (amadísima esposa de mi corazón); "darling companion" (amable compañera); "my precious *chichita*" (mi adorada chichita); "my love is too firmly grounded . . . to be shaken" (mi amor está fundada sobre una roca demasiado fuerte . . . para vacilar). Ibid.

40. "Soothing balm of her sweet advice" (el bálsamo de tus dulces consejos). Ibid.

41. Borchart de Moreno, "La imbecilidad," 171–173.

42. Thorne to Sáenz, Lima, Dec. 11, 1822, in Villalba (ed.), *Manuela Sáenz: Epistolario,* 186–188. Receipt for goods sold to Manuela Sáenz on May 22, 1822, in Lecuna (ed.), "Papeles de Manuela Sáenz," 501. The receipt reflects Sáenz's purchase of items worth a total of 3,643 pesos, including 189 yards of damask and brocade fabric; five tulle dresses; three tulle shawls; four rolls of faux pearls; 25 dozen cashmere scarves ("pañuelos casimir"), and 20 dozen cotton stockings ("de borlón superior de hilo").

43. Slave sale and manumission documents transcribed in Lecuna (ed.), "Papeles de Manuela Sáenz," 498–500.

44. Archivo Nacional de Historia del Ecuador (eds.), "Expediente . . . sobre su filiación," 90–91.

45. On the inheritance rights of illegitimate children, see Mannareli, *Pecados públicos,* 165–184; Twinam, *Public Lives,* 217–220. Mannareli also notes that, in most cases, illegitimates had to undertake legal action in order to enjoy their rights, as those rights were seldom acknowledged by others with claims to the same estate.

46. Villalba (ed.), *Manuela Sáenz: Epistolario,* 82–84; Transacción y convenio entre las Señoras Ygnacia Aizpuru y Manuela Sáenz, Quito, 31 julio 1823, Archivo Nacional de Historia del Ecuador (henceforth ANE), Quito, Notaría 1, Protocolos, vol. 481, ff. 48–52.

47. Hunefeldt, *Liberalism in the Bedroom,* 19 (table 1.1). In 1811, Mexico City had almost 169,000 inhabitants; see Arrom, *The Women of Mexico City,* 7. A good general description of Lima by the end of the colonial period appears in Klarén, *Peru,* 73–74 passim.

48. Hunefeldt, *Liberalism in the Bedroom,* 19 (table 1.1).
49. Proctor, *Narrative,* 232.
50. Ibid., 221.
51. Martín, *Daughters of the Conquistadores,* 301–304.
52. Important studies of the impact of the 1808–1810 Spanish crisis and ensuing wars for independence in Spanish America include Lynch, *The Spanish American Revolutions;* Rodríguez O., *The Independence of Spanish America;* Archer, *The Wars of Independence;* Earle, *Spain.*
53. On women's support for the insurgent cause in Gran Colombia, see Cherpak, "The Participation of Women"; Taxin, "La participación de la mujer en la independencia"; Arrom, *The Women of Mexico City,* 32–38; Kentner, "The Sociopolitical Role of Women." On women and Peruvian independence, see Prieto de Zegarra, *Mujer,* vol. 2.
54. On Salavarieta, see Cherpak, "The Participation of Women," 222; Earle, "Rape and the Anxious Republic," 139.
55. Earle, "Rape and the Anxious Republic," 129–130.
56. Rodríguez Plata, *Antonia Santos Plata,* 151.
57. Díaz, "Ciudadanas and padres de familia," 285–288.
58. Anna, *The Fall of the Royal Government in Peru,* 137, 156–157; Lynch, *The Spanish American Revolutions,* 172–173.
59. For a description of the Numancia regiment, see Chiriboga Navarro, "Los Sáenz en el Ecuador," 202–205, 217–218. On the campaign of seduction that targeted Numancia and that involved women such as Rosa Campuzano, see Prieto de Zegarra, *Mujer, poder y desarrollo en el Perú,* vol. 2, 160–163. Sáenz's friendship with Campuzano is alluded to in Palma, "La protectora y la libertadora," in *Tradiciones peruanas completas,* 962–963.
60. Chiriboga Navarro, "Los Sáenz en el Ecuador," 202–203.
61. Prieto de Zegarra, *Mujer,* 208, 223. Sáenz's name appears on two official collection lists, one for July, the other for August; in the latter list, she is cited as having donated a bolt (about two hundred yards) of "bayetón inglés," a kind of canvas or duffle.
62. "To the patriotism of the most delicate" (Al patriotismo de las más sensibles). "Institución"; January 11, 1822, Decree of San Martín and Bernardo Monteagudo, *Gaceta del Gobierno del Perú Independiente* (Buenos Aires, 1950) 2, no. 4 (Jan. 12, 1822), 3.
63. "Ministerio de Estado," *Gaceta del Gobierno del Perú Independiente* 2, no. 7 (Jan. 23, 1822), 3–4. The women's names are listed in alphabetical order, with Sáenz listed under "M."
64. Ibid.
65. Jurado Noboa, "La familia y ascendientes de Manuelita," 199. According to Jurado, María Josefa Sáenz del Campo, wife of Audiencia judge Francisco Javier Manzanos del Castillo, was imprisoned for a time (in late 1810) by Quito patriots and later escaped, for a while joining the loyalist forces of General Montes.

66. Anna, *The Fall of the Royal Government in Peru,* 158–159, 174, 198–199. A further sense of the material hardships suffered by Limeños in these years may be gleaned from contemporary travelers' accounts.

67. Jurado Noboa, "La familia y ascendientes de Manuelita," 201; Chiriboga Navarro, "Los Sáenz en el Ecuador," 202.

Chapter Two

1. Although we have little direct evidence of the trip itself, its occurrence may be inferred from extant correspondence and other available sources pointing to Sáenz's departure from Lima sometime in April and arrival in Quito by mid-June 1822.

2. Salvador Lara, *Breve historia,* 328–331; O'Leary, *Memorias,* vol. 2, 140.

3. Jurado Noboa, "La familia y ascendientes de Manuelita," 198. Sáenz de Vergara died in Spain three years later, on June 17, 1825.

4. Transacción y convenio entre las Señoras Ygnacia Aizpuru y Manuela Sáenz, Quito, 31 julio 1823, ANE, Quito, Notaría 1, Protocolos, vol. 481, ff. 48–52.

5. Standard biographies of Simón Bolívar include Masur, *Simón Bolívar;* De Madariaga, *Bolívar* (1979), and its abridged English-language version; Mijares, *El Libertador;* Bushnell, *Simón Bolívar.*

6. Detailed coverage of Bolívar's career may be found in the biographies cited in note 5.

7. Davis, "Ecuador under Gran Colombia," 70.

8. For more on Bolívar's image among his contemporaries, see Conway, *The Cult of Bolívar,* 25–26; Lecuna (ed.), "Cartas de mujeres," 335 passim.

9. Chiriboga Navarro, "Los Sáenz en el Ecuador," 206–207; Jurado Noboa, "La familia y ascendientes de Manuelita," 201.

10. A vivid description of this ball and of the couple's encounter there may be found in Von Hagen, *The Four Seasons of Manuela,* 46–48. While other biographers such as Rumazo also mention the ballroom encounter, I have found no evidence of it or of any meeting between Sáenz and Bolívar that night.

11. Twinam, *Public Lives,* 11–13, 62–63.

12. For more on the couple's relationship, see Moreno de Ángel, *Santander,* chap. 15; Duarte French, *Las Ibáñez.* The wife of a royalist official, Antonio José Caro, Nicolasa Ibáñez Arias was a native of Ocaña in Santander and eldest daughter of a respectable family of patriot sympathizers who, in 1813, had befriended both Santander and Bolívar.

13. Martínez Carreño, "Revolución," 426–427; Moreno de Ángel, *Santander,* 226–227.

14. For a brief discussion of Bolívar's marriage and affairs with various women, see Mijares, *El Libertador,* 77, 93, 378–379; on his infatuation with Bernardina Ibáñez, see Moreno de Ángel, *Santander,* 212–213. Years later, Bernardina became the wife of Florentino González, one of Bolívar's old enemies.

15. Mijares, *El Libertador,* 494–495, 82–85. See also De Madariaga, *Bolívar,* 81. De Madariaga claims that, for Bolívar, "love of woman could neither look to the

future nor be reciprocal," adding that, "for him, there were no women in the concrete; only woman in the abstract."

16. The fullest descriptions of Sáenz's physical appearance, personality, and character may be found in Boussingault, *Mémoires de Jean-Baptiste Boussingault* (Paris, 1900), vol. 3, and in Ortiz, *Reminiscencias.* (Bogotá, 1946) Both authors knew Sáenz during her years in Bogotá (1828–1830). See also Palma, "La Protectora y la Libertadora," in *Tradiciones peruanas completas,* 962–963.

17. Manuela Sáenz to James Thorne, n.p., n.d. [1829], Archivo del Libertador, reproducción [microfilm] costeada por las Fundaciones Creole, Shell, Eugenio Mendoza y John Boulton (henceforth AL), Caracas, 1961, roll 34. Although the original manuscript letter is undated, its author's reference to having been Bolívar's lover for "7 years" suggests she wrote it in or around 1829. This same letter was transcribed by Vicente Lecuna in Lecuna (ed.), "Papeles de Manuela Sáenz," 501. Lecuna hypothesized that it was written in October 1823, an unlikely event, in my opinion.

18. Boussingault, *Mémoires,* vol. 3, 215–216.

19. Ibid., 201–202.

20. "Delightful temperament" (genio encantador). Bolívar to Sáenz, Ica, Apr. 20, 1825, in *Cartas del Libertador,* 1st ed., vol. 11, 277–278.

21. "[Our] dear madwoman" (la amable loca). Bolívar to José María Córdoba, n.d. [Aug. 1, 1828?], enclosed in James Henderson to John Bidwell, Bogotá, Aug. 6, 1828, Public Record Office (henceforth PRO), Foreign Office (henceforth FO) 18/56, ff. 53. This is Córdoba's handwritten copy of the original, which apparently has not survived.

22. Sáenz to Thorne, n.p., n.d. [1829], AL, roll 34.

23. Ibid.

24. Ibid.

25. Throughout his biography of Bolívar, Salvador de Madariaga stresses the impact of Napoleon as a model and source of inspiration—one that encouraged the Liberator to think and act on the grandest possible scale and to achieve a comparable level of greatness.

26. On Bolívar's activities from his June arrival in Quito through his July meeting with San Martín in Guayaquil, see his biographies and Restrepo, *Historia de la revolución,* vol. 6, 72–77.

27. Mijares, *El Libertador,* 431, 437–438; Restrepo, *Historia de la revolución,* vol. 6, chaps. 6–7. Bolívar's initial hesitancy to go to Peru himself was the result of, among other things, caution in the face of that country's political turmoil as well as the need to secure official authorization from the government in Bogotá.

28. Sáenz to Bolívar, Dec. 30, 1822, in Lecuna (ed.), "Cartas de mujeres," 332.

29. Ibid. Sáenz's letter acknowledges her receipt of a letter from Bolívar dated Dec. 22. For a description of the Boves uprising and a detailed account of Bolívar's response to it, see Restrepo, *Historia de la revolución,* vol. 6, 127–133; O'Leary, *Memorias,* vol. 2, 171–184.

30. Sáenz to Bolívar, Dec. 30, 1822, in Lecuna (ed.), "Cartas de mujeres," 332.

31. On Vicario, see Arrom, *The Women of Mexico City*, 32–38; Kentner, "The Socio-political Role of Women."

32. Sáenz to Captain Juan José Santana, Huamachuco, May 28, 1824; and Receipt for 3,000 pesos paid by José María Romero to Manuela Sáenz . . ., Lima, Aug. 29, 1825, in Lecuna (ed.), "Cartas de mujeres," 332–333.

33. Santana's surviving letters to Sáenz have been transcribed in Lecuna (ed.), "Papeles de Manuela Sáenz," 502 passim.

34. O'Leary, *Memorias*, vol. 2, 239–244.

35. Sáenz's evacuation from the city is alluded to in Heres to Bolívar (Chanquillo), Feb. 13, 1824, as transcribed in ibid., vol. 5, 67.

36. Ibid., vol. 2, 245–249.

37. Aspects of Sáenz's Andean Campaign experience, including her journey to Huánuco, may be gleaned from extant correspondence. See Santana to Sáenz, June 23, July 18, and Aug. 28, 1824 (including editor's notes), in Lecuna (ed.), "Papeles de Manuela Sáenz," 502–506.

38. Santana to Sáenz (Huanta), Aug. 28, 1824 (and editor's note) in ibid., 506. Some authors claim that Sáenz marched with (rather than behind) the army during the Andean Campaign and that she participated in the battles fought at Junín and Ayacucho. See, for example, Rumazo González, *Manuela Sáenz*, 169–186; Álvarez Saá, *Manuela*, 80, 85, 87. These authors' claims seem baseless, however; beyond an anecdote in Boussingault's memoirs, I have found no evidence to corroborate them. Reputable scholars in the region (e.g., Jorge Villalba and Fernando Jurado in Ecuador and Pilar Moreno de Ángel in Colombia) agree that the letters and documents in Álvarez's private collection—those purported to prove Sáenz's role in battle—are apocryphal.

39. Lecuna (ed.), "Papeles de Manuela Sáenz," 496.

40. Sáenz to Santana, Huamachuco, May 28, 1824, in Lecuna (ed.), "Cartas de mujeres," 332. On Bolívar's famous (and possibly legendary) flirtation with Manuelita Madroño, see Palma, "La vieja de Bolívar," in *Tradiciones peruanas completas*, 1009.

41. Bolívar to Sáenz, Ica, Apr. 20, 1825, in S. Bolívar, *Cartas del Libertador*, vol. 11, 277–278.

42. Bolívar to Sáenz, La Plata (Bolivia), Nov. 26, 1825, in AL, roll 27, f. 160.

43. Sáenz to Thorne, n.p., n.d., in Lecuna (ed.), "Papeles de Manuela Sáenz," 501.

44. "Dreaded misfortunes" (los males que temes). Bolívar to Sáenz, Potosí, Oct. 13, 1825, in Mutis Daza Manuscript Collection, Lilly Library, Indiana University (hereafter LL).

45. Bolívar to Sáenz, Ica, Apr. 20, 1825, in S. Bolívar, *Cartas del Libertador*, vol. 11.

46. Bolívar to Sáenz, La Plata (Bolivia), Nov. 26, 1825, in AL, roll 27, f. 160.

47. Bolívar to Sáenz, n.p., n.d., AL, roll 27, f. 162. Sáenz's letter mentioning the London trip has not survived. Both Vicente Lecuna and Alfonso Rumazo have suggested that Bolívar's response was written in July 1826.

48. William Tudor to U.S. Secretary of State Henry Clay, Lima, March 23, 1827, in Despatches from U.S. Consuls in Lima, 1823–1854, 1949, microfilm roll 1. Tudor's despatch refers both to Sáenz's residence at La Magdalena and the stipend.

49. Sáenz to Bolívar, Dec. 30, 1822, in Lecuna (ed.), "Cartas de mujeres," 332.

50. Sáenz to Santana [?], Lima, Oct. 31, 1825, in Lecuna (ed.), "Cartas de mujeres," 333. The unedited microfilm copy of this letter (available in AL, roll 42) shows that, except for the signature, the original was not in Sáenz's handwriting and did not name its intended recipient—who was identified only as "mi querido amigo." It is thus possible the letter was meant for Bolívar and reflected an effort to go along with his earlier suggestion that the lovers cool their relationship.

51. See references to their greetings in Santana's letters to Sáenz in Lecuna (ed.), "Papeles de Manuela Sáenz," 504–506.

52. Sáenz to Santana [?], Lima, Oct. 31, 1825, in Lecuna (ed.), "Cartas de mujeres," 333.

53. See Santana's various letters to Sáenz in Lecuna (ed.), "Papeles de Manuela Sáenz," 502, 505.

54. Ibid.; Sáenz to Santana [?], Lima, Oct. 31, 1825, in idem, "Cartas de mujeres," 333.

55. For Bolívar's governance of Peru after his army's victory at Ayacucho, see Basadre, *Historia de la República del Perú,* vol. 1, 91–93, 104–106.

56. Heres to Bolívar, Lima, Dec. 16, 1825, in O'Leary, *Memorias,* vol. 23, 403.

57. Hints of Sáenz's role as an advocate or intercessor appear mainly in her later correspondence, including, for example, Sáenz to Bolívar, Bogotá, March 28, 1828, in Lecuna (ed.), "Cartas de mujeres," 335.

58. Ibid.; see also Bolívar to Sáenz, Ibarra, Oct. 6, 1826, in AL, roll 27, f. 161; Tudor to Clay, Lima, March 23, 1827, Despatches from U.S. Consuls in Lima, microfilm roll 1.

59. Basadre, *Historia de la República del Perú,* vol. 1, 121–123.

60. Ibid., 101–103.

61. De Madariaga, *Bolívar,* 519–521; Basadre, *Historia de la República del Perú,* vol. 1, 119–120.

62. Sáenz to Santana [?], Lima, Oct. 31, 1825, in Lecuna (ed.), "Cartas de mujeres," 333.

63. Bolívar to Sáenz, Ibarra, Oct. 6, 1826, in AL, roll 27, f. 161.

64. Basadre, *Historia de la República del Perú,* vol. 1, 122.

65. For a summary of these developments, see Moreno de Ángel, *José María Cordova,* 344; Consul-General Ricketts to Secretary of State George Canning, Lima, Feb. 6, 1827, PRO, FO 61/11, ff. 65–85.

66. Moreno de Ángel, *José María Cordova,* 345–346; Basadre, *Historia de la República del Perú,* vol. 1, 126–127. Also see despatches from Rickets to Canning for February 6 and 26, 1827, and March 31, 1827, PRO, FO 61/11, ff. 65–85.

67. Posada, "La Libertadora," vol. 15, 20; also Heres's report on the uprising in O'Leary, *Memorias,* vol. 5, 175.

68. Tudor to Clay, Lima, March 23, 1827, Despatches from U.S. Consuls in Lima, microfilm roll 1; Palma, "Doña Manuela Sáenz (La Libertadora)," in *Tradiciones peruanas completas*, 1134; Moreno de Ángel, *José María Cordova*, 350–351.

69. Sáenz to Consul Cristóbal Armero, Lima, n.d., in Lecuna (ed.), "Papeles de Manuela Sáenz," 507. Mention of Sáenz's imprisonment also appears in Tudor to Clay, Lima, March 23, 1827, Despatches from U.S. Consuls in Lima, microfilm roll 1, and in Despatch from Ricketts to Planta, Lima, March 11, 1827, PRO, FO 61/11, ff. 182–183.

70. Sáenz to Armero, Lima, n.d., in Lecuna (ed.), "Papeles de Manuela Sáenz," 507–508.

71. "No se si habrá razón para que se me juzgue como peruana, mas si la hay, que se me castiga peruanamente." Ibid.

72. Ibid.

73. Tudor to Clay, Lima, March 23, 1827, Despatches from U.S. Consuls in Lima, microfilm roll 1.

74. Moreno de Ángel, *Santander*, 351. Moreno's account includes an excerpt from an April 14 letter from Vidaurre to a friend.

75. Tudor to Clay, Lima, March 23, 1827, Despatches from U.S. Consuls in Lima, microfilm roll 1.

Chapter Three

1. Moreno de Ángel, *José María Córdova*, 353–354.

2. Sáenz to Bolívar, n.p. [Quito], Nov. 27, [1827], AL, roll 42, f. 106; also in Lecuna (ed.), "Cartas de mujeres," 334.

3. Ibid.

4. For a description of the quake, see Cordovez Moure, *Reminiscencias de Santafé y Bogotá*, 34n8; Moreno de Ángel, *José María Córdova*, 431. According to Moreno, the quake also coincided with the eruptions of the Puracé and Huila volcanoes that same year in southern Colombia.

5. For a description of the difficulties encountered by the Colombian army in its conquest of the Pasto region, see the pertinent chapters in De Madariaga's biography of Bolívar.

6. Sáenz to Colonel Tomás Cipriano de Mosquera, Pasto, Jan. 5, 1828, Sala Mosquera, Archivo Central del Cauca (henceforth ACC)-Popayán.

7. "Separate house" (casa aparte). Ibid. Sáenz's journey from Popayán to La Plata and the Magdalena River likely followed the path of the old Spanish trade route known as the Camino de Guanacas.

8. Le Moyne, *Viajes y estancias en America del Sur*, 120; Bushnell, *The Making of Modern Colombia*, 82; Safford and Palacios, *Colombia*, 159.

9. Throughout her time with Bolívar in Bogotá, Sáenz kept a separate residence located on the eastern corner of the Plazuela de San Carlos (Calle 10 between Carreras 6 and 7) whose rental apparently was handled by one of Bolívar's aides-de-camp. See Cordovez Moure 490; Lecuna (ed.), "Papeles de Manuela Sáenz," 514.

10. Le Moyne, *Viajes y estancias,* 119; Bushnell, *The Making of Modern Colombia,* 82.

11. Uribe, *Honorable Lives,* 86. See also idem, "Birth of a Public Sphere." The concept of the "public sphere" was first formulated by Jürgen Habermas as a way to explain the rise of modern bourgeois society and politics in eighteenth-century Western Europe. For a useful discussion of it in relation to the study of political life and nation-state formation in nineteenth-century Latin America, see Hilda Sábato's excellent "Review Essay: On Political Citizenship," esp. 1304–1310.

12. Moreno de Ángel, *Santander,* 358–359.

13. For a detailed description of the nature and ubiquity of the *papelucho* literature of the time, see Le Moyne, *Viajes y estancias,* 135–136; Moreno de Ángel, *Santander,* 358–359.

14. Bushnell, *Simón Bolívar,* 96.

15. See "The Jamaica Letter (1815)," reprinted in Hanke and Rausch, *People and Issues in Latin America: From Independence to the Present,* 17–26; quotation from "Message to the Congress of Bolivia (1826)," in ibid., 29.

16. "Message to the Congress of Bolivia (1826)," in ibid., 31.

17. Accounts of the ideological differences between Bolívar and his New Granadan opponents may be found in standard biographies of the hero, such as Masur's previously cited work and, more briefly, Bushnell, *The Making of Modern Colombia,* 64–65.

18. Uribe, *Honorable Lives,* 76–78, 87–89.

19. For a general explanation of the origins of the Páez rebellion, see Masur, *Simón Bolívar,* 424–429; Bushnell, *The Making of Modern Colombia,* 61–62.

20. Bushnell, *Simón Bolívar,* 168–170; quotation on 172. Bushnell portrays Bolívar's drift toward dictatorship as largely the result of political circumstances (e.g., the Páez rebellion) that led him to try to perpetuate the extraordinary political authority he had exercised earlier in his career. Salvador de Madariaga, by contrast, portrays it as a simultaneous expression of Bolívar's boundless ambition, naturally authoritarian temperament, and lack of faith in republican government; see, for example, De Madariaga, *Bolívar* (1969), 521–523.

21. Masur, *Simón Bolívar,* 430–431.

22. Moreno de Ángel, *Santander,* 402; Restrepo, *Diario político y militar,* vol. 1, 369.

23. On the personal rivalry that arose between Santander and Bolívar, see Masur, *Simón Bolívar;* Moreno de Ángel, *Santander,* chaps. 26–28; and Mijares, *El Libertador,* 513–515, 523.

24. De Madariaga, *Bolívar* (1969), 541–542.

25. Masur, *Simón Bolívar,* 434–435; Moreno de Ángel, *Santander,* 402.

26. Moreno de Ángel, *Santander,* 408–409.

27. Ibid., 403–404; Restrepo, *Diario político y militar,* vol. 1, 373.

28. Sáenz to Bolívar, Bogotá, Mar. 28, 1828, in Lecuna (ed.), "Cartas de mujeres," 335.

29. "Wicked men" (malvados). Ibid.

30. Ibid.

31. Bolívar to Manuela Sáenz, Bucaramanga, Apr. 3, 1828, AL, roll 27, f. 158. This letter likely was a response to Sáenz's of March 28, since in it Bolívar alludes to

Sr. Torres. It also comments on several of her earlier letters to him; "una de tus cartas está muy tierna y me penetra de ternura; la otra me divertió mucho por tu buen humor; y la tercera me satisface de las injurias pasadas y no merecidas," Bolívar informed his mistress. Only one of the mentioned letters seems to have survived, however.

32. Cayetano Freyre to Simón Bolívar (Lima), Jan. 26, 1830, in O'Leary, *Memorias,* vol. 10, 472–473; Sáenz to Bolívar (Bogotá), Mar. 28, 1828, in Lecuna (ed.), "Cartas de mujeres," 335.

33. Sáenz to Bolívar (Bogotá), Mar. 28, 1828, in Lecuna (ed.), "Cartas de mujeres," 335.

34. Ibid.; Bolívar to Manuela Sáenz (Bucaramanga), Apr. 3, 1828, AL, roll 27, f. 158; Sáenz to General Juan José Flores (Bogotá), Dec. 15, 1829, in Villalba (ed.), *Manuela Sáenz: Epistolario,* 95.

35. A concise description of Bolívar's and Santander's respective followers may be found in Bushnell, *The Making of Modern Colombia,* 65–68. References to Bolívar's military allies also appear in De Madariaga (1969), *Bolívar.*

36. On the circumstances behind the Bolivarians' decision to abandon the convention and declare Bolívar dictator, see De Madariaga, *Bolívar* (1969), 564–565; Masur, *Simón Bolívar,* 451–452; Bushnell, *Simón Bolívar,* 182–186. On the Ocaña Convention, see relevant chapters in Moreno de Ángel, *Santander.* For a discussion of the dictatorship and historiographical debates surrounding it, see Bushnell, "The Last Dictatorship."

37. Cordovez Moure, *Reminiscencias de Santafé y Bogotá,* 377.

38. "F.[rancisco] de P.[aula] S.[antander] dies for treason" (F. de P.S. muere por traidor). Ibid. An account of the effigy incident also appears in Moreno de Ángel, *José María Córdova,* 407–408; and, more briefly, in the police report (and deposition of witnesses) included in Pedro Herrán to secretary of interior José Manuel Restrepo, Bogotá, Aug. 5, 1828, AGN, Bogotá, Sección República, Fondo Historia, vol. 4, ff. 170–175.

39. "An assault" (un atentado). José María Córdova to Bolívar, Bogotá, Aug. 1, 1828 (enclosure in dispatch from James Henderson to John Bidwell, Bogotá, Aug. 6, 1828), PRO, FO 18/56.

40. Sáenz to Bolívar, n.p., n.d., AL, roll 42, f. 110; see transcribed versions in Lecuna (ed.), "Cartas de mujeres," 334; and in Rumazo González, *Manuela Sáenz,* 228. Lecuna suggests this note was written in March or April 1826, when Sáenz was still in Lima, whereas Rumazo suggests it was written sometime in June 1828. I believe it more likely to have been penned toward the end of July 1828, in the aftermath of the effigy scandal.

41. Sáenz to Bolívar, n.p., n.d., AL, roll 42, f. 110.

42. Córdova to Bolívar, Bogotá, Aug. 1, 1828, PRO, FO 18/56.

43. Bolívar to Córdova, n.p. [Aug. 1, 1828?] (enclosure in Aug. 6, 1828, Henderson despatch), PRO, FO 18/56, ff. 53. This letter is Córdova's handwritten copy of the original, which seems not to have survived.

44. Ibid.

45. Bushnell, *Simón Bolívar*, 186. Further discussion of the anti-Bolívar *círculos* may be found in Mijares, *El Libertador*, 522–525.
46. Bushnell, *Simón Bolívar*, 185–186.
47. Cordovez Moure, *Reminiscencias de Santafé y Bogotá*, 490–491; Rumazo González, *Manuela Sáenz*, 239–240; Von Hagen, *The Four Seasons of Manuela*, 275–276.
48. De Madariaga (1969), *Bolívar*, 566.
49. "La conspiración del 25 de septiembre 1828," in Cordovez Moure, *Reminiscencias de Santafé y Bogotá*, 699–704; Botero Saldarriaga, *El Libertador-Presidente*, 112–115; Moreno de Ángel, *Santander*, 441–446, 450.
50. Sáenz to Daniel F. O'Leary, Paita, Aug. 10, 1850, in Lecuna (ed.), "Papeles de Manuela Sáenz," 509–510. As Sáenz recalled, Bolívar later had asked one of his friends (José París) to visit the informant's home in order to query her further and thus, apparently, confirm the truth of what she had told his mistress.
51. Ibid.
52. Ibid., 510.
53. Ibid., 510–511.
54. Ibid. Other contemporary accounts of Sáenz's role in thwarting the September 25 attackers are F. Bolívar (Bolívar's nephew), "Recuerdos de Fernando Bolívar," 310; Henderson to Bidwell, Bogotá, Oct. 7, 1828 ("private"), FO 18/56, ff. 218–219. Both acknowledge that Sáenz saved Bolívar's life.
55. Sáenz to Daniel F. O'Leary, Paita, Aug. 10, 1850, in Lecuna (ed.), "Papeles de Manuela Sáenz," 509–510. Bolívar, nevertheless, omitted mention of Sáenz's role in the account of the attack that appeared the next day in the *Gaceta*, his government's official newspaper. See De Madariaga, *Bolívar* (1969), 572.
56. Sáenz to Daniel F. O'Leary, Paita, Aug. 10, 1850, in Lecuna (ed.), "Papeles de Manuela Sáenz," 509–510.
57. Masur, *Simón Bolívar*, 456–457; Cordovez Moure, *Reminiscencias de Santafé y Bogotá*, 710–711.
58. Bushnell, "The Last Dictatorship," 78–79.
59. Moreno de Ángel, *Santander*, 454–455; Cordovez Moure, *Reminiscencias de Santafé y Bogotá*, 714–743. Cordovez's thorough chronicle of the September 25 conspiracy and its aftermath includes a description of the testimony taken during the conspirators' trial.
60. Moreno de Ángel, *Santander*, 453, 456–462, 463–467; Cordovez Moure, *Reminiscencias de Santafé y Bogotá*, 745–749. In her analysis of Santander's trial, Moreno highlights Urdaneta's effort to obtain a guilty verdict against (and thus the death sentence for) the former vice president. For an insightful analysis of racial factors that contributed to the execution of the innocent Padilla, see Helg, "Simón Bolívar and the Specter of 'Pardocracia.'"
61. Sáenz to O'Leary, Paita, Aug. 10, 1850, in Lecuna (ed.), "Papeles de Manuela Sáenz," 511–512.

62. Moreno de Ángel, *Santander*, 456–457; Rojas, "El 25 de septiembre de 1828"; González, *Memorias*. Interestingly, while both men mentioned Sáenz's effort to obtain information about Santander's involvement in the conspiracy, neither one acknowledged her role in sparing him the death sentence.

63. Montebrune to Sáenz, Guaduas, Nov. 19, 1828, in Cordovez Moure, *Reminiscencias de Santafé y Bogotá*, 491–492.

64. Ibid. Montebrune also referred to Sáenz affectionately as "comadre," suggesting that the two were bound by ties of *compadrazgo*, or godparenthood. As the Libertadora herself had no known children, she may well have agreed to serve as the godmother for one of Montebrune's; Bolívar may have served as godfather.

65. A detailed account of Bolívar's activities in the final months of 1828 and during 1829 may be found in Restrepo, *Diario político y militar*, vol. 1, 396–402, and vol. 2, 9–51; also see pertinent chapters in the Bolívar biographies cited earlier.

66. Ibid., esp. Restrepo, *Diario político y militar*, vol. 1, 396–402, and vol. 2, 9–51. For a brief summary of Colombia's war with Peru, see Bushnell, *The Making of Modern Colombia*, 70.

67. In 1826, Páez suggested that Bolívar heal the nation's divisions and solve its myriad problems by assuming the powers of a monarch. Other advocates of monarchy included Juan García del Río (who had espoused the idea since 1821) along with a group of high-ranking Colombian army officers known by 1829 as "the faithful friends." On opinion favorable to constitutional monarchy, see Henderson to Bidwell, Bogotá, Dec. 4, 1828, FO/56, 305.

68. Restrepo, *Diario político y militar*, vol. 2, 20–21, 25. For brief accounts of the monarchist project, see Bushnell, *Simón Bolívar*, 196–197; Masur, *Simón Bolívar*, 468–469; for a thoroughgoing analysis, see De Madariaga, *Bolívar* (1969), chaps. 25, 26. While Bushnell and Masur stress Bolívar's ambivalence toward the project, De Madariaga stresses his desire to extend his power while also ensuring a veneer of legitimacy.

69. Ibid.

70. On the faithful friends and their role in the monarchist project, see Van Aken, *King of the Night*, 25–26. Although Sáenz's correspondence with Urdaneta has not survived (and none of her extant letters mention the project), various other sources refer to her friendship and collaboration with him.

71. Sáenz's hosting of the reception is mentioned in Henderson to Córdova, Bogotá, May 28, [1829], and in Córdova to Henderson, Popayán, June 21, 1829, both in FO 357/7. Córdova observed that Harrison and British envoy Henderson were not invited to the party ("convite") and suggested that this was because of their disagreement with the council's views.

72. Unsigned note in Sáenz's handwriting, [Bogotá], n.d., in AL, roll 34, f. 39; also in Lecuna (ed.), "Papeles de Manuela Sáenz," 512–513. The note was written on a sheet of fancy stationery complete with (now-faded) engravings of flowers and emblems on the margins. It states: "El siglo XIX es el siglo de los placeres, por tanto creo que Ud. y yo tenemos mucho placer en que el Libertador de tres Repúblicas no haya sido asesinado. ¡Y como podría morir el que ha libertado un

continente y ha llenado el otro con su nombre! Y aunque no es nada metafísica, se consuela con el mismo gusto imaginario que él le ha dado a Manuela Sáenz. Y esta misma presenta a Ud. un poco de cabello de su cabeza, la que siempre se halla ocupada de la felicidad del General Bolibar y sus fieles amigos." This note may have been addressed to one Federico de Eben y Brunnen, who, in a short letter to Sáenz, thanked her for various unidentified favors and acknowledged receipt of "your very special stationery" (muy atenta esquela). See De Eben to Sáenz, Bogotá, Sept. 14, 1829, in Lecuna (ed.), "Papeles de Manuela Sáenz," 515.

73. Boussingault, *Mémoires,* vol. 3, 216.

74. Ibid., 213.

75. Printed certificate of the Jesús, María y José de la Peña confraternity signed by Chaplain Juan Gualberto Caldas, n.d., in Lecuna (ed.), "Papeles de Manuela Sáenz," 514.

76. Rafael Gaytán to Sáenz, [Sept. 1828?], in ibid., 512.

77. Rafael de Paul to Sáenz, Sept. 26, 1829, in ibid., 515.

78. Joaquín Posada Gutiérrez, *Memorias histórico-políticas,* vol. 1, 340.

79. Ibid., 370, and vol. 2, 48–49.

80. Masur, *Simón Bolívar,* 472–476.

81. For a thorough discussion of this final phase of Bolívar's career, see De Madariaga, *Bolívar* (1969), chap. 29; on the pressures Bolívar felt from followers reluctant to see him abandon power, see Posada Gutiérrez, *Memorias histórico-políticas,* vol. 2, 46–48.

82. Bolívar to Sáenz, Guaduas, May 11, 1830, AL, roll 27, f. 163.

83. Bolívar to Juan Illingworth, Turbaco, June 9, 1830, LL.

84. Restrepo, *Diario político y militar,* vol. 2, 80–82, 84–85; Minister Plenipotentiary William Turner to the Earl of Aberdeen, Bogotá, May 10 and 14, 1830, FO 18/75, ff. 126–128, 136–142.

85. Cordovez Moure, *Reminiscencias de Santafé y Bogotá,* 66–67.

86. Restrepo, *Diario político y militar,* vol. 2, 93; Turner to Aberdeen, Bogotá, June 14, 1830, FO 18/76, ff. 217–221.

87. "Documentos inéditos," 373–402.

88. Ibid.; Sáenz to Flores, Kingston, May 6, 1839, in Villalba (ed.), *Manuela Sáenz: Epistolario,* 96.

89. "Documentos inéditos," 390–393.

90. Ibid.

91. *La Aurora,* no. 8 (June 13, 1830), 42–44 (microfilm), Hemeroteca Manuel del Socorro Rodríguez, Biblioteca Nacional de Colombia, Bogotá (henceforth BNC).

92. Follies ("imprudencias"). "Al público," Bogotá, June 20, 1830, AL, roll 34; and Lecuna (ed.), "Papeles de Manuela Sáenz," 518.

93. "Hotheadedness" (exaltación). Ibid., 518–519.

94. Ibid., 519.

95. Restrepo, *Diario político y militar,* vol. 2, 97; Turner to Aberdeen, Bogotá, July 14, 1830, FO 18/76, ff. 269–271. According to Turner, the idea of killing Urdaneta,

Castillo Rada, and some of the city's foreign residents had been proposed during one of the Liberals' nightly strategy meetings. Turner's despatch also mentions that, in response, the British had begun arming themselves and their servants and were staying in their homes at night.

96. Restrepo, *Diario político y militar*, vol. 2, 102; Turner to Aberdeen, Bogotá, Aug. 14, 1830, FO 18/77, ff. 42–55. Turner's despatch summarizes political developments since July.

97. "Carta de Manuela Sáenz," 207.

98. Sáenz to Sr. Alcalde Municipal, Bogotá, June 27, 1830, and Juan José Gómez to Prefect of Cundinamarca Cristóval de Vergara, Bogotá, June 30, 1830, AGN-Bogotá, Sección República, Fondo Historia, vol. 4, ff. 190–192.

99. "Documentos inéditos," 377.

100. Ibid., 380–385.

101. Restrepo, *Diario político y militar*, vol. 2, 102–103; Turner to Aberdeen, Bogotá, Aug. 14, 1830, FO 18/77, ff. 42–55. The *orejones* appear to have been mainly middling-size farmers of the fertile plain surrounding the capital city (the *sábana*).

102. N. R. Cheyne to Sáenz, site of "Cuatro Esquinas," Aug. 18, 1830, AL, roll 34, f. 56; also transcribed in Lecuna (ed.), "Papeles de Manuela Sáenz," 520.

103. Turner to Aberdeen, Bogotá, Aug. 14, 1830, FO 18/77, ff. 46–47.

104. "Documentos inéditos," 375.

105. Ibid., 394–395.

106. Ibid.

107. See, for example, the broadsides "El bello secso" and "A las señoras liberales," transcribed in Lecuna (ed.), "Papeles de Manuela Sáenz," 517–518. The second broadside, signed by "Unos Patriotas de Corazón," chided authorities for criminalizing Sáenz's effort to exercise her freedom of speech via distribution of the "Biba Bolibar" flyer, and so on. It concluded that "petty and ignoble passions" lay behind the "campaign raised against [her]."

108. Lecuna (ed.), "Papeles de Manuela Sáenz," 519–520.

109. Posada, "La Libertadora," vol. 17, 246. Posada's article includes excerpts from local court documents, including an August 11 memo showing Sáenz's attempt to be "recused" on one of the charges authorities apparently had brought against her. Unfortunately, I was unable to find these documents in the course of my research.

110. After having suspended action against Sáenz in late July, prefect Cristóval de Vergara ordered police to expel her from Bogotá within twenty-four hours, justifying the order on the basis of local residents' "repeated complaints . . . about [her] scandalous conduct." See "Documentos inéditos," 396–402; Vergara to Minister of Interior and Justice, Bogotá, Aug. 3, 1830, AGN-Bogotá, vol. 4, f. 198. Brief mention of the assassination attempts against Sáenz appears in Turner to Aberdeen, Bogotá, Aug. 12, 1830, FO 18/77, ff. 14–18. Reference to Sáenz's arrest and departure for Guaduas appears in Restrepo, *Diario político y militar*, vol. 2, 102.

111. Restrepo, *Diario político y militar*, vol. 2, 102–119.

112. Ibid., 120–121; Turner to Aberdeen, Bogotá, Sept. 7, FO 18/77, ff. 74–96. Restrepo found little joy in the rebels' victory and questioned the social respectability of those who celebrated it. He described the merrymakers as "el bajo pueblo" and reported that "no iban en la procesión cuatro personas decentes." Turner, by contrast, applauded the Bolivarians' victory and interpreted the latter as genuinely "popular."

113. Lecuna (ed.), "Papeles de Manuela Sáenz," 521.

114. Ibid.

115. Sáenz to Dundas Logan, Guaduas, Nov. 24, 1830, transcribed in Masur, "Documentos históricos," 280.

Chapter Four

1. A. Torres to Sáenz, Bogotá, Dec. 7, 1830, in Lecuna (ed.), "Papeles de Manuela Sáenz," 522.

2. R. S. Illingworth to Sáenz, Bogotá, Jan. 6, 1831, in ibid., 523.

3. Luis Perú de Lacroix to Sáenz, Cartagena, Dec. 18, 1830, in Villalba (ed.), *Manuela Sáenz: Epistolario*, 185.

4. Restrepo, *Diario político y militar*, vol. 2, 148–149, 157–158.

5. Receipt from Estanco Proveedor de Tabacos, Guaduas, Jan. 12, 1831, in Lecuna (ed.), "Papeles de Manuela Sáenz," 523. Cigar smoking seems to have been fairly common among upper-class Spanish American women of Sáenz's generation.

6. Boussingault, *Mémoires*, vol. 3, 216–218. Biographers such as Rumazo and Von Hagen generally have used this suicide attempt story to stress the view that, with the death of Bolívar, Sáenz's life lost meaning and purpose—a view that justifies their tendency to gloss over the last twenty-six years of her life.

7. José María Acosta and Justiano Gutiérrez to M. Sáenz, Guaduas, Mar. 4, 1831, in Lecuna (ed.), "Papeles de Manuela Sáenz," 523–524. Sáenz briefly mentions the snakebite in Sáenz to Flores, Kingston, May 6, 1834, in Villalba (ed.), *Manuela Sáenz: Epistolario*, 96.

8. Sáenz to Dundas Logan, Guaduas, Nov. 24, 1830, in Masur, "Documentos históricos," 280. In this letter, Sáenz identifies each of her maids and her servant by name and reports briefly on how each is doing.

9. This comment appears in Turner to Aberdeen, Bogotá, Aug. 14, 1830, FO 18/77, ff. 42–55.

10. Sáenz to Dundas Logan, Guaduas, Nov. 24, 1830, in Masur, "Documentos históricos," 280.

11. On the history of Cataguango, including Sáenz's possession of it, see Villalba (ed.), *Manuela Sáenz: Epistolario*, 130–134; "Sesión de remate: El Sr. General Juan José Flores a favor del Sr. Comandante del Batallón de Quito José María Sáenz," Sept. 30, 1826, ANE, Sección Judicial, Notaría 1a: Protocolos, vol. 482. This document shows that the hacienda was auctioned off for 9,908 pesos.

12. José Modesto Larrea to M. Sáenz, Quito, Nov. 6, 1831, in Villalba (ed.), *Manuela Sáenz: Epistolario,* 137–138. Sáenz's letter to Larrea has not survived.

13. Villalba (ed.), *Manuela Sáenz: Epistolario,* 134. Sáenz's desire to sell the hacienda and ongoing worries over her lack of income from it also appear in Sáenz to Flores, Kingston, May 6, 1834, in ibid., 97.

14. Manuel Vélez to M. Sáenz, Medellín, Feb. 9, 1832, in Lecuna (ed.), "Papeles de Manuela Sáenz," 524–525. Vélez's business partner was Juan de Dios Aranzazu. The fond tone of this letter also suggests the extent to which its author may have harbored romantic feelings toward its recipient: "nada puede llenar el vacío que por todas partes encuentro y el cual solo ud., mi querida amiga, puede ocupar," Vélez wrote her.

15. Moreno de Ángel, *Santander,* 547–548; Restrepo, *Diario político y militar,* vol. 2, 158–181.

16. Restrepo, *Diario político y militar,* vol. 2, 184. For a good general discussion of the Liberals' *exaltado* and *moderado* (moderate Liberal) factions and their relevance to the emergence of country's two-party system, see Safford and Palacios, *Colombia,* 135–137.

17. Restrepo, *Diario político y militar,* vol. 2, 189–196; Safford and Palacios, *Colombia,* 137.

18. Restrepo, *Diario político y militar,* vol. 2, 197–198.

19. Ibid., 201, 216. A political moderate, Restrepo worried about the implications of the June decree, remarking that "este decreto . . . consagra como virtud la máxima del tiranicidio, opuesto a la moral pública."

20. Ibid., 208. Restrepo disapproved of these festivities and denounced them as "un funesto ejemplo y triste resultado de la perversion de la moral pública!"

21. The *quinta* was located in Guanacas del Arroyo and belonged to Guillermo Wills. See receipt for thirty gold pesos paid by Sáenz to Rafaela Isari, Oct. 6, 1832, in Lecuna (ed.), "Papeles de Manuela Sáenz," 525.

22. Restrepo, *Diario político y militar,* vol. 2, 210–214.

23. Ibid., 217–218.

24. Ibid., 229; Sáenz to General J. J. Flores, Kingston, May 6, 1834, in Villalba (ed.), *Manuela Sáenz: Epistolario,* 96.

25. Restrepo, *Diario político y militar,* vol. 2, 228; Moreno de Ángel, *Santander,* 559–561.

26. Prior to his joining the Colombian army, Sardá's patriot credentials included his participation in Francisco Javier Mina's ill-fated 1817 liberation expedition in Mexico, an adventure that earned him several years in a Moroccan prison. For a summary of his career and opposition to the Santander government, see Moreno de Ángel, *Santander,* chap. 37.

27. Ibid., 587–597.

28. Ibid., 594–595. Moreno cites the officer's secondhand testimony as the basis for her assertion that Sáenz was part of the conspiracy.

29. Some sense of this may be gleaned in Sáenz to Flores, Kingston, May 6, 1834, in Villalba (ed.), *Manuela Sáenz: Epistolario,* 96. Passing mention of her alleged

involvement in the conspiracy appears in Cuervo and Cuervo, *Vida de Rufino Cuervo*, vol. 1, 193.

30. José Rafael Mosquera, Secretary of Interior and Foreign Relations, to Cundinamarca governor, Bogotá, Aug. 7, 1833, transcribed in Posada, "La Libertadora," vol. 17, 246. Mosquera was a first cousin of one of Bolívar's most ardent former followers, General Tomás Cipriano Mosquera.

31. Davis, "Acosta, Caro, and Lleras," 172–175, 182–183.

32. "Juez letrado de hacienda," *El Cachaco de Bogotá*, no. 20 (Sept. 22, 1833); "Al jefe político de Bogotá," *El Cachaco*, no. 40 (Dec. 15, 1833), in BNC, Hemeroteca Manuel del Socorro Rodríguez (microfilm collection).

33. "Al jefe político de Bogotá," *El Cachaco*, no. 40 (Dec. 15, 1833), in BNC, Hemeroteca Manuel del Socorro Rodríguez (microfilm collection).

34. Excerpt from Mar. 1834 issue of *El Cachaco*, in Posada, "La Libertadora," vol. 17, 249.

35. Sáenz to Flores, Kingston, May 6, 1834, in Villalba (ed.), *Manuela Sáenz: Epistolario*. This allegation does not seem to have been part of any formal charges made against Sáenz since her July 17, 1830, indictment by the Mosquera government; indeed, I have found no evidence of such charges being made or of any trial or lawsuit resulting from her alleged involvement in the Battle of Santuario or other crimes committed after the battle.

36. Posada, "La Libertadora," vol. 17, 249–250; Cuervo and Cuervo, *Vida de Rufino Cuervo*, vol. 1, 193–194.

37. Cuervo and Cuervo, *Vida de Rufino Cuervo*, vol. 1, 194; "Señora Manuela Sáenz," *El Cachaco*, no. 45 (Jan. 19, 1834) (letter to the editor signed by "unos testigos oculares de lo sucedido" [eyewitnesses]), in BNC, Hemeroteca Manuel del Socorro Rodríguez (microfilm collection).

38. "Señora Manuela Sáenz," *El Cachaco*, no. 45 (Jan. 19, 1834), in BNC, Hemeroteca Manuel del Socorro Rodríguez (microfilm collection).

39. Ibid.; excerpt of Apr. 3 letter from José Hilario López to Santander, in Villalba (ed.), *Manuela Sáenz: Epistolario*, 97n4.

40. Despatch from Robert B. McAfee to U.S. Secretary of State Louis McClane, Bogotá, Jan. 19, 1834, in Despatches from U.S. Ministers to Colombia, 1820–1906, microfilm roll 8.

41. Despatch from Turner to Viscount Palmerston, Bogotá, Mar. 27, 1834, FO 18/103, f. 152.

42. "Otro diálogo entre *El Cachaco* y el religionario," *El Cachaco*, no. 45 (Jan. 19, 1834), 183–184, in BNC, Hemeroteca Manuel del Socorro Rodríguez (microfilm collection). In this dialogue, "el religionario" is the voice of critics of the government.

43. Ibid.; "Señora Manuela Sáenz," *El Cachaco*, no. 45 (Jan. 19, 1834), in BNC, Hemeroteca Manuel del Socorro Rodríguez (microfilm collection), 186.

44. Sáenz to Flores, Kingston, May 6, 1834, in Villalba (ed.), *Manuela Sáenz: Epistolario*, 96–97.

45. Ibid.: "Quien sabe si monto en mi caballo y me voy de cuenta de genio y no más."

46. Ibid. Sáenz's statement likely sprang from a wish to play down conduct that, besides having attracted the criticism of her New Granadan antagonists, might have provoked a scolding from Flores.

47. Ibid.

48. Ibid.

49. Ibid.

50. For a summary of Rocafuerte's background and career, see the encyclopedia entry by Jaime E. Rodríguez, "Rocafuerte, Vicente (b. 1 May 1783, d. 16 May 1847)," in Tenenbaum, *Encyclopedia*, vol. 4, 585; idem, *The Emergence of Spanish America*.

51. On the origins and nature of the April 1834 agreement between Rocafuerte and Flores, see chap. 3 of Van Aken, *King of the Night*; Ayala Mora, *Nueva historia del Ecuador*), vol. 7, chap. 5, including the essay by Jorge Núñez.

52. Order from minister of interior José Miguel González Alminati, Quito, Oct. 14, 1835, in Villalba (ed.), *Manuela Sáenz: Epistolario*, 98–99. For a summary of José María Sáenz's career, including his role in the rebellion sponsored by the Sociedad del Quiteño Libre, see ibid., 43, 47–56.

53. Ibid., 98–99.

54. "Riffraff" (esta canalla). Sáenz to Flores, Guaranda, Oct. 19, 1835, in ibid., 97–98.

55. Ibid. Sáenz's lament concerning her brothers refers to the fact that, by 1835, both José María and Ignacio Sáenz had become opponents of Flores.

56. Flores to Sáenz, Guayaquil, Oct. 25, 1835, in ibid., 101–102. Flores already had written to Rocafuerte several days earlier expressing his disappointment at the president's decision to exile Sáenz while ignoring his recommendation to the contrary; see his Oct. 21 letter in ibid., 100–101.

57. Ibid., 102.

58. Sáenz to González, Guaranda, Oct. 20, 1835, in ibid., 105–106.

59. Ibid. Sáenz retained the original safe-conduct, explaining that she still needed it to complete her journey; this original has not survived.

60. Ibid.

61. Ibid.

62. Ibid.

63. For a discussion of the various causes behind this turmoil, see Ayala Mora, *Nueva historia del Ecuador*, 169–172; Van Aken, *King of the Night*, 90–99; Villalba (ed.), *Manuela Sáenz: Epistolario*, 57–60.

64. Villalba (ed.), *Manuela Sáenz: Epistolario*, 61. For further discussion of Rocafuerte's treatment of his opponents, see Van Aken, *King of the Night*, 98–99; Ayala Mora, *Nueva historia del Ecuador*, 175. According to Ayala, seventy-three men were executed for opposing or rebelling against the Rocafuerte government.

65. See, for example, "Otro diálogo entre *El Cachaco* y el religionario," *El Cachaco*, no. 45 (Jan. 19, 1834), in BNC, Hemeroteca Manuel del Socorro Rodríguez (microfilm collection).

66. Ibid.

67. Rocafuerte to Flores, Quito, Oct. 14, 1835, in Villalba (ed.), *Manuela Sáenz: Epistolario*, 99–100.

68. Rocafuerte to Flores, Quito, Oct. 23, 1835, in AHBC-Quito, Fondo Jijón y Caamaño, roll 55, f. 43; excerpt of letter from Rocafuerte to Flores, Quito, Oct. 28, 1835, in Villalba (ed.), *Manuela Sáenz: Epistolario*, 102.

69. Rocafuerte to Flores, Quito, Oct. 14, 1835, in Villalba (ed.), *Manuela Sáenz: Epistolario*, 99–100.

70. Rocafuerte to Flores, Quito, Oct. 23, 1835, in AHBC-Quito, Fondo Jijón y Caamaño, roll 55, f. 43

71. González to Flores, Quito, Oct. 28, 1835, in Villalba (ed.), *Manuela Sáenz: Epistolario*, 103.

72. Ibid.: "esta señora . . . es la única que en las actuales circunstancias, y cuando los cuerpos no están ni con mucho cubiertos de sus haberes, podía hacer alguna cosa y dar impulso a los constantes esfuerzos de los facciosos."

73. Chief among these opponents was Catalina Valdivieso (wife of José Félix), who lent vital financial and logistical support to the cause of the Sociedad del Quiteño Libre. For reference to her and other women's opposition to the Rocafuerte government, see Villalba (ed.), 62–63; on the Sociedad del Quiteño Libre, see Villalba (ed.), 46–60.

74. Silvia Arrom notes that, although Hispanic law gave women (especially widows and single emancipated women) the right to conduct their own legal affairs and engage in various public activities (e.g., administering a business, serving as a courtroom witness), it consistently barred them from positions of leadership or governance—even guardianship over children. See *The Women of Mexico City*, 58–62

75. Earle, "Rape and the Anxious Republic," 127–142.

76. Dore, "One Step Forward," 14–15.

77. Arrom, *The Women of Mexico City*, 264–265. Arrom explains the rise of this ideology—Marianism—as a result of Mexicans' reluctance to accept the changes in gender relations that had begun earlier and that had begun to move women toward a position of equality with men. With its glorification of motherhood, Marianism (which Arrom sees as a variant of the Victorian idea of separate spheres) represented an effort to reconcile liberalism with women's traditional gender subordination.

78. "Documentos inéditos," 394–395.

79. Rocafuerte to Flores, Quito, Oct. 14, 1835, in Villalba (ed.), *Manuela Sáenz: Epistolario*, 99–100. On French revolutionary leaders' hostility toward women in the public sphere and political arena (along with their linking of female virtue with domesticity), see Landes's path-breaking *Women and the Public Sphere;* also see Godineau, "Daughters of Liberty," 16–32; Hunt, "The Many Bodies of Marie-Antoinette," 117–138. All three works show the extent to which Rocafuerte's critical views of female influence and activism mirrored those of his counterparts in Western Europe, in effect forming part of a larger backlash against women's recent politicization.

80. Rocafuerte to Flores, Oct. 21, 1835, Fondo Jijón Caamaño, roll 55, f. 76. This letter is excerpted in Villalba (ed.), *Manuela Sáenz: Epistolario*, 100.

81. Rocafuerte to Flores, Quito, Oct. 28, 1835, in Villalba (ed.), *Manuela Sáenz: Epistolario*, 102. On Madame de Staël, see Weingarten, *Madame de Staël;* on La Güera Rodríguez, see Del Valle Arizpe, *La Güera Rodríguez.*

82. Rocafuerte to Flores, Quito, Oct. 28, 1835, in Villalba (ed.), *Manuela Sáenz: Epistolario*, 102. Rocafuerte's comments about women have a distinctly misogynist flavor. In an earlier rant against Catita Valdivieso, he not only accused her of waging a "horrible war" against him but described her as being possessed by "a uterine frenzy of silver and revolution." She "is capable of giving her soul to the devil and her body to the first person who would serve her lofty ambitions," he added. See excerpt from his September 14 letter to Flores in Villalba (ed.), *Manuela Sáenz: Epistolario*, 63.

Chapter Five

1. Lofstrom, *Paita*, 21. The quotation comes from the journal of U.S. Navy surgeon Thomas Boyd, who visited the port in 1827 while serving on the U.S.S. *Brandywine.*

2. Ibid., xii.

3. Ibid., 20.

4. Ibid., 23–24.

5. Ibid., 79–80.

6. Ibid., 6–7, 35. This population figure represents an estimate for 1833 based on travelers' accounts. Lofstrom notes that Piura River water was widely believed to be helpful for the curing of syphilis, thanks to the medicinal qualities imparted to it by nearby groves of sarsaparilla and palo santo trees.

7. Ibid., 83; Villalba (ed.), *Manuela Sáenz: Epistolario*, 65.

8. Lofstrom, *Paita*, chap. 4. The author traces Ruden's background and career, including the origins of his arrival and settlement in Paita.

9. Manuela Sáenz to Juan José Flores, Paita, July 12, 1840, in Villalba (ed.), *Manuela Sáenz: Epistolario*, 111.

10. Sáenz to Flores, Paita, Jan. 23, 1844, in ibid., 152. In this same letter, Sáenz describes her friends as "being crazy over" Flores.

11. Sáenz to Flores, Paita, June 3, 1842, in ibid., 122.

12. A fuller discussion of Sáenz's property may be found in Chap. 6 here.

13. Von Hagen, *The Four Seasons of Manuela*, 279. Scattered references to her money shortage and reliance on loans and credit appear throughout Sáenz's letters to Flores during these years. See Chapter 6 here for further discussion of this as well as of Sáenz's efforts to earn a living in Paita.

14. Reference to this sale appears in Sáenz to Flores, Paita, Apr. 22, 1843, in Villalba (ed.), *Manuela Sáenz: Epistolario*, 130. In this letter Sáenz explains that she sold the hacienda for six thousand pesos and that so far she has received only four thousand.

15. Some scholars see such feelings as symptoms of what they call the "psychopathology of migration." For further reference to this, see Fey and Racine, *Strange Pilgrimages*, xv–xvi.

16. Sáenz to Flores, Paita, Oct. 20 and Nov. 20, 1837, in Villalba (ed.), *Manuela Sáenz: Epistolario*, 108.

17. Sáenz to Flores, Paita, Nov. 20, 1837, in ibid., 109.

18. "Alone and unfortunate" (sola y desgraciada). Sáenz to Flores, Paita, May 21, 1840, and Aug. 10, 1844, in ibid., 110, 164.

19. Although most of her personal correspondence would disappear after her death—especially in the fire that destroyed her last home in Paita—extant letters show that, in addition to Flores, Sáenz stayed in touch with General Andrés de Santa Cruz (founder and Protector of the short-lived Peru-Bolivia Confederation of 1836–1839), General Tomás Cipriano de Mosquera (who, in 1845, became president of New Granada), and Juan García del Río (intellectual author of Bolívar's aborted monarchist project and later advisor to both Santa Cruz and Flores). This chapter is based largely on her surviving letters to Flores (fifty-five in all), most of which were written after her arrival in Paita and published in *Manuela Sáenz: Epistolario*. With rare exception, Flores's letters to her have not survived.

20. Chambers, "Republican Friendship," 245–246. While based on the same letters used for this chapter and interesting from a theoretical, gender-historical perspective, Chambers's analysis shows limited understanding of the uniqueness of Sáenz's friendship with Flores, including her complex motives for cultivating it.

21. Sáenz to Flores, Bogotá, Dec. 14, 1829, in Villalba (ed.), *Manuela Sáenz: Epistolario*, 95. Bolívar may have encouraged her to correspond regularly with Flores as a way of keeping tabs on the officer; he also encouraged Colonel Ferguson and other members of his inner circle to do so.

22. Sáenz to Flores, Paita, Nov. 20, 1837, in ibid., 108–109.

23. Sáenz to Flores, Dec. 25, 1837, and June 11, 1843, in ibid., 110, 138.

24. Sáenz to Flores, Nov. 20, 1837, in ibid., 108–109.

25. Sáenz to Flores, June 22, 1844, in ibid., 161.

26. Sáenz to Flores, Nov. 20, 1837, in ibid., 108–109.

27. Sáenz to Flores, Dec. 25, 1837, in ibid., 109–110.

28. Ibid.

29. Chasteen, *Heroes on Horseback*, 13.

30. Calderón and Thibaud, "La construcción del orden," 157n60. The authors stress how the idiom of friendship reflected the new norms and "horizontal links" that characterized the postindependence public sphere and that sprang from the growing influence of republican notions of fraternity and equality—notions that tended to disguise real social differences as well as persistent patron-client-type relationships.

31. Sáenz to Flores, Kingston, May 6, 1834, in Villalba (ed.), *Manuela Sáenz: Epistolario*, 97.

32. This is suggested in Sáenz to Flores, Paita, May 21, 1840, in ibid.

33. Sáenz to Flores, Paita, Nov. 20, 1837, in ibid.
34. Sáenz to Flores, Paita, May 21 and July 12, 1840, in ibid., 110–111, 111–112.
35. Calderón and Thibaud, "La construcción del orden," 156.
36. See, for example, Valencia Llano, *Mujeres caucanas,* 135–156. The author sees the political involvement of women in Cauca Department (Caucanas) in the decades after independence largely as a kind of defense strategy adopted in response to the dislocations caused by civil war, violence, and chronic political instability—factors that, besides often leaving them as the sole or de facto head of house-hold, left them vulnerable to the arbitrary actions and abuses of local officials. Such conditions, he suggests, motivated many to seek the protection of caudillos like General Tomás Cipriano Mosquera and thus to become their political clients.
37. Sáenz to Flores, Paita, May 18, 1837, in Villalba (ed.), *Manuela Sáenz: Epistolario,* 107.
38. Sáenz to Flores, Paita, Aug. 18, 1844, in ibid., 165.
39. Sáenz to Flores, Paita, Oct. 20, 1837, in ibid., 108.
40. Sáenz to Flores, Paita, Nov. 20, 1837, in ibid., 108–109.
41. Sáenz to Flores, Paita, Dec. 25, 1837, in ibid., 110.
42. Sáenz to Flores, Paita, July 12, 1840, in ibid., 111–112. Flores's letter to Sáenz, unfortunately, has not survived. Further discussion of Sáenz's hip injury appears in Chapter 6 here.
43. Sáenz to Flores, Paita, May 18, 1837, in ibid., 107.
44. Sáenz to Flores, Paita, Nov. 20, 1837, in ibid., 109.
45. Sáenz to Flores, Paita, Sept. 7, 1843, in ibid., 144.
46. Sáenz to Flores, Paita, Nov. 20, 1837, in ibid., 109.
47. Ibid.
48. Sáenz to Flores, Paita, Jan. 30, 1843, in ibid., 125–127: "Crea usted mi amigo que tengo un defecto capital, el ser tan vengativa; yo no perdono medio que esté a mi alcance. Conozco que es mala cualidad, pero no puedo prescindir, pues creo que en ello faltaría a la consecuencia y gratitud de amigos muy queridos vivos y muertos." Sáenz's comments were in reference to an article she had read in an 1843 issue of the *Gaceta de la Nueva Granada* reporting on the recent confession of Sucre's alleged assassin, one Apolinar Murillo. For further reference to Sucre's assassination and the controversy surrounding it, see Bushnell, *The Making of Modern Colombia,* esp. 89n17; Safford and Palacios, *Colombia,* 147.
49. Sáenz to Flores, Paita, Nov. 20, 1837, in Villalba (ed.), *Manuela Sáenz: Epistolario,* 109.
50. Van Aken, *King of the Night,* 125–127.
51. Ibid., 148–150.
52. Sáenz to Flores, Paita, Dec. 12, 1841, in Villalba (ed.), *Manuela Sáenz: Epistolario,* 113.
53. Basadre, *Historia de la República del Perú,* vol. 2, 161–163; Van Aken, *King of the Night,* 152. The Treaty of Guayaquil was the result of Gran Colombia's victory over the Peruvians at the Battle of Tarqui (1829).

54. Sáenz to Flores, Paita, Dec. 12, 1841, in Villalba (ed.), *Manuela Sáenz: Epistolario,* 113–114. Sáenz spoke of being "well-connected" in Peru and several times in her letters to Flores referred to unnamed friends in Lima who kept her informed of developments there as well as in southern Peru. One of these friends was Cayetano Freyre, most of whose letters to her have not survived.

55. Sáenz to Flores, Paita, Jan. 30, 1842, in ibid., 114. Until its 1820 declaration of independence (this followed by its annexation to Gran Colombia less than two years later), Guayaquil had been under the jurisdiction of the Viceroyalty of Peru and thus subject to the authority of the government in Lima. The latter's attempt to reclaim it by force in late 1828 had triggered war between Peru and Gran Colombia.

56. Ibid. Sáenz's opinion of the Peruvians seems to have been shared by compatriots such as Pedro Moncayo, Ecuador's consul in Piura, who, in explaining Peru's refusal to accept his nation's boundary claim, characterized its people as "innately insecure" as well as vain and arrogant. See Moncayo to Flores, Piura, Apr. 5, 1842, in ibid., 118–119.

57. For further information on the Peru-Bolivia Confederation, see the entry for it by William Sater in Tenenbaum, *Encyclopedia,* vol. 5, 442; Bonilla, "Peru and Bolivia," 249 passim; Bushnell and Macaulay, *The Emergence of Latin America,* 112–114.

58. Van Aken, *King of the Night,* 151–154, 165–166. As Van Aken shows, the Grand Project also included the idea of placing a revived confederation under the protection of a European monarchy, an idea that spurred Flores to launch secret negotiations with various European powers.

59. Ibid., 152–154; Basadre, *Historia de la República del Perú,* vol. 2, 96, 160–163. Although both Van Aken and Basadre refer to the filibustering expeditions organized by Santa Cruz and sponsored by Flores, Basadre offers the most detail on them and their significance for Peruvians.

60. Sáenz to Flores, Paita, Nov. 28 and Dec. 1, 1843, in Villalba (ed.), *Manuela Sáenz: Epistolario,* 149–150. Sáenz mentioned having learned of Santa Cruz's imprisonment and transfer to Cuzco from letters sent her by friends in Lima. For further details of Santa Cruz's last filibustering expedition and its consequences, see Basadre, *Historia de la República del Perú,* vol. 2, 96–98.

61. Sáenz to Flores, Paita, Jan. 23, 1844, in Villalba (ed.), *Manuela Sáenz: Epistolario,* 151–153.

62. Sáenz to Flores, Paita, Apr. 22, 1843, in ibid., 130: "Saludo al Sr. General Santa Cruz y que ya le va su salvoconducto al General Orbegoso; quien sabe si vendrá." Orbegoso was president of Peru from 1833 to 1835 and, during the Peru-Bolivia Confederation, president of the Estado Norperuano (State of Northern Peru). For further information on his career, see the Alfonso Quiroz entry on Santa Cruz in Tenenbaum, *Encyclopedia,* vol. 4, 230. Uncertainty regarding the extent of Sáenz's involvement in the Grand Project stems not only from the scant mention of it in her surviving correspondence (which does not include any of the letters she presumably received from Santa Cruz) but also from historians'

still-scanty knowledge of Peruvian politics in this period. In *Peru,* for example, Peter F. Klarén refers to the years 1824–1845 as a "scholarly black hole" while characterizing the years 1841–1845 simply as years of "political disintegration."

63. Sáenz to Flores, Paita, Feb. 4, 1842, in Villalba (ed.), *Manuela Sáenz: Epistolario,* 115–116.

64. Sáenz to Flores, Paita, Feb. 1, 1841, in ibid., 112–113.

65. Sáenz to Flores, Paita, Jan. 30, 1842, in ibid., 114–115.

66. Sáenz to Flores, Paita, Apr. 28, 1842, in ibid., 116–118.

67. Sáenz to Flores, Paita, June 3, 1842, in ibid., 120–122.

68. Ibid.

69. Sáenz to Flores, Paita, July 15, 1842, in ibid., 123. Sáenz's effort to explain the discrepancy between official and popular Peruvian sentiments toward Flores led her to state, "le tienen a usted aquí un terror pánico los mandatarios; pero los del pueblo desean mucho la venida de los ecuatorianos." Flores's plan to invade Peru apparently dissolved in the wake of news of the June 1842 peace agreement between Peru and Bolivia, since, after this agreement, tensions over the boundary also faded.

70. Sáenz to Flores, Paita, May 18, 1837, in ibid., 107.

71. Sáenz to Flores, Paita, July 15, 1842, in ibid., 122–123.

72. Sáenz to Flores, Paita, Sept. 7, 1843, in ibid., 144–145. Sáenz by then had begun closely following the career of General Manuel Ignacio Vivanco, who, on becoming president of Peru in April 1843, struck a secret deal with Santa Cruz that would have allowed the latter to head a special Peruvian mission to Europe to help Peru rebuild its naval squadron. See Basadre, *Historia de la República del Perú,* vol. 2, 96.

73. Sáenz to Flores, Paita, Aug. 9, 1842, in Villalba (ed.), *Manuela Sáenz: Epistolario,* 125.

74. Sáenz to Flores, Paita, Mar. 22, 1843, in ibid., 128. The constitutional convention had begun meeting in Quito in mid-January.

75. Van Aken, *King of the Night,* 188–190.

76. Ibid., 192–193, 201 passim.

77. Joaquín Monsalve to J. J. Flores, Piura, Sept. 7, 1843, in Villalba (ed.), *Manuela Sáenz: Epistolario,* 145n41.

78. Sáenz to Flores, Aug. 9, 1843, in ibid., 143.

79. An example was the note from Pedro Moncayo to Manuela Sáenz, Piura, July 12, 1843, in ibid., 140.

80. Sáenz to Flores, Paita, June 12, 1843, in ibid., 140.

81. Villalba (ed.), *Manuela Sáenz: Epistolario,* 73–74.

82. Sáenz to Flores, Paita, Jan. 30, 1842, in ibid., 114–115.

83. Ibid.

84. Ibid.

85. Sáenz to Flores, Paita, Jan. 30, 1843, in ibid., 126.

86. Sáenz to Flores, Paita, July 22 and 24, 1843, in ibid., 141–142. Moncayo was replaced by Joaquín Monsalve.

87. Sáenz to Flores, Paita, Jan. 30, 1842, in ibid., 114–115.

88. Sáenz to Flores, Paita, June 11, 1843, in ibid., 138–139.

89. Ibid.

90. Sáenz to Flores, Paita, Mar. 23, 1843, in ibid., 128.

91. Sáenz seems to have relied heavily on her female friends, the women of the Lamas y Godos family in particular, to fill her in on local hearsay and other developments. She especially relied on them to help her keep tabs on Moncayo (who happened to be engaged to one of the Lamas daughters) and his fellow conspirators. See, for instance, Paula Godos to Manuela Sáenz, [Paita], Nov. 30, 1844, in Fondo Jijón y Caamaño, AHBC-Quito, roll 92, ff. 519–520.

92. Sáenz to Flores, Paita, July 22 and Sept. 11, 1843, in Villalba (ed.), *Manuela Sáenz: Epistolario*, 141–142, 145. For further information on Manuel Cárdenas, see Arboleda, *Diccionario*, 95–96.

93. Sáenz to Flores, Paita, July 22, 1843, in Villalba (ed.), *Manuela Sáenz: Epistolario*, 141.

94. Sáenz to Flores, Paita, July 24, 1843, in ibid., 142–143.

95. A sense of this may be gleaned from Joaquín Monsalve to J. J. Flores, Piura, Sept. 7, 1843, in ibid., in which Monsalve refers to Sáenz not only as "mujer influyente e importante" (an influential and important woman) but as "muy ecuatoriana" (a true patriot).

96. Sáenz to Flores, Paita, July 24, 1843, in ibid., 142–143.

97. Sáenz later mentioned having agreed to forward Proaño's mail to him, although it is unclear whether he had asked her to or whether she had offered. See Sáenz to Flores, Paita, Jan. 23, 1844, in ibid., 151. Sáenz also mentions the trust the conspirators had in her, an example of which is one of Proaño's extant letters from Lima; see Víctor Proaño to Manuela Sáenz, Lima, Nov. 9, 1843, in ibid., 148.

98. Sáenz to Flores, Paita, Sept. 11, 1843, in ibid., 145–146. Other than her mention of them to Flores, I have found no trace of the letters Sáenz wrote to her compatriots in Piura. Her frustration with Cárdenas is reflected in her statement that "Cárdenas está en busca de que le den una paliza."

99. Ibid.

100. Sáenz to Flores, Paita, Oct. 22, 1843, in ibid., 146–147.

101. Ibid.

102. Ibid.

103. Sáenz to Flores, Paita, Jan. 23, 1844, in ibid., 151–153. A November 8 letter from Proaño in Lima to Moncayo in Piura—which Sáenz intercepted later that month in Paita—revealed some of the differences among the conspirators and appears in ibid., 153–154. Its interception also suggests that Sáenz's home served as a distribution point for all inbound and outbound émigré mail, at least that sent via British Pacific Steam Company packet boats, which stopped in Paita weekly.

104. See, for example, her letters to Flores in ibid., 113–118.

105. "Confidential" (reservado) or "highly confidential" (reservadísimo). Sáenz to Flores, Paita, June 11, 1843, in ibid., 138–139.

106. Ibid.

107. Sáenz to Flores, Paita, Feb. 12, 1844, in ibid., 156.
108. Sáenz to Flores, Paita, Feb. 12 and July 13, 1844, in ibid., 156, 162–163.
109. Sáenz to Flores, Paita, Jan. 23, 1844, in ibid., 151–153.
110. Sáenz to Flores, Paita, Apr. 10, 1844, in ibid., 158–159.
111. Sáenz to Flores, Paita, Feb. 7, 1844, in ibid., 154.
112. Sáenz to Flores, Paita, Jan. 23, 1844, in ibid., 151–153.
113. Sáenz to Colonel Carlos Joaquín Monsalve, Jan. 10, 1844, in ibid., 150.
114. Sáenz to Flores, Paita, Apr. 10, 1844, in ibid., 158–159: "Usted estese alerta con esa ciudad [Guayaquil], como yo oigo a los que vienen de esa, temo algun bochinche . . . bueno es evitar toda clase de insurrección."
115. Sáenz to Flores, Paita, July 20 and 27, 1844, in ibid., 163–64. Sáenz also had friends in Lima who kept her informed of developments there; see, for example, J. V. (?) to Sáenz, Lima, Dec. 8, 1844, in AHBC-Quito, Fondo Jijón y Caamaño, roll 92, ff. 525–526.
116. Sáenz to Flores, Paita, Sept. 2, 1844, in Villalba (ed.), *Manuela Sáenz: Epistolario,* 169–170.
117. Ibid. Sáenz may have feared that Wright would be vulnerable to either bribery or persuasion by the government's opponents.
118. On the March Revolution and Flores's fall, see Van Aken, *King of the Night,* 205–207. Sáenz remained in touch with Flores's wife and family.
119. For a brief overview of Vivanco's career, see the entry on Vivanco by Alfonso Quiroz in Tenenbaum, *Encyclopedia,* vol. 5, 429. A more thorough discussion may be found in Basadre, *Historia de la República del Perú,* vol. 3, 186–188.
120. Sáenz to Flores, Paita, [July or Aug.?] 1944, in Villalba (ed.), *Manuela Sáenz: Epistolario,* 166–169.
121. "Infamous and vile rebellion" (infame y vil pronunciamiento). Ibid.
122. "Twenty years of fruitless mestizo and torpid caudillo leadership" (veinte años de caudillaje estéril, mestizo e ignorante). Basadre, *Historia de la República del Perú,* vol. 3, 189–190.
123. "Nobody" (desconocida deidad). Sáenz to Flores, Paita, [July–Aug.?] 1944, in Villalba (ed.), *Manuela Sáenz: Epistolario,* 166–169.

Chapter Six

1. Sáenz to Flores, Paita, Aug. 10, 1844, in Villalba (ed.), *Manuela Sáenz: Epistolario,* 165: "Ya sabrá usted que terminó la cuestión de Vivanco, miserablemente, como terminan acá las cosas; ahora comienza la misma escena con parte de nuevos actores [y] no sé cuanto dure esta farsa or contradanza de locos." For a summary of events behind the fall of the Vivanco government, see Basadre, *Historia de la República del Perú,* vol. 3, 193–203.
2. Sáenz to Flores, Paita, Dec. 6, 1844, in Villalba (ed.), *Manuela Sáenz: Epistolario,* 171.
3. Sáenz to Roberto Ascásubi, Paita, Mar. 13, 1851, in Borja (ed.), "Epistolario," 242.

4. Sáenz to Dundas Logan, Guaduas, Nov. 24, 1830, in Masur "Documentos históricos," 280.

5. Sáenz to Flores, Paita, Jan. 30, 1842, in Villalba (ed.), *Manuela Sáenz: Epistolario,* 114–115. Freyre's statement appears in "Expediente judicial," 257–258. The reasons behind this testimony will be discussed ahead.

6. Garibaldi, *Autobiography,* vol. 2, 59. Sáenz found herself obliged to spend much time in a hammock, references to which appear in some of her letters to Flores.

7. "Crippled" (tullida). Palma, "Doña Manuela Sáenz," in *Tradiciones peruanas completas,* 1132–1135. This essay recalls the author's visit to Paita around 1856 (the last year of Sáenz's life). In Spanish: "Era una Señora abundante de carnes, ojos negros y animadísimos en los que parecía reconcentrado el resto de fuego vital que aún le quedara, cara redonda y mano aristocrática." Other references to Sáenz's heaviness in her later years appear in a few letters as well as in Ortiz, *Reminiscencias,* 108–109.

8. According to medical historian Michael Flannery (Nov. 10, 2002, phone interview with the author), the bone-repair techniques that might have restored Sáenz's physical mobility were not then widely available.

9. On Paita's American hospital, see Lofstrom, *Paita,* 49–52.

10. See, for example, Sáenz to Flores, Paita, Aug. 9, 1843, in Villalba (ed.), *Manuela Sáenz: Epistolario,* 143. Here Sáenz refers to Bonetti as a "doctor" (médico) whom she saw frequently and who was also treating a compatriot in Paita, one "Chana" Torres.

11. Sáenz to Flores, Paita, Dec. 6, 1844, in ibid., 171. Sáenz also may have gone to the beach in order to bury herself in the sand, a practice hinted at in Palma's aforementioned recollection, including his reference to "sand baths" (baños de arena) she had told him about. Palma recalled her explaining that a doctor had once recommended such baths for her "[damaged] nerves," and that this was the reason why she had chosen to live in Paita. Besides her injured hip, Sáenz likely suffered from rheumatoid arthritis, a condition suggested in a remark regarding the "unsuitability" of Quito's (relatively chilly) climate for her; see Sáenz to Flores, Paita, Jan. 30, 1842, in ibid., 114–115.

12. For a brief, useful summary of research on urban female-headed households in Latin America at this time, see Kuznesof, "Gender Ideology," 161–162. Kuznesof also mentions the limited range of occupations that were then open to women generally. On the way in which traditional notions of female respectability limited the options of white upper-class women, see Arrom's discussion in chap. 4 of *The Women of Mexico City* and Hunefeldt, *Liberalism in the Bedroom,* 18–20, 274. Hunefeldt notes, too, that "the whiter a woman's skin, the more society resisted her entrance into the public sphere" and that even by the end of the nineteenth century, when most of Lima's female population worked, women were still "largely excluded from the formal labor market."

13. Socolow, *The Women of Colonial Latin America,* 113–114; Martínez Carreño, "Mujeres y familia," 318–319; Arrom, *The Women of Mexico City,* 172–174.

Martínez notes that elite women, especially nuns, were often administrators of urban property, overseeing rent payments ("manejo de rentas") and engaging in moneylending—something Sáenz once expressed interest in.

14. This demographic preponderance is noted by Lofstrom, who explains that most of the town's male population was engaged in coastal trade and maritime activities that required them to be away from home for long stretches of time; see *Paita*, 33–34.

15. The house, retail store, and other items are mentioned in some of her extant letters to Roberto Ascásubi. See, for example, Sáenz to Ascásubi, Paita, Dec. 16, [1847], in Borja (ed.), "Epistolario," 235–236; also Sáenz to Flores, Paita, July 24, 1843, in Villalba (ed.), *Manuela Sáenz: Epistolario*, 142–143. The store apparently was located in a house that still sits on Quito's Guayaquil Street; see Jurado, Aguilar, and Moreno, *Casas de Quito Viejo*, 106.

16. Sáenz to Flores, Paita, Apr. 22, 1843, in Villalba (ed.), *Manuela Sáenz: Epistolario*, 130.

17. Sáenz to Ascásubi, Paita, Oct. 22, 1846, in Borja (ed.), "Epistolario," 238. In this letter—as well as in others written to Flores—Sáenz alludes to expenditures she had authorized in 1827 on the advice of her estate administrator (as well as, it seems, Bolívar) and that had gone toward the purchase of tools, Indian labor, and cattle for the hacienda.

18. José Modesto Larrea to M. Sáenz, Quito, Nov. 6, 1831, in Villalba (ed.), *Manuela Sáenz: Epistolario*, 137–138.

19. Sáenz to Ascásubi, Paita, Dec. 16, [1847], in Borja (ed.), "Epistolario," 235–236. The content of this letter strongly suggests that Sáenz wrote it in 1847 rather than in 1841, as Borja dates it in his transcription. The same can be said of at least two of the other letters published by Borja. The most glaring example is the one in which Sáenz informs Ascásubi of her husband's murder and which, despite the fact that this murder occurred in February 1847, is dated August 11, 1841!

20. Sáenz to Flores, Paita, May 21, 1840, in Villalba (ed.), *Manuela Sáenz: Epistolario*, 110–111.

21. Sáenz to Ascásubi, Paita, June 11, 1846, in Borja (ed.), "Epistolario," 237.

22. Sáenz to Flores, Paita, May 21, 1840, in Villalba (ed.), *Manuela Sáenz: Epistolario*, 110–111. Sáenz's quest for satisfaction from those who owed her is a major theme of the twenty-one letters of hers published in Borja (ed.), "Epistolario," most of which date from the 1840s and are addressed to Roberto Ascásubi.

23. Ibid.

24. Sáenz to Flores, Paita, Jan. 30, 1842, in ibid., 115.

25. Sáenz to Flores, Paita, Apr. 22, 1843, in ibid., 129–130.

26. Sáenz to Flores, Paita, July 24, 1843, in ibid., 143: "Ud. haga señor, por dios, que le embarguen hasta que se hagan las cuentas." Use of the word "embargar" suggests Sáenz was asking Flores to arrange for some kind of injunction or official order against her administrator, probably for a seizure of his property.

27. Sáenz to Flores, Paita, Sept. 7, 1843, in ibid., 145. An indication that Flores had offered his help appears in Sáenz to Flores, Paita, July 12, 1840, in ibid., 111–112. In

this letter, Sáenz thanks the caudillo profusely for the "interest" he has shown in her problem with her estate administrator.

28. Sáenz to Flores, Paita, Aug. 10, 1844, in ibid., 164–165.

29. Ibid. Flores's letter has not survived.

30. "Thirty gold ounces" (30 onzas de oro). Sáenz to Flores, Paita, Sept. 21 and Feb. 12, 1844, in ibid., 170, 155–157. Sáenz had justified her initial request for the loan (in a letter dated Oct. 22, 1843) by explaining that she was "very poor" (muy pobre), or cash strapped. She later reminded Flores several times of his promise to send her thirty gold ounces. The receipt included in her Feb. 12, 1844, missive reads: "Recibí del señor general Juan José Flores treinta onzas de oro en calidad de préstamo, por mis urgentes necesidades me hace este bien; las mismas que serán pagadas de lo primero que cobre mi apoderado de mis deudores."

31. Sáenz to Flores, Paita, Aug. 10, 1844, in ibid., 164. For a further glimpse into the nature of Sáenz's difficulties with her debtors, see Pedro Sanz to Manuela Sáenz, Quito, Nov. 27, 1844, in ibid., 166. I found no documents related to Sáenz's debt claims in the notarial archives located at the Archivo Nacional de Historia del Ecuador in Quito.

32. Sáenz to Flores, Paita, Aug. 10, 1844, in ibid., 164–165.

33. Sáenz to Sra. Doña Mercedes Jijón de Flores, Paita, Feb. 20, 1846, in Villalba (ed.), *Manuela Sáenz: Epistolario,* 177–178. Sáenz sent greetings to Jijón and congratulated her on the news of her husband's positive reception in Europe. She also reported on her frequent visits with Stagg, husband of the couple's daughter Amalia.

34. Sáenz to Ascásubi, Paita, Oct. 22, 1846, in Borja (ed.), "Epistolario," 238.

35. "Lima," *El Comercio* (Lima) July 19, 1847; "Comunicados: Horrendos asesinatos en la provincia de Chancay (July 17)," *El Comercio* July 21, 1847 (microfilm). Sáenz learned of the assassination from Cayetano Freyre. See Freyre to Sáenz, Lima, July 23, 1847, in Borja (ed.), "Epistolario," 246.

36. Sáenz to Flores, Paita, Jan. 30, 1842, in Villalba (ed.), *Manuela Sáenz: Epistolario,* 115. Some evidence hints that Sáenz cooperated with Thorne in his efforts to assist the charity hospital that had been established in his hometown of Aylesbury. One letter, for example, asks Flores to order her a dozen scapulars from one of the Quito convents, noting that the items were to be sent to England; see Sáenz to Flores, Paita, Jan. 23, 1844, in ibid., 152–153.

37. "This incident has left my head exploding" (mi cabeza está muy fatal con este suceso). Sáenz to Ascásubi, Paita, Aug. 11, 1847, in Borja (ed.), "Epistolario," 234.

38. Ibid. Sáenz's November 1847 granting of a power of attorney to Freyre appears in Freyre, "Expediente judicial," 256.

39. Freyre to Sáenz, Lima, July 23, 1847, in Borja (ed.), "Epistolario," 246.

40. Sáenz to Consul-General John Barton, Paita, Sept. 20, 1847, FO 177/32. Barton claimed he had nothing to tell her, given that Thorne had not died intestate; see Barton to Sáenz, Lima, Nov. 10, 1847, in FO 177/33.

41. Hunefeldt, *Liberalism in the Bedroom,* 227.

42. Arrom, *The Women of Mexico City*, 63, and on the plight of widows generally, 129–134.

43. Hunefeldt, *Liberalism in the Bedroom*, 227; Arrom, *The Women of Mexico City*, 64.

44. Testamento de Don Jayme Thornet (Oct. 25, 1847), AGN-Lima, Sección Historia, Libro de Protocolos, leg. 160, ff. 248–251. Article 3 in the will mentions the *Columbia*. A portion of this will is reproduced in Von Hagen, "Testamento de Jaime Thorne." Escobar's appointment as Thorne's executor appears in Poder de Jayme Thorne a Manuel Escobar (Aug. 17, 1835), AGN-Lima, Sección Historia, Libro de Protocolos, leg. 86, f. 462.

45. Testamento de Don Jayme Thornet (Oct. 25, 1847), AGN-Lima, Sección Historia, Libro de Protocolos, leg. 160, ff. 248–251, art. 6 passim. The will reveals that, in addition to administering the estate of Orué (who had died in 1835 and named the Englishman his chief executor), Thorne had been operating Huaito as a tenant farmer; it does not assign a specific value to any of the physical property (equipment, etc.) he had purchased for it. Thorne apparently continued to manage and reside on the hacienda after ownership had been transferred to Justo Hercelles in or around the early to mid-1840s. His will shows that he had gotten Hercelles to agree that, only after he (or his estate) had been reimbursed for the 82,000 pesos, would Huaito be turned over to Hercelles's legal descendants.

46. Ibid., art. 20. The will recognizes two other young girls—leaving each a small inheritance of two thousand pesos—and thus suggests that Thorne had other children by local women.

47. Buenaventura Concha is identified as Thorne's fellow murder victim in "Sobre la averiguación de un asesinato realizado en la Hacienda Huaito (Huacho, Aug. 21, 1851)," Criminales-Manuscritos República, Justicia (card catalog designation), Biblioteca Nacional de Perú.

48. Testamento de Don Jayme Thornet (Oct. 25, 1847), AGN-Lima, Sección Historia, Libro de Protocolos, leg. 160, ff. 248–251, arts. 20 and 12.

49. "Poverty report" (información de pobreza). Freyre, "Expediente judicial," 257.

50. Sáenz to Flores, Paita, Jan. 30, 1842, in Villalba (ed.), *Manuela Sáenz: Epistolario*, 115: "Estoy miserable como jamás lo creí; a veces me dan ganas de darme un balazo."

51. Sáenz to Flores, Paita, Apr. 23 and Oct. 22, 1843, in ibid., 129–130, 147.

52. Sáenz to Ascásubi, Paita, Sept. 20, 1847, in Borja (ed.), "Epistolario," 234.

53. References to Ruden are sprinkled throughout the letters included in the collection compiled and edited by Jorge Villalba (ed.), *Manuela Sáenz: Epistolario*. Sáenz's role as an intermediary between Ruden and others in the region may be gleaned from Moncayo to Sáenz, Piura, July 19, 1843, in ibid., 140.

54. Paula Godos to Manuela Sáenz, Paita, Nov. 30, 1844, AHBC, Fondo Jijón y Caamaño, roll 92, ff. 519–520.

55. Orejuela claimed to be one of Sáenz's *ahijadas*, or goddaughters. Her recollections were recorded during an interview in 1924 with Peruvian author Luis Alberto Sánchez during the latter's visit to Paita. For a brief discussion, see Vega,

"El largo y torturado silencio." Juana Rosa and Dominga both appear to have been the only servants Sáenz retained during her years in Paita.

56. Freyre, "Expediente judicial," 263. Witness Manuel Mújica testified: "Su pequeño arbitrio y trabajo no le sufraga para sus más precisas atenciones de la vida."

57. Ibid.

58. Ibid., 267.

59. Ibid., 263–270.

60. Klarén, *Peru,* 143–144; Basadre, *Historia de la República del Peru,* vol. 2, 203. Basadre notes that, through the early republican era, impoverished creole elites continued to wield prestige and influence.

61. Hunefeldt, *Liberalism in the Bedroom,* 239–241 passim. Hunefeldt's study also shows how women, especially of the lower classes, used their country's courts not just to defend imperiled dowry claims but also to win recognition for their contributions to household wealth, whether in the form of property or wages. For a useful survey of liberalism's mixed impact on women's lives and gender relations, see Dore, "One Step Forward," 3–32.

62. Von Hagen, "Testamento de Jaime Thorne," 581–582. This article includes excerpts from Escobar's lawsuit (referred to as "Autos seguidos por don Manuel Escobar, albacea de Don Jayme Thorne, contra Doña Manuela Sáenz, sobre cantidad de pesos provenientes de una dote paterna de 8,000 pesos y sus intereses"). Unfortunately, I was unable to find the original documents associated with this lawsuit during my forays in the AGN-Lima.

63. Ibid., 582–583.

64. Ibid., 584. Freyre's statements form part of a section entitled "Escrito de contestación de Don Cayetano Freyre, apoderado de la Señora Doña Manuela Sáenz . . . 2 de julio de 1848." Speaking of Thorne's trust in Escobar, the lawyer also noted that "le confió . . . la defensa de su buena reputación y fama, que esta identificada con la reputación y buen nombre de su esposa."

65. Ibid. Characterizing his client's dowry as "una deuda a favor de una esposa", Freyre also alleged that Escobar's "recriminations" against Sáenz were part of an effort to deprive her of her rightful property.

66. Ibid., 586–587. According to Von Hagen, the dispute between Sáenz and Escobar continued in Lima's Corte Superior de Justicia and ultimately produced a decision unfavorable to her. My own search through documents in the AGN's Sección Historia, Protocolos and Causas Civiles (which includes material from the original Corte Superior archive), however, uncovered no evidence to confirm this—or, for that matter, any further traces of the dispute.

67. Although little is known about Ascásubi generally, this summary relies on details gathered from Borja (ed.), "Epistolario," 233; Moncayo, "Una carta inédita," 146–147; "Los Ascásubi"; Villalba (ed.), *Manuela Sáenz: Epistolario,* 45, 47, 54; Loor, *Cartas,* vol. 1, 13n. Also from Sáenz to Flores, July 13, 1844, in Villalba (ed.), *Manuela Sáenz: Epistolario,* 162–163n45.

68. Sáenz to Ascásubi, Paita, Nov. 5, 1845, in Borja (ed.), "Epistolario," 236. She identified the lawyers as one Dr. Mendisábal and one Sr. Pacífico.

69. Sáenz to Ascásubi, Paita, Dec. 16, 1847, in ibid., 235. Sáenz's comments are in reference to Sra. Gangotena and Don Ignacio Sáenz. She refers to the latter as "my other heir" and as someone who "has given me an invincible desire to get well" (una invencible gana de curarme)!

70. Ibid.

71. Sáenz to Ascásubi, Paita, Nov. 15, 1849, in ibid., 239.

72. Sáenz to Ascásubi, Paita, Dec. 15, 1849, in ibid., 240.

73. Sáenz to Ascásubi, Paita, July 15, 1850, in ibid., 240: "La Sra. Gangotena hasta cuando me perjudicará, yo contando con eso quede a hacer unos pagos, no creyendo que faltase así a su palabra. . . . ¡Qué buena fe! ¡Paso por mil y más bochornos por su causa . . . por esa Señora que tiene tanto! Es el colmo de la maldad. No la considere usted más; por Dios oblígela al pago. No puedo tolerar más."

74. Sáenz to Ascásubi, Paita, Nov. 15, 1849: "A no ser por usted, no habría recibido las treinta onzas," Sáenz tells her friend. Subsequent letters show that she also sought to sue Gangotena for payment of interest on the balance due.

75. Sáenz to Ascásubi, Paita, Aug. 8, 1850, in ibid., 241.

76. Sáenz to Ascásubi, Paita, Nov. 12, 1851, in ibid., 243–244. Sáenz's letters also show that from at least 1851, she began to draw on an account her friend apparently had established for her; see, for example, her mention of two drafts she wrote in a second November 12, 1851, note to Ascásubi in ibid., 243. An example of her appeals to Mosquera for help in recovering her archive is Sáenz to Sr. Presidente General Tomás C. Mosquera, Paita, May 12, 1846, ACC, Archivo Mosquera.

77. Sáenz to Ascásubi, Paita, Mar. 13, 1851, in Borja (ed.), "Epistolario," 241.

78. Sáenz to Ascásubi, Paita, June 12, 1851, in ibid., 242; Sáenz to Ascásubi, Paita, Oct. 29, 1853, in Villalba (ed.), *Manuela Sáenz: Epistolario*, 179.

79. References to Ascásubi's sisters, to Aguirre, and to other intermediaries are scattered throughout Sáenz's letters to Ascásubi from at least 1847; see Borja (ed.), "Epistolario," 234 passim. References to the intermediary role of the Ascásubi sisters also appear in the letters Gabriel García Moreno wrote them (his sisters-in-law) during his 1853–1854 exile in Paita and Piura; see Loor, *Cartas,* vol. 1, 410 passim.

80. Loor, *Cartas,* vol. 1, 3–4.

81. Sáenz to Ascásubi, Paita, Oct. 22, 1846, in Borja (ed.), "Epistolario," 238.

82. Sáenz to Ascásubi, Paita, Nov. 12, 1851, in ibid., 243: "Mi señor, es usted una segunda providencia. Yo, sin usted, ¿cómo estaría? En fin, Dios pagará sus buenos oficios." In the same note, she acknowledges writing two drafts in accordance with instructions Ascásubi apparently had sent her.

83. Sáenz to Ascásubi, Paita, Oct. 29, 1853, in Villalba (ed.), *Manuela Sáenz: Epistolario,* 178–179.

84. Sáenz to Ascásubi, Paita, Mar. 13 and Mar. 30, 1851, in Borja (ed.), "Epistolario," 241–242.

85. Ascásubi to G. García Moreno, Piura, July 7, 1852, in Loor, *Cartas,* vol. 1, 257.

86. For a study of one of the most prominent of these clans, see Jurado Noboa, *Los Larrea*. Sáenz's personal ties to them may be gleaned from letters to Ascásubi in which she inquires after or alludes affectionately to Rosa Montúfar Larrea, daughter of Carlos Montúfar (and wife of General Vicente Aguirre); Carmen Salinas, daughter of early creole patriot leader Juan Salinas, who was married to Manuel Ascásubi; and Francisca ("Panchita") Larrea, who resided for a time with her nieces in Piura.

87. For further discussion of this, see Ayala, "La fundación de la república."

88. Van Aken, "Urbina, José María."

89. Ibid. On Urbina and his reform program, also see Ayala, "La fundación de la república," 183 passim. For brief background on the Jesuits, see Cushner, "Jesuits," in Tenenbaum (ed.), *Encyclopedia*, vol. 3, 316–319. On the Jesuits' expulsion from New Granada, see Bushnell, *The Making of Modern Colombia*, 109–110.

90. For a good, concise overview of García's life and career, see Van Aken, "García Moreno, Gabriel." A standard, if highly laudatory, biography is Pattee, *Gabriel García Moreno*. García Moreno was Ecuador's president from 1861 to 1865 and again from 1869 to 1875, during which time he became a dictator.

91. Sáenz to Ascásubi, Paita, June 14, 1853, in Moncayo, "Epistolario inédito," (1933), 23.

92. Sáenz to Ascásubi, Paita, Aug. 11, 1847, in Borja (ed.), "Epistolario," 234. For a glimpse of García's role as an intermediary between Sáenz and Ascásubi, see his 1849 letters to the latter in Biblioteca Ecuatoriana Aurelio Espinosa Polit: Cartas de Gabriel García Moreno, 1846–1854 (microfilm), roll 7315, Vatican Film Library, Special Collections. Most of García's letters in this collection have been published in Loor, *Cartas*.

93. Sáenz to Ascásubi, Paita, Oct. 29, 1853, in Villalba (ed.), *Manuela Sáenz: Epistolario*, 178–179.

94. García to sisters-in-law [Dolores, Rosario, and María Josefa Ascásubi], Paita, Nov. 22, 1853, in Loor, *Cartas,* 421.

95. Sáenz to Ascásubi, Paita, Jan. 21, 1853, in Borja (ed.), "Epistolario," 244.

96. For brief reference to Hernáez and other Jesuits who visited Sáenz in Paita (some of whom later became friends and associates of García Moreno's), see Villalba (ed.), *Manuela Sáenz: Epistolario*, 15. Alluding to her enchantment with her Jesuit visitors, Roberto Ascásubi once described Sáenz as being "enjesuitada." See Ascásubi to García Moreno, Piura, July 7, 1852, in Loor, *Cartas,* 257.

97. "Daily kindnesses" (finezas). García to Ascásubi, Paita, Oct. 29, 1853, in ibid., *Cartas,* 411.

98. Ibid.: "Soy amigo de toda confianza."

99. On the Flores naval expeditions, see Villalba, *El General Juan José Flores,* 449–454, and pertinent chapters in Van Aken, *King of the Night.* On the turmoil unleashed in Paita by the arrival of ships that formed part of the defeated 1852 squadron, see despatches from Vice-Consul Charles Higginson in Paita to

Chargé d'Affaires William Pitt in Lima, July 27 and Aug. 3, 1852, FO 177/53; Higginson to John Barton in Callao, Aug. 3, 1852, FO 177/53.

100. Sáenz to Ascásubi, Paita, Oct. 29, 1853, in Villalba (ed.), *Manuela Sáenz: Epistolario*, 179.

101. "Our good friend" (nuestra buena amiga). García to Ascásubi, Paita, Oct. 14, 1853, in Loor, *Cartas*, 406; Gómezjurado, *Vida de García Moreno*, vol. 2, 223–224.

102. García to Ascásubi, Paita, Oct. 14, 1853, in Loor, *Cartas*, 406.

103. García to sisters-in-law, Paita, Jan. 12, 1854, in Loor, *Cartas*, 440; Gómezjurado, *Vida de García Moreno*, vol. 2, 266–267. Mention of the antigovernment *pronunciamiento* and of the conflict between Castilla loyalists and authorities in Piura appears in a few of the despatches sent by British vice-consul Blacker in Paita to chargé d'affaires Sullivan in Lima. See for example, Blacker to Sullivan, Paita, May 27, 1854, FO 177/62.

104. Chambers, "Letters and Salons," 56.

105. Ibid., 59–61.

106. For a general discussion of the complex social processes behind nineteenth-century political life, see Sábato, "Review Essay," 1293 passim; and Safford, "Politics, Ideology, and Society."

107. Sáenz to Ascásubi, Paita, Oct. 29, 1853, in Villalba (ed.), *Manuela Sáenz: Epistolario*, 178: "Cuando se trata con agrado y franqueza a las personas se le da pasto al alma."

108. Sáenz to Ascásubi, Paita, June 29, 1856, in Borja (ed.), "Epistolario," 244–245.

109. García to Ascásubi, Paita, Dec. 20, 1854, Vatican Film Library, St. Louis University, Special Collections, Biblioteca Ecuatoriana Aurelio Espinosa Polit: Cartas de Gabriel García Moreno, 1846–1854, roll 7315.

110. "Countrywoman" (paisana). A brief description of Juana Rosa's role as a caretaker appears in Palma, "Doña Manuela Sáenz," 1132–1133. For passing references to Juana Rosa, see Moncayo to Sáenz, Piura, July 19, 1843, in Villalba (ed.), *Manuela Sáenz: Epistolario*, 140–141 (in which Juana Rosa is referred to as "paisana"); Paula Godos to Sáenz, Nov. 30, 1844, in AHBC-Quito, Fondo Jijón y Caamaño, roll 92, ff. 519–520. Sáenz's tendency to share her letters with Juana Rosa appears in Sáenz to Monsalve, Paita, Jan. 10, 1844, in Villalba (ed.), *Manuela Sáenz: Epistolario*, 150–151, where she mentions reading Monsalve's letter to the servant and announces that "one of these days" the latter intended to write the consul.

111. Sáenz to Ascásubi, Paita, June 29, 1856, in Borja (ed.), "Epistolario," 244–245. This last letter was dictated.

112. Passing reference to an 1856 diphtheria epidemic in the region (in Guayaquil and/or northern Perú) appears in Rolando, "La fecha de la muerte de la Libertadora," 164. Unfortunately, I have found no further references to this either in general works on epidemic disease or in e-mail consultation with Marcos Cueto, an expert on the history of science, medicine, and public health in modern (mainly twentieth-century) Peru. For brief mention of this pandemic, see Kohn, *Encyclopedia of Plague and Pestilence;* and Hoff and Smith, *Mapping*

Epidemics, 24–25. According to these sources, diphtheria appeared in England in the mid-1850s, spreading later to the rest of Europe and the world.

113. Hoff and Smith, *Mapping Epidemics,* 24–25; author's Nov. 7, 2002, phone conversation with Michael Flannery, director of the Reynolds Historical Library, University of Alabama at Birmingham; e-mail from Flannery to author, Jan. 14, 2003. In 1894, an antitoxin was developed by bacteriologist Pierre Roux.

114. Rolando, "La fecha de la muerte de la Libertadora," 164. This article includes an excerpt from a December 5, 1856, letter written by General Antonio de la Guerra to his wife in Lima.

Chapter Seven

1. Epigraph: "In Paita, we asked about her, the Dead Woman, so that we could touch, could feel the earth of the Buried Woman's radiance. They did not know" (Neruda, "The Unburied Woman of Paita," 18–55). The poem was published for the first time in 1962 in the original Spanish. In this 1996 edition, the Spanish original and its English translation appear side by side.

2. Any burial records that might have been kept in the parish church of San Francisco de Paita apparently were destroyed in the same fire that, according to William Lofstrom, destroyed the church's baptismal records in the 1880s; see *Paita,* 37. On the mystery of Sáenz's burial site, see Vega, "El largo y torturado silencio"; Godos Curay, "Manuela Sáenz"; Ayala Marín, "Doña Manuela Sáenz." According to Vega and Godos Curay (a native of Paita), Sáenz likely was buried at the top of a small hill that Paita lore has identified as the site of the mass grave of victims of the diphtheria epidemic. Although the Peruvian government's search for her remains led to a report submitted to one General Arciniegas Hueby of the Centro de Estudios Históricos Militares del Perú in Lima, it appears to have been inconclusive.

3. One of Sáenz's reputed godchildren was Paula Orejuela a mulatta known locally as "La Morito." As an old woman, she recalled going to Sáenz's home when she was little. Orejuela also recalled helping to make "rag flowers" whose sale (possibly to sailors and other visitors to Paita), she added, helped support Sáenz and her two female servants. Her recollections were part of an interview given to Luis Alberto Sánchez during the latter's 1924 visit to Paita. See Vega, "El largo y torturado silencio," 4–5.

4. An early roundup of the abundant Saenz literature (212 books and articles) may be found in Aljure Chalela, "Bibliografía de Manuela Sáenz," which includes many of the historical writings surveyed and analyzed in Murray, "'Loca' or 'Libertadora'?" For a discussion of the various, mostly fictional, works that have appeared more recently—including the 2000 Venezuelan film produced by Diego Rísquez—see Hennes, "The Spaces of a Free Spirit."

5. For a fuller discussion of Rumazo's book in the context of the Sáenz historiography, see Murray, "'Loca' or 'Libertadora'?"

6. Rumazo, *Manuela Sáenz*, 175.

7. The various editions of Rumazo's biography have been published in Spain, Argentina, Venezuela, Colombia, and Ecuador. The 2003 Ecuadorian edition (sponsored in part by Quito's Casa de la Cultura Ecuatoriana) includes an introduction by historian Jorge Núñez Sánchez.

8. "Pure smuggler" (contrabandista pura); "guerrilla" (guerrillera). Neruda, "The Unburied Woman of Paita," 29, 49 passim.

9. Ibid., 41. This view of Sáenz and her significance brings to mind Joanne Rappaport's observation regarding the difference between "popular" and "professional" history. Rappaport notes that the former has become the domain of Latin American novelists and Third World writers generally (a group that includes poets like Neruda), for whom "the locus of historical memory is not the past but the present and future." See Rappaport, *The Politics of Memory*, 16–17.

10. By the early 1970s, a number of Latin American writers and intellectuals had begun to see their region's struggles for independence—and the struggle led by Bolívar in particular—as an aborted social revolution. See, for example, Aguirre, *Bolívar*.

11. García Márquez, *The General in His Labyrinth*, trans. Edith Grossman (New York: Penguin Books, 1991), 6–7.

12. Arciniegas, *El libertador y la guerrillera*. More recent fictional works such as Jaime Manrique's 2006 novel, *Our Lives Are the Rivers*, tend to deemphasize the heroic-revolutionary dimension in favor of stressing Sáenz as a free spirit and earthy iconoclast.

13. Martínez, "Cual rostro." This anthology includes poems, short essays, and sketches dedicated to Sáenz. Feminist views of Sáenz are discussed in Mogollón and Narváez, *Manuela Sáenz*, 145–155.

14. Ayala Marín, "Doña Manuela Sáenz." This article is a newspaper clipping provided to me by Juan José Vega of Lima. Unfortunately, the clipping from Lima's *El Nacional* does not include page numbers from the original paper.

15. Ibid.

16. Ibid. Quotations are from Martínez's speech in Spanish as transcribed by Ayala.

17. Ibid. It also was announced that Peruvian president Alan García had authorized the conversion of Sáenz's Paita home into a museum and library—a project that was delayed until recently. According to an April 1, 2001, report in Lima's *El Comercio* (http:/www.elcomercioperu.com), Peruvian and Ecuadorian authorities have signed an agreement with the mayor of Paita that allows the Ecuadorians to take charge of "rehabilitating" the house in which Sáenz supposedly resided. Paita lore has identified at least three such houses, yet, it is likely that the one she was occupying at the time of her death was destroyed in the 1884 fire that burned some fifty homes in Paita. See Vega, "El largo y torturado silencio," 5.

18. Another example of Sáenz as a rallying point and symbol for activists is a 1996 radio documentary that summarizes her life and portrays it as an example for contemporary women struggling against the effects of sexism, racism, and other

forms of prejudice and injustice. See "En las huellas de Manuela Sáenz," documentary produced by Iris Disse et al. of the Centro de Educación Popular, Quito.

19. Lind, "Gender and Neoliberal States," 193.

20. *La esposa del doctor Thorne* was the first Latin American winner of Spanish publisher Tusquets's annual prize for best erotic novel, the Premio Sonrisa Vertical. Depicting Sáenz as a restless, sexually insatiable woman, it sparked a firestorm of controversy throughout Spanish America. A summary of this controversy appears in Valero Martínez, *En defensa de Manuela Sáenz*—which brings together the reactions of thirty-six authors—as well as in Mogollón and Narváez, *Manuela Sáenz*, 156–161. On Romero's provocative depiction of the sexual relationship between Sáenz and Bolívar, see the enlightening discussion in Conway, *The Cult of Bolívar*, chap. 4.

21. "Manuela Sáenz es la nueva generala de Ecuador," *El Universo* (May 24, 2007; www.eluniverso.com/2007); "Generala Manuela Sáenz, una deuda con la historia," *Agencia Latinoamericana y Caribeña de Comunicación* (May 29, 2007; www.alcnoticias.org/). I thank John Sanbrailo for bringing this news to my attention.

22. María Josefa Sáenz del Campo (1788–1844?) was known for her strong royalist sentiments and, like Manuela's younger half-sister, María Manuela, left Quito in 1822 in order to settle in Spain permanently with her husband and children. For details, see Jurado Noboa, "La familia y ascendientes de Manuelita," 199.

23. For a brief summary of scholarship on the theme of intergenerational and family conflict as part of the Age of Revolution, see Earle, "Rape and the Anxious Republic," 130–132. On Chile specifically, see Felstiner, "Family Metaphors" and "Kinship Politics."

24. Sáenz's references to the Godos y Lamas women are woven into a fair number of her letters to Flores. See, for example, Sáenz to Flores, Paita, Jan. 23 and Feb. 7, 1844, in Villalba, *Manuela Sáenz: Epistolario*, 151–153, 154–155.

25. Valencia, *Mujeres caucanas*, 150–154. According to Charles F. Walker, *caudillismo* and caudillo politics represent "a unique type of state formation." For further discussion of this idea based on an innovative study of early national Peru, including the popular, regional basis of the Gamarra movement, see Walker, *Smoldering Ashes*, 123 passim.

Archival and Manuscript Sources

Archivo Arzobispal de Lima.
Archivo Central del Cauca, Popayán. Archivo Mosquera.
Archivo del Libertador. Caracas, Casa Natal, 1961. Microfilm rolls 27, 34, 42.
Archivo General de la Nación, Bogotá. Sección República, Fondo Historia. Vol. 4.
Archivo General de la Nación, Lima. Sección Historia, Protocolos and Causas Civiles.
Archivo Histórico del Banco Central, Quito. Fondo Jacinto Jijón y Caamaño, 1ᵃ Serie: Documentos Misceláneos; 5ᵃ Serie: Documentos del General Juan José Flores, Col. 7 (microfilm).
Archivo Nacional de Historia del Ecuador, Quito. Sección General, Testamentarías; Sección Judicial, Notaría 1ᵃ: Protocolos. Vols. 481–485.
Despatches from U.S. Consuls in Lima, 1823–1854. Washington, D.C.: National Archives and Records Administration, 1949. Microfilm roll 1.
Despatches from U.S. Consuls in Paita, 1833–1874. Washington, D.C.: National Archives and Records Administration, 1961. Microfilm roll 1.
Despatches from U.S. Ministers to Colombia, 1820–1906. Washington, D.C.: National Archives, 1955. Microfilm roll 8.
Lilly Library, Indiana University. Illingworth Manuscript Collection; Ecuador Collection; Mutis Daza Manuscripts.
United Kingdom National Archives (formerly Public Record Office), Kew. Foreign Office Section, including FO 18: General Correspondence before 1906, Colombia; FO 135: Correspondence of Embassy & Consular Archives, Colombia (1823–1918); FO 61: General Correspondence before 1906, Peru; FO 177: Correspondence of Embassy & Consular Archives, Peru (1836–1940); FO 357: Henderson Papers.
Vatican Film Library, St. Louis University. Special Collections, Biblioteca Ecuatoriana Aurelio Espinosa Polit: Cartas de Gabriel García Moreno, 1846–1854 (microfilm).

Published Sources

Primary Sources

COLLECTED LETTERS AND DOCUMENTS

Academia Colombiana de Historia (comp.). "Documentos inéditos: Sumaria información instituída por orden del Supremo Gobierno para averiguar los hechos escandalosos y criminales con que Manuela Sáenz ha tratado de perturbar el orden y tranquilidad públicas (julio–agosto 1830)." *Boletín de Historia y Antigüedades* (Bogotá) 47 (May–June 1960), 373–402.

Archivo General de la Nación (comps.). "Expediente judicial de información de pobreza seguido en nombre de Doña Manuela Sáenz, 'la Libertadora del Libertador,' 1847–1848." *Revista del Archivo General de la Nación* (Lima) 3 (1975), 256–270.

Archivo Nacional de Historia del Ecuador (eds.). "Expediente promovido por Doña Manuela Sáenz sobre su filiación y calidad [y] poder general [de] Manuela Sáenz y Thorne al Presbítero Don José Manuel Flores." *Arnahis: Órgano del Archivo Nacional de Historia* (Quito) 3 (1970), 87–91.

Bolívar, Simón. *Cartas del Libertador*. 1st ed. New York, 1948; 2nd ed. Caracas: Fundación Vicente Lecuna & Banco Central de Venezuela, 1970.

Borja, Luis F. (ed.). "Epistolario de Manuela Sáenz." *Boletín de la Academia Nacional de Historia* (Quito) 26, no. 48 (July–Dec. 1946), 228–246.

"Carta de Manuela Sáenz al Sr. Ministro del Interior Alejandro Osorio." *Boletín de Historia y Antigüedades* 19, no. 219 (Apr. 1932), 207.

Gómezjurado, Severo, S.J. *Vida de García Moreno*. 10 vols. Cuenca: Editorial El Tiempo, 1954–.

Grases, Pedro. *El archivo de Bolívar (manuscritos y ediciones)*. Caracas: Equinoccio, 1978.

Lecuna, Vicente (ed.). "Cartas de mujeres." *Boletín de la Academia Nacional de la Historia* (Caracas) 16, no. 62 (Apr.–July 1933), 332–398.

———. "Papeles de Manuela Sáenz." *Boletín de la Academia Nacional de la Historia* (Caracas) 28 (Oct.–Dec. 1945), 494–525.

Loor, Wilfredo (ed.). *Cartas de Gabriel García Moreno (1846–1854)*. 2nd. ed. 2 vols. Quito: La Prensa Católica, 1956.

Masur, Gerhard. "Documentos históricos: Una carta desconocida de Manuela Sáenz." *Boletín de la Academia Nacional de Historia* (Quito) 29, no. 74 (July–Dec. 1949), 277–280.

Moncayo, Hugo. "Epistolario inédito de Doña Manuela Sáenz." *Boletín del Instituto Nacional Mejía* (Quito) 1, no. 3 (1933), 21–29.

———. "Epistolario inédito de Doña Manuela Sáenz." *Boletín del Instituto Nacional Mejía* (Quito) 2, no. 1 (Jan.–Feb. 1934), 59–68.

Posada, Eduardo. "La Libertadora." *Boletín de Historia y Antigüedades* (Bogotá) 15, no. 169 (Aug. 1925), 17–38.

———. "La Libertadora." *Boletín de Historia y Antigüedades* (Bogotá) 17, no. 196 (Nov. 1928), 237–250.

Rolando, Carlos. "La fecha de la muerte de la Libertadora del Libertador." *Boletín del Centro de Investigaciones Históricas de Guayaquil* 9, nos. 21–22 (1952), 164.

Villalba, Jorge F. (ed.). *Manuela Sáenz: Epistolario*. Quito: Banco Central del Ecuador, 1986.

Von Hagen, Victor W. (ed.). "Testamento de Jaime Thorne y pleito con Manuela Sáenz sobre devolución de su dote [May–June 1848]." *Boletín de Historia y Antigüedades* (Bogotá) 41 (Sept.–Oct. 1954), 574–586.

Bolívar, Fernando. "Recuerdos de Fernando Bolívar, sobrino y último secretario del Libertador." *Boletín de la Academia Nacional de la Historia* (Caracas) 25 (Oct.– Dec. 1942), 296–314.

Boussingault, Jean-Baptiste. *Mémoires de Jean-Baptiste Boussingault.* 3 vols. Paris: Chamerot & Renouard, 1900.

Cuervo, Ángel, and José Rufino Cuervo. *Vida de Rufino Cuervo y noticias de su época.* 2 vols. Paris: Roger & Chernoviz, 1892.

De LaCroix, Luis Perú. *Diario de Bucaramanga.* 2nd ed. Bogotá: Editorial Cromos, 1945.

Garibaldi, Giuseppe. *Autobiography of Giuseppe Garibaldi.* 3 vols. A. Werner (trans.). New York: H. Fertig, 1971.

González, Florentino. *Memorias.* Medellín: Editorial Bedout, 1971.

Hall, Basil. *Extracts from a Journal Written on the Coasts of Chile, Peru, and Mexico in the Years 1820, 1821, and 1822.* 2 vols. Edinburgh: Constable, 1824.

Le Moyne, Auguste. *Viajes y estancias en América del Sur: La Nueva Granada, Santiago de Cuba, Jamaica y el Istmo de Panamá.* Bogotá: Biblioteca Popular de Cultura Colombiana, 1945.

Miller, John. *Memoirs of General Miller in the Service of the Republic of Peru.* 2 vols. London: Longman, Rees, 1828.

Ortiz, Juan Francisco. *Reminiscencias* [1907?]. Bogotá: Ministerio de Educación, 1946.

Posada Gutiérrez, Joaquín. *Memorias histórico-políticas del General Joaquín Posada Gutiérrez.* 2nd ed. 4 vols. Bogotá, 1929.

Proctor, Robert. *Narrative of a Journey across the Cordillera of the Andes and of a Residence in Lima and Other Parts of Peru in the Years 1823 and 1824.* London: Constable, 1825.

Restrepo, José Manuel. *Diario político y militar.* 4 vols. Bogotá: Imprenta Nacional, 1954.

Rojas, Ezequiel. "El 25 de septiembre de 1828." In Jorge Roa (ed.), *Biblioteca popular: Colección de grandes escritores.* Bogotá: Librería Nueva, 1894.

Stevenson, W. B. *An Historical and Descriptive Narrative of Twenty Years' Residence in South America.* London: Longman, Rees, 1825.

Biblioteca Nacional de Colombia, Bogotá. Hemeroteca Manuel del Socorro Rodríguez. *La Aurora* (Apr. 15–Aug. 15, 1830), microfilm roll 0148; *El Cachaco* (May 1833–Apr. 1834), microfilm.

El Comercio (Lima), 1846–1848; 1856–1857. Microfilm.

Gaceta del Gobierno del Perú Independiente, vols. 1–3 (July 1821–Dec. 1822). Buenos Aires: Ministerio de Educación, 1950.

Suplemento a la Gaceta del Gobierno del Perú Independiente 30 (Oct. 21, 1821). Buenos Aires: Ministerio de Educación, 1950, 143–146.

Secondary Sources

BOOKS, ARTICLES, DISSERTATIONS

Aguirre, Indalecio Liévano. *Bolívar* [1971]. 6th ed. Bogotá: Editorial Oveja Negra, 1987.

Aljure Chalela, Simón. "Bibliografía de Manuela Sáenz." *Boletín Cultural y Bibliográfico* 18, no. 2 (1981), 234–253.

Álvarez Saá, Carlos (comp.). *Manuela: Sus diarios perdidos y otros papeles.* Quito: Imprenta Mariscal, 1995.

Andrien, Kenneth. *The Kingdom of Quito, 1690–1830: The State and Regional Development.* Cambridge: Cambridge University Press, 1995.

Anna, Timothy. *The Fall of the Royal Government in Peru.* Lincoln: University of Nebraska Press, 1979.

Applewhite, Harriet, and Darline Levy (eds.). *Women and Politics in the Age of the Democratic Revolution.* Ann Arbor: University of Michigan Press, 1990.

Arboleda, Gustavo. *Diccionario biográfico y genealógico del Antiguo Departamento del Cauca.* Bogotá: Librería Horizontes, 1962.

Archer, Christon (ed.). *The Wars of Independence in Spanish America.* Wilmington, Del.: Scholarly Resources, 2000.

Arciniegas, Germán. *El libertador y la guerrillera.* Carlos Milla Batres (ed.). Bogotá: Editorial Milla Batres, 1990.

Arrom, Silvia. *The Women of Mexico City, 1790–1857.* Stanford, Calif.: Stanford University Press, 1985.

Ayala Marín, Alexandra. "Doña Manuela Sáenz, la libertadora: 'Soy ciudadana de América.'" *El Nacional* (Lima) (Dec. 3, 1989).

Ayala Mora, Enrique. "La fundación de la república: Panorama histórica, 1830–1859." In Enrique Ayala Mora (ed.), *Nueva historia del Ecuador,* vol. 7, 145–185.

——— (ed.). *Nueva historia del Ecuador.* 15 vols. Quito: Corporación Editorial Nacional: Grijalbo, 1983–1995.

Basadre, Jorge. *Historia de la República del Perú, 1822–1933.* 7th ed. 11 vols. Lima: Editorial Universitaria, 1983.

Bethell, Leslie (ed.). *The Independence of Latin America.* Cambridge: Cambridge University Press, 1987.

Bonilla, Heraclio. "Peru and Bolivia." In Leslie Bethell (ed.), *Spanish America after Independence, c. 1820–c. 1870,* 239–282. Cambridge: Cambridge University Press, 1987.

Borchart de Moreno, Christiana. "La imbecilidad y el coraje: La participación femenina en la economía colonial de Quito, 1780–1830." *Revista Complutense de Historia de América* 17 (1991), 167–182.

Botero Saldarriaga, Roberto. *El Libertador-Presidente.* Bogotá: Editorial Kelly, 1969.

Brungardt, Maurice. "Tithe Production and Patterns of Economic Change in Central Colombia, 1764–1833." Ph.D. dissertation, University of Texas at Austin, 1974.

Bushnell, David. "The Last Dictatorship: Betrayal or Consummation?" *Hispanic American Historical Review* 63, no. 1 (Feb. 1983), 65–105.

————. *The Making of Modern Colombia: A Nation in Spite of Itself.* Berkeley & Los Angeles: University of California Press, 1993.

————. *Simón Bolívar: Liberation and Disappointment.* New York: Pearson-Longman, 2004.

————, and Neill Macaulay. *The Emergence of Latin America in the Nineteenth Century.* 2nd ed. New York: Oxford University Press, 1994.

Calderón, María Teresa, and Clément Thibaud. "La construcción del orden en el paso del antiguo régimen á la república: Redes sociales e imaginario político del Nuevo Reino de Granada al espacio grancolombiano." *Anuario Colombiano de Historia Social y de la Cultura* (Bogotá) 29 (2002), 135–165.

Chalus, Elaine, and H. Barker (eds.). *Gender in Eighteenth-century England: Roles, Representations, and Responsibilities.* London: Longman, 1997.

Chambers, Sarah. *From Subjects to Citizens: Honor, Gender, and Politics in Arequipa, Peru, 1780–1856.* University Park: Penn State University Press, 1999.

————. "Letters and Salons: Women Reading and Writing the Nation." In Sara Castro-Klarén and John C. Chasteen (eds.), *Beyond Imagined Communities: Reading and Writing the Nation in Nineteenth-Century Latin America,* 54–83. Washington, D.C.: Woodrow Wilson Center & Johns Hopkins University Press, 2003.

————. "Republican Friendship: Manuela Sáenz Writes Women into the Nation, 1835–1856." *Hispanic American Historical Review* 81, no. 2 (May 2001), 225–257.

Chasteen, John. *Heroes on Horseback: A Life and Times of the Last Gaucho Caudillos.* Albuquerque: University of New Mexico Press, 1995.

Cherpak, Evelyn. "The Participation of Women in the Independence Movement in Gran Colombia, 1780–1830." In Asunción Lavrin (ed.), *Latin American Women: Historical Perspectives,* 219–234. Westport, Conn.: Greenwood Press, 1978.

Chiriboga Navarro, Ángel I. "Los Sáenz en el Ecuador." *Boletín de la Academia Nacional de Historia* (Quito) (July–Dec. 1942), 200–241.

Conway, Christopher B. *The Cult of Bolívar in Latin American Literature.* Gainesville: University Press of Florida, 2003.

Cordovez Moure, José María. *Reminiscencias de Santafé y Bogotá.* 3rd ed. Bogotá: Gerardo Rivas Moreno, 1997.

Davis, Robert H. "Acosta, Caro, and Lleras: Three Essayists and Their Views of New Granada's National Problems, 1832–1854." Ph.D. dissertation, Vanderbilt University, 1969.

Davis, Roger. "Ecuador under Gran Colombia, 1820–1830: Regionalism, Localism, and Legitimacy in the Emergence of an Andean Republic." Ph.D. dissertation, University of Arizona, 1983.

Delpar, Helen. "Bogotá, Santa Fe de." In Barbara Tenenbaum (ed.), *Encyclopedia of Latin American History and Culture,* vol. 1, 355–356. New York: Charles Scribner's Sons, 1996.

Del Valle Arizpe, Artemio. *La Güera Rodríguez.* Mexico City: Editorial Diana, 1977.

De Madariaga, Salvador. *Bolívar.* 2 vols. Madrid: Espasa-Calpe, 1979.

————. *Bolívar.* Eng.-lang. ed. New York: Schocken Books, 1969.

Descola, Jean. *Daily Life in Colonial Peru, 1710–1820.* New York: Macmillan, 1968.

Díaz, Arlene Julia. "Ciudadanas and Padres de Familia: Liberal Change, Gender, Law, and the Lower Classes in Caracas, Venezuela, 1786–1888." Ph.D. dissertation, University of Minnesota, 1997.

———. *Female Citizens, Patriarchs, and the Law in Venezuela, 1786–1904.* Lincoln: University of Nebraska Press, 2004.

Dore, Elizabeth. "One Step Forward, Two Steps Back: Gender and the State in the Long Nineteenth Century." In Elizabeth Dore and Maxine Molyneux (eds.), *Hidden Histories of Gender and the State in Latin America,* 3–32. Durham, N.C.: Duke University Press, 2000.

———, and Maxine Molyneux (eds.). *Hidden Histories of Gender and the State in Latin America.* Durham, N.C.: Duke University Press, 2000.

Duarte French, Jaime. *Las Ibáñez.* 3rd ed. Bogotá: El Áncora Editores, 1987.

Duby, Georges, and Michelle Perrot (eds.). *A History of Women in the West.* 4 vols. Cambridge, Mass.: Belknap Press of Harvard University Press, 1993.

Earle, Rebecca. "Letters and Love in Colonial Spanish America." *The Americas: A Quarterly Review of Interamerican Cultural History* 62, no. 1 (July 2005), 17–46.

———. "Rape and the Anxious Republic: Revolutionary Colombia, 1810–1830." In Elizabeth Dore and Maxine Molyneux (eds.), *Hidden Histories of Gender and the State in Latin America,* 127–146. Durham, N.C.: Duke University Press, 2000.

———. *Spain and the Independence of Colombia, 1810–1825.* Exeter, U.K.: University of Exeter Press, 2000.

Ellis, Joseph. "Get a Life! Reflections on Biography and History." *Historically Speaking: The Bulletin of the Historical Society* 5, no. 5 (May/June 2004), 1–3.

Felstiner, Mary Lowenthal. "Family Metaphors: The Language of an Independence Revolution." *Comparative Studies in Society and History* 25 (1983), 154–180.

———. "Kinship Politics in the Chilean Independence Movement." *Hispanic American Historical Review* 56, no. 1 (1976), 58–80.

Fey, Ingrid, and Karen Racine (eds.). *Strange Pilgrimages: Exile, Travel, and National Identity in Latin America, 1800–1990s.* Wilmington, Del.: Scholarly Resources, 2000.

Flores Galindo, Alberto. *La ciudad sumergida: Aristocracia y plebe en Lima, 1760–1830.* 2nd ed. Lima: Editorial Horizonte, 1991.

Flores y Caamaño, Alfredo. "Origen de Manuela Sáenz: Unos breves reparos." *Boletín de la Academia Nacional de la Historia* (Caracas) 36, no. 143 (July–Sept. 1953), 342–346.

Galvis, Luis (ed.). *Historia extensa de Colombia.* 40 vols. vol. 7: *La Gran Colombia, 1819–1830.* Bogotá: Lerner, Plaza & Janès, 1965–1986.

Gangotena y Jijón, C. "Los Ascásubi (genealogía)." *Boletín de la Academia Nacional de Historia* (Quito) 7, no. 19 (Sept.–Oct. 1923), 241–247.

García Márquez, Gabriel. *El general en su laberinto.* Bogotá: Editorial Oveja Negra, 1989.

Godineau, Dominique. "Daughters of Liberty and Revolutionary Citizens." In Genevieve Fraisse and Michelle Perrot (eds.), *A History of Women in the West.*

Vol. 4: *Emerging Feminism from Revolution to World War*, 16–32. Cambridge, Mass.: Belknap Press of Harvard University Press, 1993.

Godos Curay, Miguel. "Manuela Sáenz: Una extraordinaria devoción por Bolívar." *Suceso* (Piura) (July 14, 1996), 6–7.

González Suárez, Federico. *Historia general de la República del Ecuador.* 7 vols. Quito: Imprenta del Clero, 1894.

Goodman, Dena (ed.). *Marie-Antoinette: Writings on the Body of a Queen.* New York: Routledge, 2003.

Guy, Donna. "Biography." In K. Lynn Stoner (ed.), *Latinas of the Americas: A Source Book,* 41–60. New York: Garland, 1989.

Hanke, Lewis, and Jane M. Rausch (eds.). *People and Issues in Latin America: From Independence to the Present.* Princeton, N.J.: Princeton University Press, 1992.

Helg, Aline. "Simón Bolívar and the Specter of 'Pardocracia': José Padilla in Post-independence Cartagena." Paper presented at Conference on Latin American History, Chicago, Jan. 2003.

Hennes, Heather R. "The Spaces of a Free Spirit: Manuela Sáenz in Literature and Film." Ph.D. dissertation, Florida State University, 2005.

Hoff, Brent, and Carter Smith III. *Mapping Epidemics: A Historical Atlas of Disease.* New York: Franklin Watts, 2000.

Hufton, Olwen H. *Women and the Limits of Citizenship in the French Revolution.* Toronto: University of Toronto Press, 1992.

Hunefeldt, Christine. *Liberalism in the Bedroom: Quarreling Spouses in Nineteenth-century Lima.* University Park: Pennsylvania State University Press, 2000.

Hunt, Lynn. "The Many Bodies of Marie-Antoinette: Political Pornography and the Problem of the Feminine in the French Revolution." In Dena Goodman (ed.), *Marie Antoinette: Writings on the Body of a Queen.* New York: Routledge, 2003.

Jurado Noboa, Fernando. "La familia y ascendientes de Manuelita: Las raíces hispánicas, americanas y judías en Manuela Sáenz y Aizpuru." In Jorge Villalba (ed.), *Manuela Sáenz: Epistolario,* 191–218. Quito: Banco Central del Ecuador, 1986.

———. *Los Larrea: Burocracia, tenencia de la tierra, poder político, crisis, retorno al poder y papel en la cultura ecuatoriana.* Quito: Sociedad Ecuatoriana de Amigos de la Genealogía, 1986.

———, Rocío Aguilar, and Vicente Moreno. *Casas del Quito Viejo.* Vol. 1. Quito: Colección Medio Milenio, 1992.

Kentner, Janet. "The Sociopolitical Role of Women in the Mexican Wars of Independence." Ph.D. dissertation, Loyola University–Chicago, 1975.

Klarén, Peter F. *Peru: Society and Nationhood in the Andes.* New York: Oxford University Press, 2000.

Kohn, George Childs (ed.). *Encyclopedia of Plague and Pestilence: From Ancient Times to the Present.* Rev. ed. New York: Facts on File, 2001.

Kuznesof, Elizabeth Anne. "Gender Ideology, Race, and Female-headed Households in Urban Mexico, 1750–1850." In Víctor Uribe (ed.), *State and Society in Spanish America during the Age of Revolution,* 149–170. Wilmington, Del.: SR Books, 2001.

Landes, Joan B. *Women and the Public Sphere in the Age of the French Revolution.* Ithaca, N.Y.: Cornell University Press, 1988.

Lavrin, Asunción. "Female Religious." In Susan Socolow and Louisa Hoberman (eds.), *Cities and Society in Colonial Latin America,* 166–177. Albuquerque: University of New Mexico Press, 1986.

——— (ed.). *Sexuality and Marriage in Colonial Latin America.* Lincoln: University of Nebraska Press, 1989.

———. "Women in Spanish America." In Leslie Bethell (ed.), *Cambridge History of Latin America,* vol. 2, 321–356. Cambridge: Cambridge University Press, 1984.

LeGoff, Jacques. "Writing Historical Biography Today." *Current Sociology* 43, nos. 2/3 (Autumn/Winter 1995), 11–17.

Leguía y Martínez, Germán. *Historia de la emancipación del Perú.* 7 vols. Lima: Comisión Nacional del Sesquicentenario de la Independencia del Perú, 1972.

Lind, Amy. "Gender and Neoliberal States: Feminists Remake the Nation in Ecuador." *Latin American Perspectives* 30, no. 1 (Jan. 2003), 181–207.

Lofstrom, William F. *Paita, Outpost of Empire: Impact of the New England Whaling Fleet on the Socioeconomic Development of Northern Peru, 1832–1865.* Mystic, Conn.: Mystic Seaport Museum, 1996.

Londoño, Jenny. *Entre la sumisión y la resistencia: Las mujeres en la Audiencia de Quito.* Quito: Abya-Yala, 1997.

Lovera de Sola, R. J. *La larga casa del afecto: Historia de las relaciones afectivas del Libertador.* Caracas: RILDS, 1994.

Lynch, John. *Simón Bolívar: A Life.* New Haven, Conn.: Yale University Press, 2006.

———. *The Spanish American Revolutions, 1808–1826.* 2nd ed. New York: Norton, 1986.

Mannareli, María Emma. *Pecados públicos: La ilegitimidad en Lima en el siglo XVII.* Lima: Editorial Flora Tristán, 1994.

Manrique, Jaime. *Our Lives Are the Rivers.* New York: HarperCollins, 2006.

Margadant, Jo Burr (ed.). *The New Biography: Performing Femininity in Nineteenth-century France.* Berkeley & Los Angeles: University of California Press, 2000.

Martín, Luis. *Daughters of the Conquistadores: Women of the Viceroyalty of Peru.* Dallas, Tex.: Southern Methodist University Press, 1983.

Martínez, Nela. "Cual rostro, cual retrato de Manuela?" In Eugenia Viteri (ed.), *Manuela Libertad.* Quito, 1983.

Martínez Carreño, Aida. "Mujeres y familia en el siglo XIX." In Magdala Velásquez Toro (ed.), *Las mujeres en la historia de Colombia.* 3 vols. Vol. 2: *Mujeres y sociedad,* 292–321. Bogotá: Grupo Editorial Norma, 1995.

———. "Revolución, independencia y sumisión de la mujer colombiana en el siglo XIX." *Boletín de Historia y Antigüedades* (Bogotá) 76, no. 765 (May–June 1989), 415–430.

Masur, Gerhard. *Simón Bolívar.* 2nd ed. Albuquerque: University of New Mexico Press, 1969.

Mendíburu, Manuel. *Diccionario histórico-biográfico del Perú*. 2nd ed. 11 vols. Lima: Evaristo San Cristóbal, 1934.

Mijares, Augusto. *El Libertador*. Caracas: Academia Nacional de la Historia, 1987.

Minchom, Martin. *The People of Quito, 1690–1810: Change and Unrest in the Underclass*. Boulder, Colo.: Westview Press, 1994.

Miramón, Alberto. *La vida ardiente de Manuelita Sáenz*. Bogotá: Editorial ABC, 1944.

Mogollón, María, and Ximena Narváez. *Manuela Sáenz: Presencia y polémica en la historia*. Quito: Corporación Editora Nacional, 1997.

Monteón, Michael. "Biography and Latin American History." *Latin American Research Review* 40, no. 2 (2005).

Moreno de Ángel, Pilar. *José María Córdova*. Bogotá: Kelly, 1977.

———. *Santander*. Bogotá: Planeta, 1989.

Murray, Pamela. "Female Citizenship in Post-independence Spanish America: The Career of Manuela Sáenz, c. 1821–1835." Paper presented at Latin American Studies Association meeting, Washington, D.C., Sept. 7, 2001.

———. "'Loca' or 'Libertadora'?: Manuela Sáenz in the Eyes of History and Historians, 1900–c.1990." *Journal of Latin American Studies* 33 (May 2001), 291–310.

———. "Of Love and Politics: Reassessing Manuela Sáenz and Simón Bolívar, 1822–1830." *History Compass* 5, no. 1 (Jan. 2007), 214–237. http://www.blackwell-compass.com/subject/history/article.

Neruda, Pablo. "La insepulta de Paita: Elegía dedicada a la memoria de Manuela Sáenz, amante de Simón Bolívar." In Pablo Neruda, *Obras completas*. 3rd ed. 2 vols. Buenos Aires: Losada, 1967.

———. "The Unburied Woman of Paita: Elegy Dedicated to the Memory of Manuela Sáenz, Lover of Simón Bolívar." In Neruda, *Ceremonial Songs/Cantos Ceremoniales* [English and Spanish], trans. María Jacketti, 18–55. Pittsburgh, Pa.: Latin American Literary Review Press, 1996.

Núñez, Jorge. "El Ecuador en Colombia." In Enrique Ayala Mora (ed.), *Nueva historia del Ecuador*. Quito: Corporación Editora Nacional: Grijalbo, 1989, vol. 6.

O'Leary, Daniel F. (ed.) *Memorias del general O'Leary, pub. por su hijo, Simón B. O'Leary, por orden del gobierno de Venezuela y bajo los auspicios de su presidente, General Guzmán Blanco*. 32 vols. Caracas: Imprenta Nacional, 1879–1888.

Painter, Nell Irvin. "Writing Biographies of Women." *Journal of Women's History* 9, no. 2 (Summer 1997), 154–163.

Palma, Ricardo. *Tradiciones peruanas completas*. 6th ed. Edith Palma (ed.). Madrid: Aguilar, 1968.

Pattee, Richard. *Gabriel García Moreno y el Ecuador de su tiempo*. 3rd. ed. Mexico City: Editorial Jus, 1962.

Paz Soldán, Mariano F. *Historia del Perú independiente (1822–1827)*. 2 vols. Madrid: Editorial América, 1919.

Pérez Vita, Manuel (comp.). *Índice de los documentos contenidos en las memorias del General Daniel Florencio O'Leary*. 2 vols. Caracas: Imprenta Departamental, 1956.

Pineo, Ronn F. "Quito." In Barbara Tenenbaum (ed.), *Encyclopedia of Latin American History and Culture*, vol. 4, 516–517. New York: C. Scribner's Sons, 1996.

Prieto de Zegarra, Judith. *Mujer, poder y desarrollo en el Perú*. 2 vols. Lima: Editorial Dorhca, 1980.

Public Record Office (Great Britain). *Guide to the Contents of the Public Record Office*. Vol. 2: *State Papers and Departmental Records*. London: H.M. Stationery Office, 1963.

Rappaport, Joanne. *The Politics of Memory: Native Historical Interpretation in the Colombian Andes*. Durham, N.C.: Duke University Press, 1998.

Restrepo, José Manuel. *Historia de la revolución de la República de Colombia en la América meridional*. 6 vols. Bogotá: Ministerio de Educación Nacional, 1942–1945.

Robalino Dávila, I. *Orígenes del Ecuador de hoy*. 8 vols. Puebla, Mex., 1966.

Rodríguez, Pablo. "Las mujeres y el matrimonio en la Nueva Granada." In Magdala Velásquez Toro (ed.), *Las mujeres en la historia de Colombia*. 3 vols. Vol. 2: *Mujeres y sociedad*, 240–249. Bogotá: Editorial Norma, 1995.

Rodríguez O., Jaime. *The Emergence of Spanish America: Vicente Rocafuerte and Spanish Americanism, 1808–1832*. Berkeley & Los Angeles: University of California Press, 1975.

Rodríguez Plata, Horacio. *Antonio Santos Plata: Genealogía y biografía*. Bogotá: Editorial Kelly, 1969.

Romero, Denzil. *La esposa del doctor Thorne*. Barcelona: Tusquets, 1988.

Rumazo González, Alfonso. *Manuela Sáenz: La Libertadora del Libertador* [1944]. 2nd ed. Buenos Aires: Almendros y Nieto, 1945.

Sábato, Hilda. "Review Essay: On Political Citizenship in Nineteenth-century Latin America." *American Historical Review* (Oct. 2001), 1290–1315.

Safford, Frank. "Politics, Ideology, and Society." In Leslie Bethell (ed.), *Spanish America after Independence, c. 1820–c. 1870*, 48–122. Cambridge: Cambridge University Press, 1987.

———, and Marco Palacios. *Colombia: Fragmented Land, Divided Society*. New York: Oxford University Press, 2002.

Salvador Lara, Jorge. *Breve historia contemporánea del Ecuador*. Mexico City: Fondo de Cultura Económico, 1994.

San Cristóbal, Evaristo. *Manuela Sáenz Aispuru: La Libertadora del Libertador*. Lima, 1953.

Socolow, Susan. "Acceptable Partners: Marriage Choice in Colonial Argentina, 1778–1810." In Asunción Lavrin (ed.), *Sexuality and Marriage in Colonial Latin America*, 209–246. Lincoln: University of Nebraska Press, 1989.

———. *The Women of Colonial Latin America*. Cambridge: Cambridge University Press, 2000.

———, and Louisa S. Hoberman (eds.). *Cities and Society in Colonial Latin America*. Albuquerque: University of New Mexico Press, 1986.

Stoner, K. Lynn. "Directions in Women's History, 1977–1985." *Latin American Research Review* 22, no. 2 (1987), 101–134.

Taxin, Amy. "La participación de la mujer en la independencia: El caso de Manuela Sáenz." *Procesos: Revista Ecuatoriana de Historia* 14, sem. 2 (1999), 85–108.

Tenenbaum, Barbara (ed.). *Encyclopedia of Latin American History and Culture.* 5 vols. New York: C. Scribner's Sons, 1996.

Tristán, Flora. *Peregrinations of a Pariah.* Trans., ed., intro. Jean Hawkes. Boston: Beacon Press, 1987.

Twinam, Ann. "Honor, Sexuality, and Illegitimacy in Colonial Spanish America." In *Sexuality and Marriage in Colonial Latin America,* 118–155. Lincoln: University of Nebraska Press, 1989.

———. *Public Lives, Private Secrets: Gender, Honor, Sexuality, and Illegitimacy in Colonial Spanish America.* Stanford, Calif.: Stanford University Press, 1999.

Uribe, Víctor M. "The Birth of a Public Sphere in Latin America during the Age of Revolution." *Comparative Studies in Society and History* 42, no. 3 (Apr. 2000), 425–457.

———. *Honorable Lives: Lawyers, Family and Politics in Colombia, 1780–1850.* Pittsburgh: University of Pittsburgh Press, 2000.

——— (ed.). *State and Society in Spanish America during the Age of Revolution.* Wilmington, Del.: SR Books, 2001.

Valencia Llano, Alonso. *Mujeres caucanas y sociedad republicana.* Cali: Universidad del Valle, 2001.

Valero Martínez, Arturo (ed.). *En defensa de Manuela Sáenz.* Guayaquil: Editorial Pacífico, 1988.

Van Aken, Mark. "García Moreno, Gabriel." In Barbara Tenenbaum (ed.), *Encyclopedia of Latin American History and Culture,* vol. 3, 29–30. New York: Charles Scribner's Sons, 1996.

———. *King of the Night: Juan José Flores and Ecuador, 1824–1864.* Berkeley & Los Angeles: University of California Press, 1989.

———. "Urbina, José María." In Barbara Tenenbaum (ed.), *Encyclopedia of Latin American History and Culture,* vol. 5, 310–311. New York: Charles Scribner's Sons, 1996.

Vargas Martínez, Gustavo. "Bolívar y Manuelita: Con los puntos sobre las íes." *Boletín de Historia y Antigüedades* 81, no. 784 (Jan.–Mar. 1994), 127–138.

Vasco de Escudero, Grecia. *Los archivos quiteños.* Quito: Instituto Panamericano de Geografía & Historia, 1977.

Vega, Juan José. "El largo y torturado silencio de Manuelita Sáenz." *La República* (Lima) (Nov. 30, 1984), 2–5.

Velásquez Toro, Magdala (ed.). *Las mujeres en la historia de Colombia.* 3 vols. Bogotá: Editorial Norma, 1995.

Villalba, Jorge F. *El General Juan José Flores, fundador de la República del Ecuador.* Quito: Centro de Estudios Históricos del Ejército, 1993.

———. *Manuela Sáenz en la leyenda y en la historia.* Caracas: Sociedad Bolivariana de Venezuela, 1988.

Von Hagen, Victor W. *The Four Seasons of Manuela: A Biography (The Love Story of Manuela Sáenz and Simón Bolívar)*. Boston: Little, Brown, 1952; London: J. M. Dent & Sons, 1952.

Walker, Charles F. *Smoldering Ashes: Cuzco and the Creation of Republican Peru, 1780–1840*. Durham, N.C.: Duke University Press, 1999.

Zúñiga, Neptalí. *Juan Pío Montúfar y Larrea*. 2 vols. Quito: Talleres Gráficos Nacionales, 1945.

Lightning Source UK Ltd.
Milton Keynes UK
UKHW010438150121
377088UK00002B/60